# Praise for
## *Outside the Green Box*

D1259984

"Steve Goreham lays out the evolution of environmental hysteria—from the population bomb of the 1960s to catastrophic global warming of today. He makes a strong case for the good news of technology-aided human progress and he arms us with the information to defend it. *Outside the Green Box* is a fact-filled and readable challenge to the popular delusions that guide liberal environmental policies."

— David Kreutzer, PhD, Senior Research Fellow, The Heritage Foundation

"*Outside the Green Box* is a handbook for those who would reassess their personal and business/professional commitment to the concept of sustainability. It takes a comprehensive look at the economic, cultural, political and science issues, identifying the faulty assumptions and rationales for sustainability and green projects, debunking population myths as well as the scare mongering about pesticides, herbicides and genetic modification of crops. Economic issues are addressed head on, crushing the end-of-the-world fears that are always the lead argument for fanatic environmentalists. The book also lays out a sensible approach to resource preservation and good conservative approaches to environmental policy. The graphics are outstanding and make the reading a pleasant and stimulating experience. Thanks for this extraordinary book."

— John Dale Dunn, MD, JD, Physician, Attorney, and
   Policy Advisor, The Heartland Institute

"*Outside the Green Box* tells the real inconvenient truth about how a powerful and corrupt climate industrial complex is thriving at the expense of all who depend upon affordable, reliable energy. This well-researched and information-packed book is a must read for those who are tired of being boxed in by green propaganda marketeers."

— Larry Bell, Columnist, Professor, University of Houston

"Goreham pulls no punches, making the systematic fallacies of green thinking clear to lay readers and experts alike. *Outside the Green Box* is a vital contribution to our energy debate."

— Robert Zubrin, PhD, Founder and President, The Mars Society

"Steve Goreham is feisty. Steve Goreham is funny. And Steve Goreham is factual. Want a feisty, funny, factual exposé and correction of environmentalism's fables and fallacies—from too many people to too few polar bears, from sagging resources to surging seas, from too much heat to too little ice? *Outside the Green Box* is just what the doctor ordered. Especially useful to businessmen pressured to 'go green' despite hurting their stockholders, the book makes the case clearly and concisely on why 'sustainability' is hypocritical nonsense. He even provides a checklist of wise and foolish corporate environmental policies."

> — E. Calvin Beisner, PhD, Founder and National Spokesman,
> The Cornwall Alliance for the Stewardship of Creation

"The news media and schools have indoctrinated society with a false sustainable ideology that has caused politicians to impose huge costs and regulatory burdens on us. Steve Goreham's new book shows that, contrary to the green narrative, population growth is slowing, pollution has declined dramatically, climate change is dominated by natural factors, and resource availability is increasing. The book is an easy and delightful read, packed with great graphics and numerous facts with 828 references. If you are concerned that our modern lifestyles are unsustainable, this book will eliminate those fears."

> — Ken Gregory, Ba.Ap.Sc, Friends of Science Society

"Lots of intellectual heft and fun illustrations make this book friendly for classrooms, waiting rooms, and boardrooms. And just in time for the new energy policy era!"

> — Robert Bradley, Jr., PhD, CEO and Founder, Institute for Energy Research

"The antidote for green ideology!"

> — Stephen Moore, Economist, Distinguished Fellow, The Heritage Foundation

"*Outside the Green Box* is a scathing, fun-to-read indictment of political correctness and renewable-energy tomfoolery. Steve debunks the Malthusians, peak oilers, and climate catastrophists with gleeful prose and a fusillade of graphics, charts, and footnotes. Buy this book and read it."

> — Robert Bryce, Journalist, Senior Fellow, Manhattan Institute

# OUTSIDE THE GREEN BOX

## Rethinking Sustainable Development

### STEVE GOREHAM

New Lenox Books

# OUTSIDE THE GREEN BOX
## Rethinking Sustainable Development

ISBN:  978-0-9824996-4-1
Library of Congress Control Number:  2017900748

www.stevegoreham.com

New Lenox Books, Inc.
New Lenox, IL USA  60451
newlenoxbooks@comcast.net

Printed in China

*Credits*
Cover Design by Monica Thomas, TLC Graphics, www.tlcgraphics.com
Cartoons by Bob Lynch

# CONTENTS

# FOREWORD

*Outside the Green Box—Rethinking Sustainable Development* is an important book that will be credited with having brought free speech and open debate back to environmentalism, a topic that has been hijacked by politicians for their own benefit. This book demonstrates with hard data (828 references) how major environmental decisions are often made today on the basis of politics rather than on what is best for the environment.

In 2009, the Oregon Institute of Science and Medicine published a petition with signatures from 31,478 scientists and engineers, one-third PhDs, challenging the theory of human-caused or anthropogenic global warming (AGW), a theory aggressively promoted by the Intergovernmental Panel on Climate Change (IPCC) of the United Nations. Nonetheless, politicians continue to declare that the "debate on climate change is over," shouting down credible scientists. To add insult to injury, those who disagree with the AGW theory are smeared with the Holocaust-derived term "climate deniers"—often by zealots who would fail a basic test on climate science. The press has unthinkingly adopted this totalitarian mindset. For example, the *LA Times* refuses to print any opinion piece critical of AGW.

I am an engineer and free-market libertarian who founded the $2 billion Silicon Valley chip company Cypress Semiconductor in 1982 and ran it for 34 years. None of us in Silicon Valley—at least not those who want to be successful—would ever start a company based on advice from politicians. There are no liberal or conservative electrons, only those that obey the laws of physics. And, when those laws are violated, a corporate fatality almost always results. Yet, in the environmental field today, good science often gives way to political pressure.

Silicon Valley's world-transforming success comes from the confluence of smart people from great universities, the availability of smart venture money and—most importantly—a culture focused on the data-driven pursuit of technology and business. Yet, the "green" start-up companies in Silicon Valley on whose boards I have served are forced to waste precious time and funding chasing the whims of politicians. In 2000, I wrote an essay for the Cato Institute titled "Why Silicon Valley Should Not Normalize Relations With Washington, D.C." It warned of the destructive nature of "free money" from government, which has been lavished disproportionately on green companies—which, in aggregate, has been a financial bust. For example, Solyndra, the bankrupt solar energy company, was funded with $249 million by the Obama administration, even though other experts and I knew that Solyndra was doomed from the start because its technology was only one-third as efficient as that of the leader, SunPower.

My research on the environment started with a re-reading of two famous books from my college years, *The Population Bomb* by Stanford Professor Paul Ehrlich and *Limits to Growth* by an MIT team. While these works were compelling to me as an undergraduate in 1969, their poor science shocked me in 2010. For example, on the basis of simplistic modeling in *The Population Bomb*, Ehrlich jumped to the wild conclusion that "The battle to feed all of humanity is over. In the 1970s and 1980s, hundreds of millions of people will starve to death in spite of any crash program embarked upon now." Since then, world population has almost doubled, but the percentage of starving people has dropped by a factor of four. Unembarrassed by his colossal errors, Ehrlich still pushes the same dogma and remains an icon of the environmental movement. Bad modeling also plagued *Limits to Growth*, which erroneously predicted that almost all commodities, even oil, would be depleted by the late twentieth century.

There are also gaping holes in the AGW theory of global warming that are ignored by the press. For example, the US National Oceanic and Atmospheric Administration gives data on Earth's temperature going back 400,000 years, as inferred from an isotope analysis of Antarctic ice cap core borings, which literally freeze information on the temperature and carbon dioxide content of the atmosphere in time. This data shows that Earth has periodically heated and cooled and has actually been hotter than it is today on several occasions, centuries before fossil fuel use. These records confirm the existence of the Medieval Warm Period (MWP) from 900 to 1300 AD, when Greenland warmed enough to be settled and farmed, as ruins there show. In its 1990 report, the IPCC actually confirmed that Earth was indeed warmer during the MWP than it is today. However, in its 2001 report, the IPCC eliminated MWP temperature data because it contradicted AGW theory!

Finally, there was the famous "Climategate" incident. Leaked e-mails from Britain's University of East Anglia, the IPCC's provider of global temperature data, exposed discussions between senior researchers on how to manipulate temperature data to make global warming appear stronger.

Read on. Both sides of this story really do need to be told. The debate is not over.

T.J. Rodgers, PhD          Founder, Cypress Semiconductor
                           IPO-Chairman, SunPower

# ACKNOWLEDGEMENTS

*Outside the Green Box* stands on the shoulders of many notable scientists and economists of recent decades. A cacophony of warnings from doomsayers predicted a rising level of environmental destruction, catastrophic global warming, and inevitable resource exhaustion wrought by our supposedly out-of-control human society. Governments and businesses rushed to embrace sustainable development, forgoing science, economics, and common sense to please an increasingly green-eyed public. Against this overwhelming tide of green propaganda, a few courageous thought leaders spoke out for the importance of human ingenuity, the benefit of improving technology, and the power of free markets to better society.

A giant above all was the late free-market economist Julian Simon, author of *The Ultimate Resource II* (1997). Simon argued powerfully that population growth was good for society and that, because of human ingenuity, resources were effectively limitless. Economist Stephen Moore, a disciple of Simon and a change-maker in his own right, followed with *It's Getting Better All the Time* (2000), providing 100 trends showing the steady improvement of the human condition. In an attempt to disprove Simon, but becoming a convert instead, Bjorn Lomborg compiled *The Skeptical Environmentalist* (2001), a huge volume of data and trends showing continued progress for civilization, rather than pending calamity. Matt Ridley's *The Rational Optimist* (2011) celebrated the benefits of trade, technology, and innovation and the resultant improvement in human prosperity. *Outside the Green Box* draws heavily from these works.

The data for graphs was gathered from previous publications by Indur Goklany, Angus Maddison, Vaclav Smil, and others. Max Roser's excellent website *Our World in Data* was also a valuable resource.

Regarding overpopulation, in addition to Simon's efforts, this book relies on Robert Zubrin's *Merchants of Despair* (2012). Zubrin shines a light on a dark stain in twentieth century history, the horrific population control efforts implemented in the name of sustainability.

Our discussion on global warming relies on the work of a growing number of skeptical scientists who challenge the theory of human-caused climate change. Dennis Avery, Tim Ball, the late Bob Carter, John Christy, Judith Curry, Will Happer, Craig Idso, Dick Lindzen, Fred Singer, Roy Spencer, and others have courageously spoken out for sound science, risking political attacks and damage to their careers. They will be vindicated when the theory of human-caused warming is discarded on the trash heap of history. The superb website of Anthony Watts, *Watts Up With That*, provided a comprehensive source of climate news and analysis from a skeptical point of view. *CO2Science*, the website of Craig Idso, provided data on historical temperatures, ocean acidification, and other topics. The Heartland Institute, a free-market think tank based in Illinois, has led the fight for sound climate science for more than a decade and provided input for this book.

A number of energy experts continue to point out the limits of renewable energy, the essential value of hydrocarbon fuels, and the powerful impact of the shale revolution. The writings and analysis of Robert Bradley, Robert Bryce, Mark Mills, and Thomas Stacy provided data and input for the conclusions herein.

Special thanks go to Dennis Avery, Robert Bryce, Don Dears, John Dunn, Ken Gregory, and Howard Hayden for technical review and correction of the text. Thanks to T.J. Rodgers for writing the Foreword. Thanks to my editor, Janet Weber, and my cover designer and style consultant, Monica Thomas, for their professionalism and patience with me. The great cartoons at the start of each chapter came from professional cartoonist Bob Lynch.

Oh, and let's not forget Rachel Carson, Paul Ehrlich, Al Gore, James Hansen, Lester Brown, Maurice Strong, David Suzuki, The Club of Rome, The United Nations, and many others who have laid the foundation for the misguided acceptance of environmental sustainable development by businesses and governments. This book aims to refute their dire warnings and to argue for rollback of foolish policy remedies.

I dedicate this book to my wife, Sue, who takes care of me and who has endured my endless frustrations with sustainability and environmental trends for almost a decade. Thanks also my family and friends for their valuable inputs and inspiration.

# INTRODUCTION

*"… because the resources that we all depend upon—fresh water, thriving oceans, arable land, a stable climate—are under increasing pressure. And that is why in the twenty-first century, the only viable development is sustainable development."*
—SECRETARY OF STATE HILLARY RODHAM CLINTON (2012)[1]

Modern society is beset by green ideology, possibly the greatest delusion in recent history. Schools teach children that carbon dioxide is a pollutant, that polar bears are endangered, that population growth is harmful, that pesticides cause cancer, that energy use is destroying the environment, that warm climate is bad for humanity, and that crude oil is all but exhausted. Further, we can save the planet if we change our light bulbs, plant a tree, forego eating meat, and drive a Prius.

Green ideology is embodied in the doctrine of environmental sustainable development. Sustainable development contends that the growth in human population, production, consumption, and energy use over the last 200 years is "unsustainable." For 30 years, proponents of sustainable development have warned that without radical changes to modern society, our planet's environment will be destroyed, with the resultant decline of human civilization. To avoid the coming catastrophe, companies are told that they must adopt sustainable business practices.

International business has embraced sustainable development, hook, line, and ledger. Today, every major company must be green. Sustainability has become an integral part of corporate strategy. Businesses rush to purchase carbon credits, contract for renewable energy, and adopt organic materials. New buildings must meet energy efficiency and

1

## A GREEN MARKET IN HERE SOMEWHERE?

**Golf Ball With
Carbon Dioxide Absorbents**
US 20120046126 A1

"This disclosure provides a golf ball that includes carbon dioxide absorbents in order that the golf ball may reduce atmospheric carbon dioxide levels to aid in alleviating global warming."
—Nike Inc. patent application
February 23, 2011[2]

environmental standards. Corporate goals include reducing energy use and shrinking the firm's "carbon footprint." Suppliers must accept sustainability as a vendor requirement. Good corporate citizens hire green consultants, donate money to environmental organizations, and volunteer their carbon emissions statistics to watchdog groups. Annual reports, corporate social responsibility reports, and press releases boast about being green and sustainable. And billions can be added to the top line by producing and marketing green products and services.

The doctrine of environmental sustainable development is based on four ideological foundations, all of which are fears about the direction of modern society. These are overpopulation, rising pollution, climate destruction, and resource depletion. Green proponents warn that, driven by rising human population and without major societal changes, our planet's environment will be polluted, the climate will be destroyed, and the natural resources that we depend on will be exhausted.

But economic trends and empirical scientific data show that these foundations are false. The last century of rapid global population growth is strongly correlated with improvements in human lifespan, living conditions, human rights, and education, along with accelerating innovation in agriculture, energy, industry, medicine, and science. It's also clear that, as national income levels rise, population growth slows, and national birth rates decline. Rising incomes allow countries to reduce air and water pollution and regrow forests, so concerns about increasing global pollution are exaggerated. After 25 years of apocalyptic warnings, it's apparent that the climate models are wrong, that human effects on the climate are small, and that climate change is overwhelmingly due to natural factors. Finally, there is no evidence of global resource depletion. Instead,

## This Isn't the Warming You're Looking For

Frozen Great Lakes, Feb. 19, 2014
(NASA satellite image)[3]

economic trends show that access to resources continues to increase.

As a result, it is likely that measures recommended for your company by your green consultant are misguided. Aside from possible public relations benefits and requirements to meet regulatory statutes, counting carbon emissions is, frankly, a waste of time and money. Reduction in energy consumption is as valuable as reducing labor, materials, overhead, or other factors in a production or service process, but saving energy provides negligible benefits for the environment. Buying carbon credits or purchasing high-priced renewable energy flushes investor money down a green drain.

Beyond wasting time and money at an individual company level, green ideology drives distortion of economic activity on a massive scale. The billions of dollars being poured into renewable energy are destroying the reliability of electrical grid systems and the solvency of national budgets. Agriculture, energy, transportation, engineering, and financial industries are skewed toward irrational behavior and away from sound business and economic policy.

In the first part of this book, we'll discuss green business and the false foundations of sustainable development. Chapter 1 discusses the almost unanimous acceptance of environmental sustainable development by the world's businesses. Chapters 2-6 discuss the creation of the doctrine of sustainable development by the United Nations and the feared foundations of the coming environmental apocalypse: overpopulation, pollution, climate destruction, and resource depletion. We'll provide scientific evidence and data on economic trends to show that these foundations are false.

The second part of the book discusses the role of green ideology in major industries. Chapters 7–9 talk about questionable company environmental efforts in energy, agriculture, and other industries. Chapter 9 also proposes "sensibly green," a common-sense environmental policy for business. Chapter 10 summarizes our conclusions and predicts the coming upheaval in climate and energy regulations.

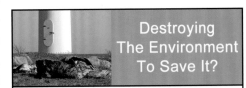

This book is written for business leaders, political leaders, and everyday people who want to sort fact from fiction about environmental issues. It's for corporate directors who want a second opinion about that advice from the green consultant. It's for C-level executives who are considering the best way to give back to the community. But it's also for anyone who wants to understand how green ideology is distorting international business and global economies.

This book is a minority report. Today, most national leaders say they believe in the theory of man-made climate change. The vast majority of the Fortune 500 companies not only pursue sustainable development, but together spend billions to do so. But this report is backed by empirical evidence and economic trends. The evidence shows that nations solve pollution problems as a normal part of economic and societal growth. Climate change is natural, not human-caused, and thousands of climate regulations across  hundreds of nations will fail to produce a measurable change in global temperatures. Finally, human ingenuity continues to expand the resources available to drive our modern society.

Readers will gain a new perspective on environmental sustainable development from this book. Advice herein can save at the bottom line and make company philanthropic effects more meaningful. Along the way, we'll poke some fun at international business and green policies. It's time for businesses and consumers to think "outside the green box."

CHAPTER 1

# THE CAPTURE OF GLOBAL BUSINESS

*"Men, it has been well said, think in herds; it will be seen that they go mad in herds, while they only recover their senses slowly, and one by one."*
—SCOTTISH JOURNALIST CHARLES MACKAY (1841)[1]

The scene was the 2014 annual Apple Corporation shareholder meeting in Cupertino, California. Apple Chief Executive Officer Tim Cook addressed a packed audience of hundreds of stockholders. While answering questions at the end of the meeting, CEO Cook was challenged by Justin Danhoff of the conservative group National Center for Public Policy Research.

Danhoff asked whether the company's environmental investments increased or decreased the bottom line. Would Apple amend its corporate documents to state that the company would not pursue environmental initiatives without a reasonable return on

### Saving the Planet: One PR Pitch At A Time

"Continued to be the largest voluntary purchaser of green power in the U.S. according to the U.S. Environmental Protection Agency (EPA), and received the EPA's Sustained Excellence in Green Power Award."
—Intel Corporation, 2012 Corporate Responsibility Report[2]

investment (ROI)? Cook angrily replied, "If you want me to make decisions on ROI only, you should get out of the stock."[3] Former United States Vice President Al Gore, a director on the Apple board since 2003, joined other shareholders in applause for Cook's response.[4]

Apple and Google, the darling companies of the millennial generation, have spent billions trying to halt global warming. Apple brought us the Mac personal computer, the I-Phone, the I-Pad, and other trend-setting devices, becoming the world's highest-valued company. Google has been called the most innovative technology company in the world, delivering the Google search engine that revolutionized use of the Internet, Google Books, Google Maps, and now a self-driving car. But these and other leading companies have swallowed the misguided theory of human-caused climate change—hook, line, and sinker.

Apple's 2015 Environmental Responsibility Report states, "We don't want to debate climate change. We want to stop it." The firm boasts that it measures its carbon footprint "rigorously."[5] Apple is spending more than two billion dollars on renewable energy to power its data centers. In February, 2015, the firm announced an investment of $848 million for electricity from the California Flats solar farm from electricity provider First Solar.[6] Apple claims that it now purchases 100 percent renewable energy for all of its US operations and 87 percent for worldwide operations.[7] But the firm is paying a sizeable premium for solar electricity over the price of traditional electricity.

Google has reportedly committed more than $1.8 billion to renewable energy projects.[8] But these renewable projects typically provide little actual electricity output at very high prices. An example is the Ivanpah Solar Electric Generating System in the California Mojave Desert. Google invested $168 million in the Ivanpah project, which began operations in January, 2014.[9] Ivanpah is a concentrating solar facility that has made headlines for its tendency to ignite birds in flight near its towers.[10] In addition to scorching more than 1,000 birds a year, in 2014 Ivanpah delivered only about half of the electricity it was designed to deliver, which is only about one-tenth of the output of a typical gas-fired power plant. The Ivanpah electrical output is sold at the whopping price of 16–17 cents per kilowatt-hour, four times the California wholesale price of 4 cents per kilowatt-hour.[11]

Apple, Google, and most global companies have accepted the idea that purchasing renewable energy provides environmental benefits. Corporate commitments to purchase renewable energy may be good public relations, but as we'll discuss, the total use of renewables worldwide has a negligible effect on global temperatures and the environment.

## HOOK, LINE, AND LEDGER

Results from the 2013 United Nations Climate Conference in Warsaw were less than spectacular. Like the previous annual UN conferences in Doha, Durban, Cancun, and Copenhagen, attending national representatives failed to agree on mandatory greenhouse gas emissions limits. Nor did they develop a successor to the Kyoto Protocol treaty that expired at the end of 2012. But the conference did issue a report titled, "Guide for Responsible Corporate Engagement in Climate Policy: A Caring for Climate Report."[12]

The report calls on businesses to urge their national governments to support a "global legal agreement on climate change." Companies should also push for "a carbon price throughout the global economy." The report was developed by three UN organizations, two environmental groups, the World Wildlife Fund and the World Resources Institute, and three business alliances, The Climate Group, Ceres, and CDP.

Business has embraced green directives. In November 2012, prior to the opening of the climate conference in Doha, Qatar, a coalition of investor groups, representing hundreds of banks and financial institutions and over $22.5 trillion in assets, issued a letter stating:

"Institutional investors understand that climate solutions will require close co-operation between governments and investors.

**CO₂ Is Green!**

**Deserts 'Greening' from Rising CO2**

"Increased levels of carbon dioxide (CO2) have helped boost green foliage across the world's arid regions over the past 30 years through a process called CO2 fertilisation, according to CSIRO research."
—Commonwealth Scientific and Industrial Research Organization, July 3, 2013[13]

**ANNUAL REPORT** **Green Drivel for Shareholders?**

**Chipotle Says Global Warming May Mean the End of Guacamole**

"Increasing weather volatility or other long-term changes in global weather patterns, including any changes associated with global climate change, could have a significant impact on the price or availability of some of our ingredients.... we may choose to temporarily suspend serving menu items, such as guacamole or one or more of our salsas ..."
—Chipotle 2013 Annual Report[14]

## GREEN LEADERS OF GLOBAL BUSINESS

"Now, we put out a lot of carbon dioxide every year, over 26 billion tons.... And, somehow, we have to make changes that will bring that down to zero."
—Bill Gates, founder,
Microsoft Corporation (2010)[15]

"Business as usual is wrecking our planet. Resources are being used up. Air, sea, and land are heavily polluted.... We must work hard to change all this."
—Sir Richard Branson, founder,
Virgin Group (2013)[16]

"Green equals growth. Sustainability equals jobs. Climate equals competitive-ness.... And we've got to really inspire in business, a clean energy future."
—Jeffery Immelt, CEO,
GE Corporation (2010)[17]

"Climate change poses clear, catastrophic threats. We may not agree on the extent, but we certainly can't afford the risk of inac-tion."
—Rupert Murdoch, founder,
News Corporation (2007)[18]

"We started in sustainability 20 years ago.... Basically it was all about footprint reduction. You think about it now with the stressors on the world, sustainability is really important for the future of civilization ..."
—Ellen Kullman, CEO,
DuPont Corporation (2014)[19]

Accordingly we call for a new dialogue with the governments of the world's largest economies on climate policy and the development of workable frameworks that will reduce climate risk and support low carbon investment."[20]

Today, every major corporation must be green. A look through the websites of the world's largest firms shows extensive commitment to sustainable development. The vast majority of companies on Fortune's Global 500 list have goals and programs to reduce energy usage and reduce their carbon footprint. Many post a scorecard comparing green goals and company performance to goals. Websites and reports trumpet each firm's efforts to save the environment.

Leading firms issue sustainability reports, that require man-years of effort to develop. Pharmaceutical giant Merck issued a 309-page Corporate Responsibility Report in 2013, with a focus on access to health care, environmental sustainability, employee policies, and ethics and transparency.[22] Energy leader BP's 52-page 2014 Sustainability Review calls for "govern-

**To Die a Green Death**

Wood-Burning Stove

**EPA's Wood-Burning Stove Ban Has Chilling Consequences for Many Rural People**
—*Forbes*, February 10, 2014[21]

ments to apply a carbon price."[23] Swiss corporation Nestlé, a world leader in food and beverage products, wins the prize for size with a 404-page "Creating Shared Value" report in 2013, including a 70-page section on environmental sustainability.[24]

"Sustainability" has become the ultimate corporate buzzword. Today's corporate sustainability covers much more than environmental issues. Sustainability now includes human rights, empowerment of women, diversity, fair employment practices, ethics and anti-corruption, access to products and services, job safety, philanthropy, and community service. It seems that each company defines sustainability in its own way. But as we discuss in Chapter 2, adoption of sustainability by international business grew from the doctrine of environmental sustainable development that was created by the UN several decades ago.

## CAUTION: FAULTY LOGIC AHEAD

**Sen. Boxer Links Keystone Pipeline to Cancer**

"How are more Americans with cancer in the national interest?... Children and families in the US have a right to know now before any decision to approve the Keystone tar sands pipeline is made how it would affect their health."

—Senator Barbara Boxer, *CNS News*, February 27, 2014[25]

World business leaders speak with an almost unanimous voice in favor of green policies, using phrases that have become dogma. Climate change poses "catastrophic threats." Our firm must count carbon emissions and work toward a "smaller carbon footprint." Society and business are "addicted to fossil fuels." "Green materials" must be substituted for petroleum-based materials. Our air and water is "heavily polluted." Energy use is "destroying the environment," so companies must use less energy. Renewable energy is "good for the planet," so businesses should purchase electric vehicles and electricity from wind and solar sources. The common-sense question, "Exactly how much do these measures help the environment?," is rarely asked publicly.

For more than 30 years, business has been the target of a withering barrage of green ideology, coercion, regulation, and persuasion from the UN, the European Economic Community, environmental groups, government officials, the news media, scientific and commercial interests, and increasingly from consumers and the public. Today, the capitulation of business is almost complete. Even the American Petroleum Institute urges its members to reduce greenhouse gas emissions.[26] Companies adopted the doctrine of environmental sustainable development for a combination of reasons: 1) the desire to do the right thing, 2) uncertainty about environmental issues, 3) to meet regulatory requirements, 4) to achieve top-line growth from green product or service sales, 5) to avoid conflict with environmental groups, and 6) to improve public relations.

## LET'S DO THE RIGHT THING

Business leaders, by and large, want to do the right thing. Philip Clarke, CEO of Tesco, the international food retailer headquartered in the United Kingdom, said,

> I'm determined that every Tesco store and every Tesco business is valued and trusted by local people because we do the right thing.[27]

Konosuke Matsushita, founder of consumer electronics corporation Panasonic of Japan, stated in 1978:

> There is much discussion today regarding "social responsibility," but while the meaning of that concept can be wide-ranging depending on social conditions at a particular time, the fundamental social responsibility of a corporation, in any era, should be to improve society through its business activities. It is extremely important to manage all business activities based on this sense of mission.[28]

But what is the right thing to do regarding the environment? As we'll discuss, environmental business policy is often based on a shaky foundation of false assumptions. News reports, college lectures, and even scientific papers are filled with misinformation about pollution, climate change, weather and disaster trends, and health issues. Corporations, in trying to do the right thing, spend large amounts without tangible environmental benefit.

## FEAR, UNCERTAINTY, DOUBT, AND "ACCEPTED SCIENCE"

Uncertainty plays a major role in corporate decisions about the environment. Environmental issues are multifaceted. Determining human-caused impacts is difficult. Mankind's role in global climatic systems is undetermined. The effects of industrial pollution on human health and natural ecosystems are complex. These uncertainties aid adoption of green policies by international business.

In 1975, computer architect Gene Amdahl left IBM Corporation to found Amdahl Corporation, his IBM plug-compatible computer company. Amdahl commented on the subsequent use of fear, uncertainty, and doubt (FUD) by IBM, his former company:

> FUD is the fear, uncertainty, and doubt that IBM sales people instill in the minds of potential customers who might be considering [Amdahl] products.[29]

Customers were urged to choose "safe" IBM products rather than "risky" equipment from Amdahl and other competitors.

FUD is used frequently to promote environmental concerns. After a hurricane or tornado, media interviews typically feature scientists proclaiming that the weather incident was in

"Now, it's difficult to attribute a particular event to climate change, but it's the frequency, and therefore the patterns, of weather that we're actually seeing.... we have an expectation that things are actually going to get worse, in terms of the frequency of these extreme events."
—Sir John Beddington, former UK government chief scientist, April1, 2014[30]

part human-caused. These "experts" are quick to point out that "no one weather event" can be attributed to anthropogenic (man-made) causes. But, they imply that human industries may be the reason for the storm. No empirical evidence is ever offered that shows that weather events are increasing in frequency or severity.

Businesses look to the scientific community for answers about environmental issues. All of the world's major scientific organizations have adopted the position that humans are causing dangerous global warming. US-based organizations such as American Physical Society, the National Oceanic and Atmospheric Administration, and the American Meteorological Society are joined by the Royal Society and the Royal Meteorological Society of Britain, the European Academy of Sciences and Arts, and the Canadian Meteorological and Oceanographic Society in advocating for reductions in greenhouse gas emissions. But as we'll discuss in Chapter 5, mounting evidence shows that these scientific organizations are fundamentally wrong on the cause of global warming. Nature is not cooperating with the "accepted science" of the theory of man-made climate change.

Other fears such as acid rain and pesticide-caused cancer became accepted science, are taught in schools, and are publicly adopted. Business policy must react to these concerns. But, as we will discuss, these and other fears are unsupported by actual empirical data.

The UN elevated fear, uncertainty, and doubt to a whole new level. The 1992 Rio de Janeiro Earth Summit institutionalized FUD into the Precautionary Principle:

> In order to protect the environment, the precautionary approach shall be widely applied by States according to their capabilities. Where there are threats of serious or irreversible damage, lack of full scientific certainty shall not be used as a reason for postponing cost-effective measures to prevent environmental degradation.[31]

In other words, the Precautionary Principle directs that green measures be adopted, even if the scientific community doesn't know whether such measures will provide any benefit for the environment.

Businesses seeking to do the right thing are susceptible to FUD. Expertise in manufacturing or marketing is of little help regarding questions about complex environmental issues such as ocean acidification or global deforestation. Well-meaning company efforts to reduce greenhouse gas emissions or expensive purchases of renewable energy are examples of the wasteful result.

CHICKEN LITTLE
The Original Disciple
of the
Precautionary Principle[32]

## GOVERNMENT REGULATIONS AND MANDATES

Climate laws form the vanguard of global environmental legislation. The Grantham Research Institute on Climate Change at the London School of Economics publishes the GLOBE Climate Legislation Study, an annual review of climate legislation around the world. The 2015 report covered 99 nations responsible for "93 per cent of world emissions" of greenhouse gases. The report states that "the pace and breadth of climate action identified provides cautious cause for optimism."[33]

At the end of 2014, 804 national climate change laws or executive policies were operating in the 99 nations covered in the GLOBE study. Thousands of additional laws are in place at the state, provincial, and local level. Carbon pricing and carbon dioxide ($CO_2$) emissions trading laws operate in 39 nations. Feed-in tariffs, subsidies, and mandates to promote renewable energy have been adopted in at least 89 nations. Laws to reduce energy demand, such as bans on incandescent bulbs, have been enacted in 86 nations. Promotion of biofuels, vehicle emissions limits, and other transportation regulations have been established in 45 nations.[34]

Many companies are now required to report their greenhouse gas emissions to government agencies. The 2008 Climate Change Act of the United Kingdom requires UK companies listed on the London Stock Exchange, the New York Stock Exchange, or the NASDAQ to report emissions as part of their annual directors' report.[35] The US Environmental Protection Agency requires emissions reporting from over 8,000 US companies.[36]

Of course, the blizzard of environmental regulations covers much more than climate change. All firewood sold in the state of California must now carry a warning label about the risks of cancer and birth defects if the wood is burned. Twenty-one nations and the European Union (EU) require mandatory labeling of foods with genetically-modified ingredients.[37] Hundreds of cities across the world have banned plastic bags and many have banned plastic water bottles, even though these products are recyclable.

California Proposition 65
**WARNING**

"Combustion of this product results in the emission of carbon dioxide, soot and other combustion byproducts which are known by the State of California to cause cancer, birth defects or reproductive harm."[38]

Most businesses want to get ahead of the regulatory curve. Rather than dragging their feet, firms map trends in environmental regulation and try to move toward future requirements before they are mandated. While many regulations have tangible human health or environmental benefits, other regulations are foolish or even destructive to health and the environment. Businesses have no choice but to comply with environmental regulations, no matter how absurd.

But the trend of growing of climate and energy legislation appears to be changing. A dark cloud of reality grows over the crusade to fight global warming. As we'll discuss in Chapters 7 and 10, climate and energy regulations are being rolled back across major nations of the world. The failure of renewable energy, the abundance of low-cost hydrocarbons, flat to cooling global temperatures, and changing world leadership point to an upheaval in global environmental regulation.

## BILLIONS IN GREEN BUSINESS

Green products and services are big business. The United Nations Environment Programme reports that global investment in renewable energy totaled $286 billion in 2015.[39] Renewable investment flattened since a 2011 total of $279 billion, but vast amounts continue to be spent each year on wind turbines, solar systems, biofuels, and other renewable sources.

**Follow The Money**

"He [Al Gore] impressed us all at Deutsche Bank Asset Management. We invited him to an internal meeting in April 2007 during which we discussed the issue of climate change extensively. A few months later, he received the Nobel Peace Prize for his commitment. We then created a fund that invests in companies that position themselves as climate-neutral. Within two months almost 10 billion dollars flowed into this fund. Can you imagine? 10 billion! There has never been such an overwhelming success."

—Kevin Parker, Director of Deutsche Bank Global Asset Management, 2010[40]

The 2012 global wind turbine market totaled $73 billion, the largest segment of world investment in renewable energy. Market leaders GE of the United States and Vestas of Denmark sold more than $10 billion in wind equipment in 2012.[41] Siemens of Germany was only the third-ranked wind turbine manufacturer but boasted that 43 percent of its fiscal year 2013 revenues were "environmental portfolio revenues," a whopping $43 billion.[42]

Global financial corporations invest heavily in the green revolution. In 2007, Bank of America set a goal of investing $20 billion in projects to "address global climate change and demands on global resources" by 2016.

By 2012, the firm reported that they had surpassed the goal four years early, lending $21.6 billion to clients for energy efficiency, renewable energy, hybrid cars, and other green projects. The firm announced a new goal to invest $50 billion in green projects over the next ten years.[43] Citibank has a similar $50 billion investment program for "advancing environmental sustainability."[44] Morgan Stanley reported that their "clean technology investment banking team" intermediated more than $6 billion in "IPOs, advisory, and other financing transactions" in the green sector in 2012.[45]

More than six billion metric tons of carbon were traded on world markets in 2015 at a value of over $50 billion. Trading on the European Emissions Trading System accounted for 77 percent of world value. Carbon trading value has fallen even more steeply than renewables investment, down 70 percent from a 2011 world peak of $176 billion.[46] We'll discuss more about this downward trend in Chapter 10.

Green products and service markets are measured by Lifestyles of Health and Sustainablility (LOHAS) statistics. US LOHAS markets are estimated at about $300 billion, with segments totaling $100 billion for green buildings and $40 billion for eco-tourism. International LOHAS markets are likely to be at least double the US totals. About one in five consumers of industrialized nations say they are willing to pay more for green products.[47]

**A GREEN MARKET IN HERE SOMEWHERE?**

No-Petroleum Sunglasses Crafted From Castor Bean Oil
—*Treehugger.com*, April 17, 2014[48]

To support corporate efforts to pursue markets for renewable energy, electric cars, green buildings, and other sustainable products and services, we now have a huge industry of green consultants. McKinsey & Company has a "sustainability and resource productivity practice."[49] Booz Allen Hamilton has an energy and environment practice, covering "regulatory compliance, natural resource management, greenhouse gas reduction, and sustainability."[50] Thousands of other consultants offer advice to firms on the best way to be sustainable. These advisors provide guidance to the vice president of sustainability, now a key officer at major firms.

Green programs are big business for colleges, media organizations, and governments. Environmental science has become a favorite course at major universities, rivaling courses in the hard sciences of biology, chemistry, and physics. Colleges charge a sustainability fee as part of student tuition, administered by the dean of sustainability. Major news organizations employ environmental editors. Development and enforcement of environmental policy provides thousands of jobs for inspectors, agents, regulators, and administrators at local, state, provincial, and national governments across the world.

Not only is green business great for corporate top and bottom lines, but sustainable practices can also motivate employees to higher levels of performance and aid in employee hiring. According to GE CEO Jeff Immelt:

> Our employees love working on sustainability. They love working on clean energy. We have in our factories what we call treasure hunts, where employees go and look for energy efficiency ideas…. As a 130-year-old company you have to constantly be thinking about what's next. In the eyes of young engineers who are graduating from college today, this is what's next.[51]

## BE GREEN OR ELSE

If revenue growth from green products is the carrot, attacks from environmental groups are the stick. Today, major corporations are not free to pursue enterprise without embracing sustainable development. Green organizations are very effective at the demonization and coercion of business.

In 2013, Richard Heede of the Climate Accountability Institute published a paper in the Journal of Climatic Change, titled, "Tracing anthropogenic carbon dioxide and methane emissions to fossil fuel and cement producers, 1854-2010." The paper points out that 90 investor-owned or nation-state producers of oil, natural gas, coal, and cement are responsible for a combined 63 percent of human greenhouse gas emissions. Heede argued that responsibility for "climate destabilization" should be shifted from nation states to corporate entities. He named the top six emitters to be Chevron, ExxonMobil, Saudi Aramco, BP, Gazprom, and Royal Dutch Shell. Heede's work was funded by the Climate Justice Program of Sydney and Greenpeace International of Amsterdam.[53]

In May 2014, Greenpeace International, World Wildlife Fund, and the Center for International Environmental Law combined to send letters to CEOs, directors, and officers of 35 hydrocarbon energy companies,

**The Sins of Big Carbon**

**Eroding Alaska Town Sues Oil, Power Companies**

"A tiny Alaska village eroding into the Arctic Ocean sued two dozen oil, power and coal companies, claiming that the large amounts of greenhouse gases they emit contribute to global warming that threatens the community's existence.

—*NBCNews.com*, February 27, 2008[52]

referencing the Heede paper. They also sent letters to 45 insurance firms that provide key man coverage for the officers of the energy companies. The letter threatened future civil and criminal litigation regarding:

> … development, sponsorship or dissemination of false, misleading or intentionally incomplete information about the climate risks associated with fossil fuel products and services….[54]

The Greenpeace letter also threatened corporate officers with personal liability.

For the last 20 years, companies have been subjected to growing attacks from environmental organizations. Boycotts, negative publicity campaigns, protests, efforts to disrupt business operations, and lawsuits are major tools used by environmental groups. Greenpeace, Rainforest Action Network, Sierra Club, BankTrack, and dozens of other non-governmental organizations (NGOs) engage in aggressive tactics to force firms to toe the green line.

ForestEthics, an activist organization with a mission to "protect endangered forests, wildlife, and human well-being," states on its website:

> Sometimes companies need a little encouragement. When companies refuse to change their harmful practices, ForestEthics holds them publicly accountable. We get creative with online and offline actions, including protests, websites, email campaigns and national advertisements. No corporation can afford to have its brand be synonymous with environmental destruction.[56]

**Faulty Forecast**

**Arctic Summers Ice-Free "by 2013"**
"… you can argue that maybe our projection of 2013 is already too conservative."
—Professor Wieslaw Maslowski,
  *BBC News*, December 12, 2007[55]

**ECO-INSIGHT?**

**Washing Hands in Hot Water Wastes Energy, Study Says**
"Although the choice of water temperature during a single hand wash may appear trivial, when multiplied by the nearly 800 billion hand washes performed by Americans each year, this practice results in more than 6 million metric tons of $CO_2$ equivalent emissions annually."
—*National Geographic*,
  December 12, 2013[57]

In 2000, ForestEthics and the Dogwood Alliance launched a campaign against office products retailer Staples, demanding that the company stop selling paper produced from old growth forests. After 18 months of protests, Staples surrendered and agreed to phase out purchases of paper products from endangered forests and to use an average of 30 percent

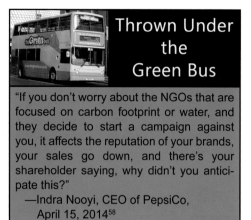

**Thrown Under the Green Bus**

"If you don't worry about the NGOs that are focused on carbon footprint or water, and they decide to start a campaign against you, it affects the reputation of your brands, your sales go down, and there's your shareholder saying, why didn't you anticipate this?"

—Indra Nooyi, CEO of PepsiCo, April 15, 2014[58]

recycled paper across all paper products.[59] As we'll discuss in Chapter 8, forests are expanding in all of the world's developed nations. Raising the income levels of people in developing nations will eventually achieve worldwide forest growth, providing a better path than coercive actions against corporations.

Many environmental advocacy campaigns have been warranted. Companies certainly need to reduce discharge of real pollutants into the environment (not carbon dioxide), to restore the land after mining operations, to use sensible methods to harvest forests and promote forest regrowth, and to control chemicals that can harm citizens. A positive example is marine group Oceana's 2004 organized boycott of Royal Caribbean Cruises. The cruise line agreed to install wastewater purification systems on all ships and to stop discharge of waste water and chemicals into the ocean.[60] But many environmental campaigns are based on false assumptions about carbon dioxide emissions, renewable energy, resource depletion, and health problems from synthetic chemicals.

In 2000, Rainforest Action Network (RAN) began a four-year campaign against Citigroup, concerned that the financial giant was "the leading financier of some of the most environmentally-destructive projects on Earth."[61] RAN organized a letter-writing campaign from college students and protests at 50 campuses, pressuring college administrators to cancel contracts with the company. In February 2003, a RAN activist suspended a banner across the street from the Citibank Wall Street headquarters, which read: "Forest Destruction and Global Warming? We're banking on it! Citi Ethically Bankrupt."[62] RAN announced that 20,000 credit cards had been cut up and mailed to RAN's offices to show displeasure with Citigroup. TV ads followed, starring celebrities such as Susan Sarandon, Ali MacGraw, and Ed Asner, criticizing the firm.[63]

Citigroup capitulated in 2004, despite the fact that Rainforest Action Network's $1.2 million in net assets was tiny compared to Citigroup's $1.2 trillion. The company announced a new set of environmental policies, including a halt to financing of logging operations in tropical rainforests, new guidelines for mining projects, a pledge to invest in green energy, and publication of greenhouse gas emissions data from lending projects. Bank of America, Goldman Sachs, and JP Morgan Chase agreed to similar policies during the next year.[64]

Chemicals has become a toxic word, courtesy of the environmental movement. The presence of synthetic chemicals at any detectable level can trigger an activist reaction. An example is the 2013 attack on Revlon by The Campaign for Safe Cosmetics and the Breast Cancer Fund. Revlon was accused of using cancer-causing chemicals in its cosmetics, namely butylated compounds in hair dyes, Quaternium-15 in mascaras, carbon black found in eyeliners, and others. Shaunna Thomas, co-founder of Ultraviolet, a women's rights group, stated:

> If soaring rates of cancer in young women aren't enough to make Revlon change their mind about lacing their products with toxic chemicals, hopefully outrage from their consumer will be. We demand Revlon take a stand against cancer and drop these chemicals from their products immediately.[65]

This all sounds very concerning, except that smoking-adjusted and age-adjusted cancer rates are not rising. It is true that high doses of the compounds in question have been linked to cancer when ingested by rats and hamsters. But compound levels in cosmetics are too low to pose a risk to humans even when eaten, and few people are eating their hair dye,

---

### Clorox Green Works:
### It's Not How Well Your Product Cleans, But How Green It Is

In 2008, Clorox introduced Green Works, its line of environmentally-friendly housecleaning products. The Green Works family included a glass cleaner, bathroom cleaner, toilet bowl cleaner, dishwasher liquid, laundry detergent, and other products that were "at least 97% naturally derived." Clorox paid $1.3 million to put the Sierra Club logo on Green Works products. The Green Works line was priced 20 percent higher than traditional housecleaning products.[66]

Clorox spent $25 million per year in television and magazine advertising in 2008 and 2009. Annual sales soared to $53 million. Clorox reduced advertising to about $1 million per year and sales fell to $32 million in the year ending May, 2012.

In 2008, competitor SC Johnson challenged the Clorox claim that "Green Works cleaning products work just as well as traditional cleaners." In 2009, the National Advertising Division (NAD) of the Council of Better Business Bureaus found that several of Clorox claims about Green Works were misleading. The NAD recommended that Clorox discontinue the claim that Green Works products were "biodegradable" and that they "clean with the power of Clorox." Clorox disagreed with the findings of NAD but decided not to appeal the NAD decision.[67]

Clorox launched a new 2014 advertising program for Green Works. Marketing slogans included "You Don't Have to Be Perfect to Be Green" and "The Power of Nature in Every Bottle." Saving the planet, one PR pitch at a time.[68]

mascara, or eyeliner.[69] However, when a scare is manufactured using the words "chemicals" and "cancer," science and common-sense go out the window.

Many corporations provide funding to environmental groups, and the level of funding has been growing. Why provide philanthropic funds to the Sierra Club, rather than the Girl Scouts? It's because the Girl Scouts won't attack your business if you don't adopt green dogma.

We're talking big dollars here. Corporate funding of environmental groups amounts to hundreds of millions of dollars per year. In 2007, the World Wildlife Fund (WWF) and Coca-Cola announced a multi-year partnership worth over $20 million to WWF.[70] Home improvement retailer Lowe's contributes more than $1 million each year to The Nature Conservancy for conservation projects in North America.[71] In 2013, Wells Fargo bank provided "$21.8 million in grants to nearly 500 environmental nonprofits."[72] The Nature Conservancy received millions in contributions from oil giant BP.[73] Boeing, Chevron, Clorox, ExxonMobil, Monsanto, Shell, Starbucks, and Walmart, are just a few of the global corporations partnering with environmental groups. Saving the world has become big business for environmental NGOs, courtesy of contributions from corporate partners.

## GOOD PUBLIC RELATIONS

Being green is good public relations. Customers, suppliers, shareholders, and employees expect it. Today, companies strive to establish a more environmentally friendly market image than their competitors.

Some firms have run high-profile marketing campaigns or changed their corporate slogan to appear more sustainable. In 2000, British Petroleum changed its name to BP and its slogan to "Beyond Petroleum" to reflect a new emphasis on renewable energy.[74] IBM launched its "Smarter Planet" marketing campaign in 2008, stating that efforts were needed to help solve new problems:

> The problems of global climate change and energy, global supply chains for food and medicine, new security concerns ranging from identity theft to terrorism—all issues of a hyperconnected world—have surfaced since the start of this decade.[75]

The use of renewable energy must be a big hit with the public. Apple, Best Buy, Cisco, FedEx, Google, Intel, Lockheed Martin, MetLife, Safeway, Walmart, and many other firms boast about using wind or solar energy in sustainability reports and press releases. Who would have thought that the type of energy you use can be good for company sales?

Many firms crow about use of ethanol or biodiesel to fuel company vehicles. But as we'll discuss in Chapter 7, scientific studies show that the use of biofuels does not reduce $CO_2$ emissions when compared to gasoline or diesel fuel. After twenty years of promotion by governments, solar use remains so small that it is absolutely trivial in the global energy picture. Renewable projects may be cost-effective due to large government subsidies or artificial above-market feed-in tariffs, but any additional benefit is only public relations. As we'll discuss, renewable use provides negligible environmental benefit.

Firms purchase carbon credits to try to establish their climate credentials. Under the Clean Development Mechanism (CDM) established by the United Nations, companies can invest in CDM $CO_2$ abatement projects in developing nations to earn tradeable emissions credits. German energy utility RWE has invested in more than 70 CDM projects in Brazil, China, Costa Rica, India, Panama, Peru, and Vietnam. Projects include "wind, biomass, small-scale hydro, and energy efficiency."[76] RWE's budget for investing in CDM projects is €150 million per year.[77] Software leader Microsoft and insurance giant Allianz SE purchase carbon offsets to be able to claim that their companies are "carbon neutral."

A good way to show your green pedigree is to register your company with one of the leading environmental business alliances. The largest of these groups is the United Nations Global Compact, which defines itself as:

> "… a strategic policy initiative for businesses that are committed to aligning their operations and strategies with ten universally accepted principles in the areas of human rights, labour, environment and anti-corruption."

The Global Compact claims more than 12,000 participating companies from more than 145 nations.[78]

Ceres is a US-based business alliance working to "find sustainable solutions to the serious threats to our economic future from climate change, water scarcity, and depletion of natural resources." Ceres developed the Global Reporting Initiative, now used by more than 1,800 firms worldwide to self-report on their environmental, social, and economic performance.[79] CDP, formerly the Carbon Disclosure Project, is a UK-based organization

**Drinking The Green Cool-Ade**

"Thanks to successful reductions in our carbon emissions and offsetting through forest and climate protection projects in Kenya, Indonesia, and India, Allianz has been operating on a carbon-neutral basis since 2012."
—Michael Diekmann, Chairman of the Board of Allianz SE, 2014[80]

that reports on greenhouse gas emission levels for major corporations. More than 700 financial institutions and thousands of firms provide information for CDP reports on climate change and water and forest resources.[81] The Climate Group is a fourth alliance that works internationally with businesses, states, regions, and cities to drive a "clean revolution."[82] Corporations participating with these organizations contribute financially, disclose data about greenhouse gas emissions, water usage, and company processes, and are expected to adopt the principles of the joined alliance. Firms join more than one environmental business alliance to demonstrate their sustainable commitment.

Carbon and energy counting is now standard procedure at most major firms. HP provides a "Carbon Footprint Calculator For Printing" on their website as part of "HP Eco Solutions."[83] This is great public relations, but because the human impact on global warming is insignificant, history will judge carbon counting to be a complete waste of time. As we'll show in Chapters 4–6, empirical trends show that energy usage is not polluting the planet, nor is conventional energy in short supply.

Many companies push for climate regulations for other industries. Apple, Google, Facebook, and Oracle signed a 2014 letter to US Secretary of State John Kerry, urging him to block the Keystone XL pipeline.[84] In 2012, Microsoft and communications giant Sprint urged the US Congress to extend the Production Tax Credit (PTC) for wind farms, stating:

> Eliminating the PTC will sharply increase prices for wind energy and particularly affect the many large and influential companies that are already committed to buying and using wind energy.[85]

In other words, taxpayers should subsidize wind energy so that Microsoft and Sprint can present their green image to the public without paying the real costs of green electricity.

## THE GLOBAL COST OF GREEN BUSINESS POLICIES

The global cost of green business policies is huge. According to Bloomberg New Energy Finance, the world is spending almost one billion dollars per day on renewable energy investments alone.[86] More than $1 trillion has been invested in renewables over the last ten years, but in 2012 renewables supplied only about one percent of global energy consumption, excluding biomass burning in developing nations.[87]

Tens of thousands of firms spend thousands of hours each year counting carbon dioxide emissions, publishing sustainability reports, and advertising their green credentials.

Companies pursue extensive programs to cut energy use, when there is little evidence that energy use hurts the environment. Voluntary purchases of carbon credits and use of expensive green energy are corporate initiatives that provide no measurable environmental benefit.

Compliance with environmental regulations across the globe costs hundreds of billions of dollars each year. The American Action Forum places the US business cost for compliance with US energy and environmental regulations at $398 billion over the last ten years.[89] While some regulations for air and water pollution improve the environment, others, such automobile mileage standards, light bulb bans, and carbon emission regulations provide negligible benefit.

**Wonderfully Sustainable!**

**Extreme Green: Reusable Toilet Wipes**
"They're comfy and environmentally friendly. You can use them wet, and they won't fall apart. It's a lot more comfortable and soft on your most delicate body parts."
—*Livescience*, February 27, 2009[88]

A simple example out of thousands is the substitution of the air conditioner refrigerant HFO-1234yf for the existing refrigerant R-134a by automakers. EU regulations require that all automobiles use a "climate-friendly" refrigerant by 2017. The change requires new factories to be built in several locations around the world, purchase of new equipment for automobile repair shops, and substitution of the new refrigerant in air conditioner systems of all automobiles by major car manufacturers. But the new refrigerant provides only doubtful climate benefits, with no benefits in air conditioning efficiency or cost.[90]

On a larger scale, the push for biofuels by a number of governments has been a massive misdirection of resources. Ethanol production consumed 42 percent of the US corn crop in 2012 to provide only 6.6 percent of US vehicle fuel.[91] Natural forests in Indonesia are cut down and replaced by palm oil plantations to enable shipment of biodiesel fuel 10,000 miles for use by cars in Europe. World corn and soybean prices have doubled since 2001, driven by a sevenfold increase in world biofuel production.[92] But studies now show that production of biofuels uses more water and does not reduce $CO_2$ emissions when compared to vehicle fuel from petroleum.

Adding it all up, the world is spending about one-half trillion dollars per year on environmental initiatives. Most of this spending has little positive effect on the environment. Misguided environmental efforts come at the expense of creating the best products and services for customers.

## INSIDE THE GREEN BOX

Enterprise is captured in the green box of sustainable development. Green products and services are delivered to markets, supported by green supply chains and green advertising campaigns. Shareholders are wooed with sustainable development reports and press releases, backed by impressive purchases of renewable energy and carbon credits. Corporations mollify environmental groups by direct cash contributions and by membership in climate certification groups. The business world has become one big, environmentally happy party.

**A GREEN MARKET IN HERE SOMEWHERE?**

**Swiss Chocolatier Barry Callebaut Creates Heat-Resistant Chocolate to Survive Global Warming**
—*The Daily Meal*, December 28, 2015[93]

Who can blame them? Companies want to do the right thing but are beset by environmental uncertainty, hammered by environmental regulations, and enticed by the lure of profits from green products and services. Customers believe that green is good and are willing to pay for it. And if your firm doesn't toe the green line, get ready for boycotts, lawsuits, and negative publicity from environmental groups. It's easier to join 'em than beat 'em.

But, as we'll discuss in the next few chapters, the foundations of sustainable development are based on deep underlying assertions about the environmental impact of human society that are fundamentally in error. Companies have been sold green ideology based on faulty scientific and economic data. Let's look more closely at these environmental fears.

CHAPTER 2

# ENVIRONMENTAL APOCALYPSE
# OR GOLDEN AGE?

*"As we watch the sun go down, evening after evening, through the smog across the poisoned waters of our native earth, we must ask ourselves seriously whether we really wish some future universal historian on another planet to say about us: 'With all their skill, they ran out of foresight and air and food and water and ideas,' or, 'They went on playing politics until their world collapsed around them.'"*

—U THANT, UNITED NATIONS SECRETARY GENERAL (1970)[1]

Are we on the verge of environmental collapse? Or do we live in a golden age of humankind? Today's green ideology is based on deep underlying philosophies that raise alarm about the growth of civilization and our impact on Earth's environment. These philosophies paint the dark picture that the improving prosperity of humanity is destroying the planet.

Thought leaders warn that humans must change direction or suffer a ruinous fall. Further, we are told that civilization will not adjust to changing conditions as a natural part of societal development. Instead, governmental and international organizations must force severe changes to move society away from the path of "business as usual." These concepts drive the ideology of environmental sustainable development that is accepted by today's international business community.

But contrary to the dark predictions by many, societal and even environmental trends do not show cause for alarm. Let's first examine concerns about environmental collapse and then compare this to historical trends over the last two centuries.

## FOUR HORSEMEN OF ENVIRONMENTAL APOCALYPSE

Today's environmental movement is based on four underlying philosophical fears that we'll call the Four Horsemen of the Environmental Apocalypse. These are overpopulation, rising pollution, climate destruction, and natural resource exhaustion. These four fears are the basis for United Nations claims that developed nations are engaged in "overproduction" and "overconsumption" and warnings that human society is on an unsustainable course.

Overpopulation is less of a headline issue today than in the past, but population growth is considered to be an underlying cause of each of the other Horsemen, a driver of increased pollution, climate destruction, and resource exhaustion. The rapid growth of human population from about one billion in 1800 to over seven billion today spawned predictions of doom by many. From Thomas Malthus, the 18th Century Anglican minister, to modern scholars such as Dr. Paul Ehrlich, thought leaders have warned that human population is expanding at an uncontrollable rate. Presidents, princes, popes, and professors have raised the alarm. The 14th Dalai Lama of Tibet warned in 2000:

> One of the greatest challenges today is the population explosion. Unless we are able to tackle this issue effectively we will be confronted with the problem of the natural resources being inadequate for all the human beings on this earth.[2]

It seems intuitive doesn't it? How can human population continue to increase without reaching the limits of a finite planet?

The second of the Horsemen is the concept that humanity is increasingly polluting our world. Too many people and too much production, consumption, and energy use, and synthetic pesticides, chemicals, and plastics are fouling our air and water and endangering human health. Author Rachel Carson, in her 1962 book *Silent Spring*, stated:

The most alarming of all man's assaults upon the environment is the contamination of air, earth, rivers, and sea with dangerous and even lethal materials.[3]

Former US Vice President Al Gore, in his 1992 book *Earth in Balance*, concluded:

Modern industrial civilization, as presently organized, is colliding violently with our planet's ecological system.[4]

Humans have struggled with control of pollution throughout history. The Roman philosopher Seneca wrote about "the heavy air of Rome and the stench of its smoky chimneys" as early as 61 AD,[5] and civil claims about air pollution were heard by Roman courts almost 2000 years ago.[6] Smelting operations for copper, lead, and other metals were located outside cities not only to access wood fuel, but also to reduce the impact of smoke and smell. The Greek historian and geographer Strabo (64 BC–23 AD) wrote how emissions from smelter furnaces were discharged into the air from "high chimneys."[7]

The concentration of population in urban areas during the Middle Ages and coal combustion during the Industrial Revolution exacerbated air and water pollution. Contaminated fogs of London reached their peak at the end of the 1800s. Air laden with ammonia and sulfide wastes from horse-drawn carriages tarnished silverware in Paris.[8] The discharge of untreated human waste fouled rivers, streams, and municipal waterways.

The twentieth century produced a new set of environmental concerns from synthetic chemicals, plastics, nuclear energy, and the rapid growth of global industry. Water quality in the Rhine River, the Great Lakes, and other fresh water bodies degraded seriously before measures were established to begin recovery. Industrial disasters, such as the Bhopal, India, chemical leak of 1984, the Chernobyl, Russia, nuclear meltdown in 1986, and the Exxon Valdez oil spill in 1989, showed the impact of modern technology on society and the environment when safety measures fail.

Pollution remains a key challenge for modern society. Controls for industrial emissions into the atmosphere, solutions to agricultural and municipal runoff into water systems and oceans, and safe disposal of waste are critical for today's communities. Protection of endangered species and ecosystems is vital for preserving the beauty and health of the natural environment. But are we headed for "world

Industrial pollution in Widnes, Cheshire, England, in the late 1800s[9]

collapse" as Secretary General U Thant warned in 1970, or is humanity winning the battle to control pollution?

Climate change is the third and the most feared of the Four Horsemen. A modern textbook on environmental science states:

> Most scientists now regard anthropogenic (human-caused) global climate change to be the most important environmental issue of our times.[10]

**Faulty Forecast**

"By 1985, air pollution will have reduced the amount of sunlight reaching earth by one half ..."
—*Life Magazine*, January 30, 1970[11]

Today, more than 190 national heads-of-state say they believe in the theory of man-made climate change. All major scientific organizations, most leading universities, the United Nations, the European Union, most of the news media, and your local women's bridge club fear that humans are destroying the climate. As we discussed last chapter, global business is "all in" as a partner in the fight against global warming.

Like the case for the other Four Horsemen, environmental leaders warn that pursuing a policy of business as usual regarding climate change will lead to catastrophe. Melting ice caps will produce rising oceans that flood our coastal cities. Stronger and more frequent hurricanes and storms will result from inaction. Species extinction and polar bear calamity await in the future. Adaptation to climate change is not an option, we are warned. Instead, we must radically alter our industrial society if we are to avoid future climate disaster.

Human-caused climate change has become the final answer for all environmental arguments. When agricultural food production outpaced population growth, the last word was "But what about the greenhouse gas emissions from the rising population?" After coal-fired power plants reduced emission of harmful pollutants, such as lead, mercury, sulfur dioxide, and nitrous oxides, the next concern became $CO_2$ emissions, which are not harmful to humans or the biosphere. If evidence shows that society has centuries of oil, natural gas, and coal remaining, and that we are not exhausting hydrocarbon energy resources in the near term, fear of global warming requires a switch from hydrocarbon fuels anyway.

The last of the Four Horsemen of the Environmental Apocalypse is resource depletion. Environmental science teaches that we live on a finite planet. We are warned that agricultural land, fresh water, energy, and natural resources are limited and soon to run out.

The 1972 book *Limits to Growth* captured this fear about resource exhaustion. The book was authored by Donella Meadows and others and funded by the Club of Rome, an organization of wealthy business owners and influential politicians. Based on a computer model study at Massachusetts Institute of Technology, the authors claimed:

> If the present growth trends in world population, industrialization, pollution, food production, and resource depletion continue unchanged, the limits to growth on this planet will be reached sometime within the next one hundred years. The most probable result will be a rather sudden and uncontrollable decline in both population and industrial capacity.[12]

*Limits to Growth* was one of the most influential environmental books of all time, selling over 30 million copies. The Club of Rome has been an advisor to the UN for decades.

These Four Horsemen, the fears of overpopulation, rising pollution, climate destruction, and natural resource exhaustion, are the foundation of today's green movement. Almost all environmental legislation, taxation, subsidies, mandates, and regulations are justified by these four concepts. Hydrocarbon fuels are viewed as finite, polluting, and emitters of greenhouse gases, so they must be eliminated. Energy from wind farms and solar plants is labeled renewable, non-polluting, and climate friendly. Biofuels are promoted by the European Union, the US, and other nations, despite the fact that biofuel production and use has many negative environmental impacts. Policies promoting sustainable urban communities, residential smart meters, vehicle fuel economy standards, electric cars, high-speed rail, bans on incandescent light bulbs, and even "meatless Mondays" can be traced to one of these four concepts.

**Wonderfully Sustainable!**

**The Norwegian Military Is Fighting Climate Change With "Meatless Mondays"**

"We need to get our soldiers to understand why they should eat more environmentally friendly."
—*The Atlantic*, November 21, 2013[13]

## THE UNITED NATIONS AND SUSTAINABLE DEVELOPMENT

The United Nations has been the champion for an environmentally sustainable society. In June 1972, the United Nations Environment Programme (UNEP) was founded as a UN agency by Maurice Strong, the organization's first director. From the UNEP website:

The United Nations Environment Program (UNEP) is the leading global environmental authority that sets the global environmental agenda, that promotes the coherent implementation of the environmental dimensions of sustainable development within the United Nations system and that serves as an authoritative advocate for the global environment.[14]

The phrase "sustainable development" was defined by the Brundtland Commission. In 1983, Javier Pérez de Cuéllar, Secretary General of the United Nations, asked Gro Harlem Brundtland, Prime Minister of Norway, to form an organization independent of the UN to study environmental and organizational issues. Ms. Brundtland organized and led the World Commission on Environment and Development, also to be called the Brundtland Commission. In 1987, the Commission issued its report, titled *Our Common Future*, defining sustainable development as:

> … meeting the needs of the present without compromising the ability of future generations to meet their own needs.[15]

The report warned:

> Many present efforts to guard and maintain human progress, to meet human needs, and to realize human ambitions are simply unsustainable—in both the rich and poor nations. They draw too heavily, too quickly, on already overdrawn environmental resource accounts to be affordable far into the future without bankrupting those accounts. They may show profit on the balance sheets of our generation, but our children will inherit the losses.[16]

The conclusion of the Brundtland Commission, and the emerging position of the UN, was that humanity could not be trusted to solve the problems of growing population, growing incomes and affluence, pollution, and resource management. As we'll discuss later this chapter, the twentieth century provided a revolution in human health, personal income, trade, food and energy availability, education, and democratic government that is unprecedented in human history. But the UN and many environmental organizations came to view these advances as unsustainable. Human progress and population growth was to be suppressed to avoid collapse of the environment and future society.

By the late 1980s, human-caused global warming emerged as the greatest of environmental concerns. In November 1988, the UN formed the Intergovernmental Panel on Climate Change (IPCC). In August 1990, after only two years at work, the IPCC issued its First Assessment Report, concluding that human activities were causing dangerous climate change and calling on nations to reduce greenhouse gas emissions by over 60 percent immediately.[17]

The doctrine of sustainable development was established as part of Agenda 21 at the UN Conference on Environment and Development in 1992, also known as the Rio de Janeiro Earth Summit. The 350-page Agenda 21 was adopted by 172 participating nations. It covered inequality, poverty, health, hunger, illiteracy, international finance and trade, as well as environmental issues.

Among the more radical Agenda 21 conclusions were:

> ... the major cause of continued deterioration of the global environment is the unsustainable pattern of consumption and production, particularly in industrialized countries .... Developing countries should seek to achieve sustainable consumption patterns in their development process, guaranteeing the provision of the basic needs of the poor, while avoiding those unsustainable patterns, particularly in industrialized countries, generally recognized as unduly hazardous to the environment, inefficient and wasteful, in their development processes.[18]

So, what are some of the practices that the United Nations would like to end in the industrialized countries and prevent in the developing countries? A 2005 paper from The Marrakech Process, an effort launched by the UN in 2003 to promote sustainable production and consumption, spells it out:

> These Western lifestyles of consumerism are spreading all around the world through products and services, media and trade policies. Western type restaurants and coffee shops are as common on the streets of Beijing, as international brands of clothing and other products.... Goods and services previously seen as luxuries—TVs, mobile phones and cars–have now become necessities. The supply of goods from exotic locations is increasing, as well as the consumption of processed food and meat.[19]

The Seeds of Our Destruction

"Central to the issues we are going to have to deal with are: patterns of production and consumption in the industrial world that are undermining the Earth's life-support systems; the explosive increase in population, largely in the developing world, that is adding a quarter of a million people daily; deepening disparities between rich and poor that leave 75 per cent of humanity struggling to live; and an economic system that takes no account of ecological costs or damage–one which views unfettered growth as progress. We have been the most successful species ever; we are now a species out of control. Our very success is leading us to a dangerous future."

—Maurice Strong, Conference Secretary General, Rio de Janeiro Earth Summit, June 3, 1992[20]

According to the UN, restaurants, coffee shops, international brands of clothing, TVs, mobile phones, cars, and consumption of processed food and meat are just a few of the practices that are unsustainable.

## EVERYONE KNOWS THE PLANET IS ILL

International filmmaker Alejandro Jodorowsky said, "The planet is ill, everyone knows that."[21] According to advice columnist Ann Landers, "The air is polluted, the rivers and lakes are dying, and the ozone layer has holes in it."[22] In his 1981 farewell speech, US President Jimmy Carter stated:

> There are real and growing dangers to our simple and most precious possessions: the air we breathe; the water we drink; and the land which sustains us. The rapid depletion of irreplaceable minerals, the erosion of topsoil, the destruction of beauty, the blight of pollution, the demands of increasing billions of people, all combine to create problems which are easy to observe and predict but difficult to resolve. If we do not act, the world of the year 2000 will be much less able to sustain life than it is now.[23]

The fear of environmental apocalypse is rooted in our educational systems. Ask today's US high school students about the environment and most will tell you that pollution is getting worse. Young people believe that our environment is in danger, but if we pursue green policies together we can save the planet. A geography course at the London School of Economics asks the question, "Is development sustainable?"[24] An environmental sciences course description at Harvard University reads, "We need an army of skilled change managers to navigate the complexity and urgency of our global environmental crisis."[25]

The Next Generation Science Standards was created in 2013 by the US National Research Council to serve as a guideline for US grade school and high school science curricula. Middle school students are to be taught that:

> "Human activities, such as the release of greenhouse gases from burning fossil fuels, are major factors in the current rise in Earth's mean surface temperature ('global warming')."[26]

By the end of the twelfth grade, students should know that "overpopulation" and "overexploitation" are practiced by humanity and that Earth's "natural capital" must be preserved.[27]

But do we see evidence that human society is headed for a fall? Is population growth exceeding our ability to produce food? Is pollution reducing life expectancy? Are resource shortages reducing global incomes? Let's look at some trends.

## THE GOLDEN AGE OF HUMANKIND

Contrary to warnings of apocalypse, overwhelming evidence shows that the last 200 years have been a golden age for mankind, unmatched in history. Beginning about 1800, human society achieved unprecedented advances in income growth, life expectancy, and poverty reduction, with remarkable gains in health, nutrition, education, social condition, and access to consumer goods and services. These improvements accelerated during the twentieth century with participation by the majority of the world's nations and show no sign of stall or reversal as we move through the twenty-first century.

The golden age started in the second half of the 1700s with the Industrial Revolution, when humankind learned to build machines and drive them with energy from hydrocarbon fuels. The invention of the steam engine led to advances in transportation and trade, including the railroad, steamship, automobile, and airplane. Industrial productivity gains boosted the daily time available for scientific research, delivering world-changing inventions such as antibiotics, electricity, the microchip, and the computer. Communications approached the instantaneous with radio, television, and the Internet. Revolutions in agriculture and health care improved the lives of the rapidly growing world population.

Arguably the greatest recent societal achievement is the increase in human longevity. For the majority of history, average human life spans were only 20 to 30 years.[28] Over the last 200 years, life expectancy has more than doubled to 70 years for persons born in 2010. Life spans for Americans rose to 79 years. Life spans for citizens of Britain and France

**Human Life Expectancy Improvements 1810–2010.** Remarkable gains in human life expectancy at birth over the last 200 years. (Kertzer and Laslett, 1995; World Bank 2014; Human Life-Table Database and official national statistics, 2014)[29]

increased from under 40 years in 1810 to over 80 years today. Life expectancy in India increased even faster, from about 24 years in 1910 to 66 years in 2010.[30]

My wife, Sue, and I are enjoying our first grandchild, Anna Grace, a remarkable little girl who began walking at only eight months of age. But had we been born around the year 1900, one of us probably would have passed away before Anna was born. Life span for Americans born in the year 1900 was only 48 years.

Elimination of pathogens from drinking water and food has been a major factor in improved longevity. Victory over infectious diseases through improved sanitation, improved hygiene, vaccination, and antibiotic drugs has been an astounding success in developed nations. Although disease, lack of sanitation, and lack of clean drinking water continue to be major problems in much of the developing world, these problems are steadily being solved. World life expectancy at birth has risen about one year per decade since 1970 with no sign of stopping. This is powerful evidence that the apocalyptic warnings about the environment are not impacting society—at least not yet.

"No one should have to bury their child," is a common line from a modern movie tragedy. But in fact, burying your child was a common event in the recent past. US President Abraham Lincoln had four children, but only one survived childhood. His second child Edward Baker died in 1850 at age four from tuberculosis. His third child, William Wallace, died from a fever at age 12 in 1862 in the middle of his presidency.[31]

A major reason for past low life expectancies was the high rate of infant mortality. During the 1800s, every fifth child died in the first year of life, or about 200 deaths per 1,000 births. Advances in better education, disease prevention, improved nutrition, and health care made great strides in reducing infant death. Today, global infant mortality rates are down by more than a factor of five to about 35 deaths per 1,000 births. As a remarkable example, infant mortality in Chile dropped from 250 per 1,000 births in 1900 to 6 per 1,000 in 2012.[32]

Growth in individual incomes is only a recent trend in history. According to economist Bradford DeLong, income levels were flat at about $115 per person in today's dollars for thousands of years prior to the year 1500.[33] Historian Angus Maddison estimates that the per capita economic growth rate prior to the industrial revolution was "virtually nonexistent."[34] By 1800, world per-person income was still small at $700 per year in 1990 dollars.[35]

Since 1800, world income levels have exploded, rising ten times to over $7,000 per person. Income levels in the US rose by sixteen times since 1820.[36] While the US, Canada,

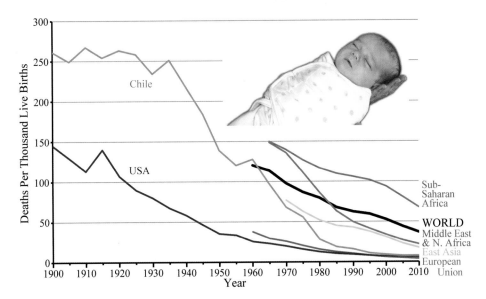

**Infant Mortality 1900–2010.** Number of deaths in the first year of life per thousand live births for selected regions and nations. (Abouharb and Kimball 2007; World Bank, 2014)[37]

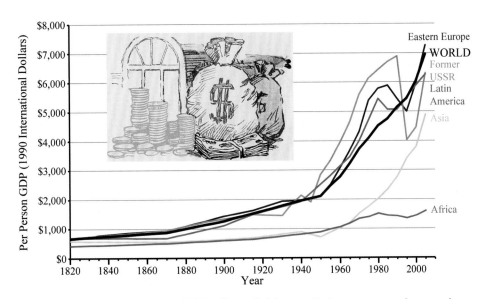

**World Income Growth 1820–2005.** Remarkable growth in per-person income (per capita Gross Domestic Product) for the world and selected regions over the last 200 years. (Maddison, 2010)[38]

"We need to change the value sets. For instance, currently a reduction in GDP is seen as a sign of government failure. In the future, reduction in GDP, while improving quality of life, could be seen as a success."
—*Vision 2050*, World Business Council for Sustainable Development, 2010[39]

Australia, Japan, and Western Europe achieved the highest income gains, per-person incomes rose rapidly in all major world regions except Africa. But today, Africa shows signs of closing the gap, with strong Gross Domestic Product (GDP) growth over the last decade and an expanding middle class.[40]

The current golden age has been characterized by an astounding growth in international trade. World exports totaled about $10 billion in 1900. By 2013, exports increased to over $18 trillion, up over 1,800 times in inflation-adjusted dollars in the last 113 years.[41] This growth in world trade is enjoyed by both developed and developing nations and it's not slowing down.

International trade is the foundation of modern business. Software from India, electronics from China, clothing from Bangladesh, petroleum from the Middle East, machinery from Germany, and many other goods are shipped in huge volumes around the world. But many in today's green movement condemn the expansion of global trade. They worry about emissions of greenhouse gases and energy consumption associated with shipment of goods. They urge consumers to "buy locally" to reduce the impact on the environment.

Agricultural food production is our most basic resource. Overpopulationists of the last century warned that food production would be unable to keep up with population growth. Since 1950, world population increased from 2.5 billion to over 7 billion today. But agricultural output increased even faster. Since 1950, world food production per person increased 47 percent from about 1,900 kilocalories per day to over 2,800 kilocalories per day. In 1950, roughly 30 percent of world population was malnourished. Today about 11 percent of the population is classified as malnourished by the UN Food and Agriculture Organization.[43] Although the number of hungry people is shrinking, still more than 800 million people today are not getting enough to eat.[44]

"Buy locally grown food. It takes much less fuel to transport local foods to your farmers' market or local store than to import food from other countries or states."
—*101 Ways to Save the Planet* by Deborah Underwood, 2012[42]

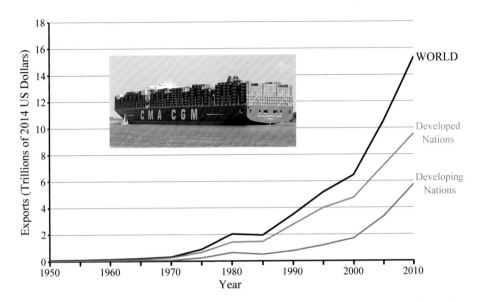

**World Trade Growth 1950–2010.** Accelerating growth in world trade (exports) over the last 60 years. (World Trade Organization, 2014)[45]

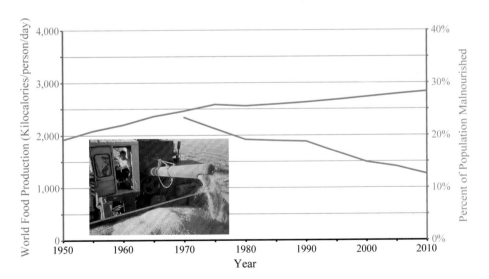

**World Food Production and Malnourishment 1950–2010.** Since 1950, world food production per person has risen steadily, with the percent of global population that is malnourished declining since 1970. (Food and Agriculture Organization, 2010, 2013, 2014; Goklany, 1999; US Department of Agriculture, 1981)[46]

For most of history, people relied on primitive forms of energy in the struggle to survive. Fields were worked with human muscle power or domesticated animals. Horses pulled wagons and wind propelled sailing ships. Wood was the world's dominant fuel for combustion until 1900. The harnessing of hydrocarbon energy, coal, oil, and natural gas, and the refinement of energy into electricity, should be regarded as miracles.

Hydrocarbons and electricity power modern society. Oil fuels global transportation. Natural gas heats homes. Electricity produced largely from coal and natural gas drives computers, communications, and all modern offices, factories, and residences.

From 1800 to 2010, world energy consumption increased by 26 times.[47] In 2012, 82 percent of global energy came from oil, coal, and natural gas, largely unchanged from the 87 percent provided by hydrocarbons in 1973.[48] Energy consumption increased even faster in developing nations. United States energy consumption today is 40 times larger than it was in 1850.[49] Low-cost energy and electricity provided the foundation for the revolutions in agriculture, health care, industry, trade, science, and technology.

So, life span, personal income, trade, energy, and the food supply are improving, but what about the quality of life? One measure of quality of life is education level. Better-educated communities tend to produce higher-value goods and services and enjoy higher levels of income, more leisure time, and improved health care. Education of women is also considered essential for stronger families and reduced population growth rates.

Driving the revolution in science, technology, health, and industry over the last century has been an increasing level of education. The average number of years of education for people around the world more than doubled from an estimated 3.2 years in 1950 to 7.8 years in 2010.[50] Years of education has been rising in all regions. For example, in 1900, the average Brazilian had fewer than two years of education, but Brazilians now have an average of almost eight years of eduction. Over 80 percent of the world's population now has a basic ability to read and write, up from under 40 percent at the start of the 1900s. Literacy expansion in developing nations has been especially remarkable. Only 35 percent of Brazilians had basic reading skills in 1900, but today nine out of ten Brazilians can read.[51]

Throughout most of history, humanity lived under dictatorships, monarchies, and other forms of totalitarian government. With the exception of citizens of ancient Greece and the Roman Republic, few people in history have enjoyed the benefits of democratic government. Slavery, indentured servitude, feudalism, and gender inequality characterized most societies.

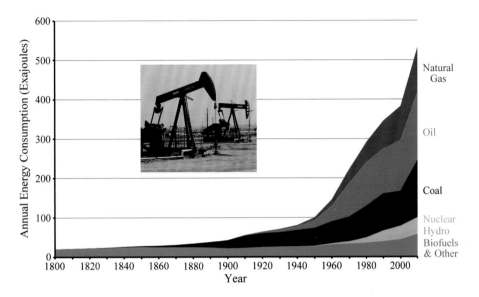

**World Energy Consumption 1800–2010.** Annual world energy consumption, measured in exajoules. Each exajoule is equivalent to the energy from about 24 million metric tons of oil. (Smil, 2010; International Energy Agency, 2012)[52]

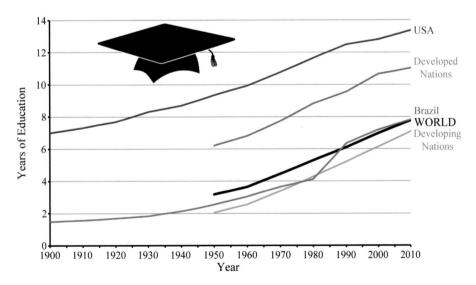

**Years of Education 1900–2010.** Increasing years of education of populations 15 years and older.  (Morrison & Murtin, 2009; Barro & Lee 2010)[53]

The Declaration of Independence and the American Revolution began a new age of democratic government. The number of democracies rose from zero in the mid-1700s to almost 90 today, encompassing almost half of the world's nations. The benefits of legal equality, freedom of speech and religion, rule of law, elimination of slavery, woman's suffrage, and personal property rights followed the establishment of democracy.

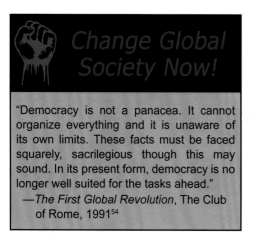

"Democracy is not a panacea. It cannot organize everything and it is unaware of its own limits. These facts must be faced squarely, sacrilegious though this may sound. In its present form, democracy is no longer well suited for the tasks ahead."
—*The First Global Revolution*, The Club of Rome, 1991[54]

Despite gains over the last 200 years, much remains to be done to improve the lives of people in the least-developed countries. According to the United Nations, about 800 million people today are chronically undernourished. Two-thirds of the undernourished reside in Asia, but sub-Saharan Africa has the highest percentage of undernourished, where one in four people is chronically hungry.[55] Twenty-two percent of the world's population, or 1.2 billion people, try to survive on less than $1.25 per day.[56] One-third of global population, about 2.4 billion people, do not use modern sanitation. An estimated 663 million do not have access to clean drinking water.[57] According to the International Energy Agency, more than 1.2 million do not have access to electricity. More than 2.6 billion people, one-third of the world, do not have access to modern energy, continuing to use traditional biomass for cooking.[58] Millions die each year from disease, with AIDS, malaria, tuberculosis, and diarrheal diseases the leading killers.

The good news is that steady progress continues. Since 1990, the number of hungry people has fallen by 200 million,[59] over 2 billion people gained access to clean drinking water, and almost 2 billion gained access to improved sanitation.[60] Electrification rates are rising, modern energy sources for cooking are expanding, and disease rates are falling.

## THE ULTIMATE RESOURCE AND EXCHANGE OF IDEAS

So why the astounding advances over the last 200 years? The late economist Julian Simon explained:

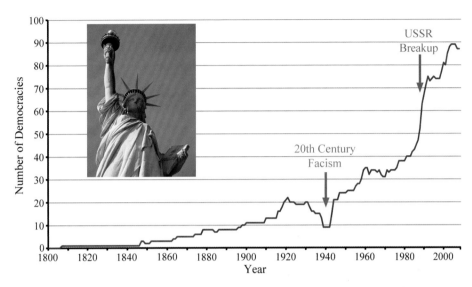

**The Rise of Democracy 1800–2009.** Number of nations with a democratic government and a population of over 500,000. (Roser, 2014; Center for Systemic Peace, 2014)[61]

The ultimate resource is people—especially skilled, spirited, and hopeful young people endowed with liberty—who will exert their wills and imaginations for their own benefits, and so inevitably they will benefit the rest of us as well.[62]

Author Matt Ridley attributes human progress to specialization and the free exchange of ideas, which leads to the creation of yet more ideas. Ridley argues that, because of specialization and exchange, "The secret of human prosperity is that everybody is working for everybody else."[63] Both Simon and Ridley would agree that the growth in world population, the explosion in trade, and the rise of democracy have been drivers of our current golden age and that human prosperity is likely to continue.

## LIVING ON BORROWED TIME?

By all reasonable accounts, human advances over the last 200 years have been both remarkable and unprecedented. But the sustainability movement warns that humans are living on borrowed time, and that our time is running out. They warn that our achievements were gained at the expense of the environment. According to many, overpopulation, rising pollution, global warming, and resource exhaustion will soon put an end to the golden age. Environmentalist Lester Brown warned:

As to how much time we have left with business as usual, no one knows for sure. We are handicapped by the difficulty of grasping the dynamics of exponential growth in a finite environment–namely, the earth. For me, thinking about this is aided by a riddle the French use to teach schoolchildren exponential growth. A lily pond has one leaf in it the first day, two the second day, four the third, and the number of leaves continues to double each day. If the pond fills on the thirtieth day, when is it half full? The twenty-ninth day. Unfortunately for our overcrowded planet, we may now be beyond the thirtieth day.[64]

So which is it? Will our golden age continue throughout the twenty-first century and beyond, or will our expanding society destroy the environment with the resultant collapse of modern civilization? Or to put it another way, will history judge humans to be creators or destroyers?

**Signs of the End Times?**

Climate Change and Air Pollution Will Lead to Famine by 2050, Study Claims —*MailOnLine*, July 28, 2014[65]

The answers to these questions are fundamental for business. If sustainable development is the solution to averting a looming global crisis, then companies need to redouble efforts to reduce energy use, eliminate hydrocarbon fuels, embrace renewable energy, curb greenhouse gas emissions, and follow the advice of today's green consultants. But if the four foundations of sustainable development are wrong, most current business environmental polices will have a negligible effect on the environment. Companies should instead pursue "sensibly green" policies, adopting a more discerning posture with regard to environmental and philanthropic investments.

Let's examine the four foundations of sustainable development—the fears of overpopulation, rising pollution, climate destruction, and resource exhaustion—over the next four chapters in the light of scientific evidence and economic trends.

# CHAPTER 3

# OVERPOPULATION FEAR

*"Population, when unchecked, increases in a geometrical ratio. Subsistence*
*increases only in an arithmetical ratio. A slight acquaintance with numbers*
*will show the immensity of the first power in comparison of the second."*
—THOMAS ROBERT MALTHUS (1798)[1]

Overpopulation is the first Horseman of the doctrine of sustainable development. For the last 200 years, the expansion of human population has been a major concern for opinion leaders. The growth of cities and the concentration of population in cities has exacerbated pollution, congestion, and overcrowding. Today's environmental groups also consider overpopulation as a root cause of climate change and exhaustion of Earth's natural resources. But contrary to apocalyptic warnings, the evidence shows that the recent rise in population has been of tremendous benefit. In addition, slowing population growth rates and declining fertility rates point to a soft landing for the "population crisis."

## POPULATION GROWTH

Thomas Malthus, a nineteenth century Anglican minster, published *An Essay on the Principle of Population* in 1798. The essay discussed the relationship between population growth and the resources needed to support the population. Malthus asserted that, if left unchecked, population would increase geometrically (i.e. 1, 2, 4, 8, ...), while the food supply increased arithmetically (i.e. 1, 2, 3, 4, ...).[2]

Malthus recommended that population be limited by public policy or it would eventually be constrained by famine, which he called "the last, the most dreadful resource of nature."[3] As we discussed in Chapter 2, human society has been beset by short life spans and high levels of infant mortality throughout most of history. Indeed, population growth was constrained by poor nutrition, poor hygiene, and the prevalence of disease up until the time of Malthus. Crop failures and primitive transportation systems resulted in local food shortages and famine. Millions of people died early in life from malnutrition and infectious disease.

But Malthus was wrong. World population rose from about 170 million in year one, to about 425 million by year 1500, and then soared to over 7 billion today.[4] Population ballooned, little constrained by disease and famine that Malthus predicted.

A huge factor in population growth, and one of mankind's greatest achievements, has been the conquest over infectious disease. Bubonic plague, a bacterial disease transmitted by the fleas of rodents, has been a major historical killer. An estimated one-third of the population of Europe died from the plague in the mid-1300s.[5] Smallpox (variola) surpassed bubonic plague as Europe's greatest epidemic disease in the 1700s, killing an average of 400,000 per year of the 200 million European population, many of them children.[6] Diseases carried by European settlers to the New World, including smallpox, influenza, and measles, are believed to have killed up to 95 percent of the native population of the Americas during the 1500s through 1700s.[7] A turning of the tide began with the introduction of the first smallpox vaccine in England by Edward Jenner in 1798.[8] By the late 1800s, improved hygiene, rudimentary sanitation systems, and the filtering of water supplies began to reduce the prevalence of infectious disease in industrial nations. From 1900 to 1970, cases of smallpox, whooping cough (pertussis), typhoid fever, diphtheria,

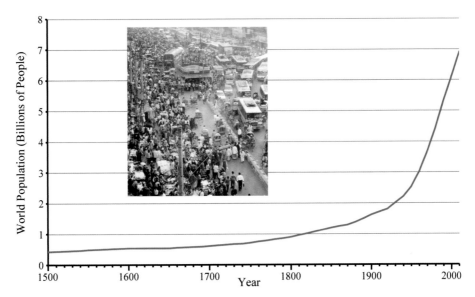

**World Population Growth 1500–2010.** Estimated world population increase since 1500. Crowd image from Dhaka, Bangladesh. (Kremer, 1993; UN Population Division, 2012)[9]

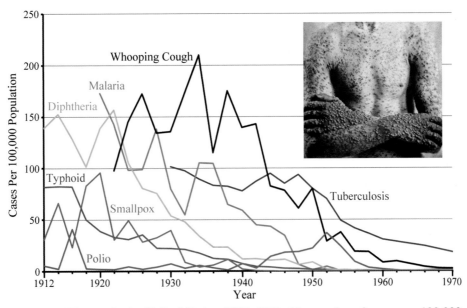

**Decline in Disease in the United States 1912–1970.** The number of cases per 100,000 population for selected diseases in the United States. Image of a smallpox (variola) victim. (US Census Bureau, 1975)[10]

malaria, cholera, and tuberculosis were all but eliminated in the US, primarily through the invention and application of vaccines, antibiotics, and other modern medicines. By 2000, most infectious diseases had been eliminated from industrial nations and many diseases were in steep decline in developing nations. More than any other reason, the rapid growth of world population in the 1800s and 1900s was due to the increase in life expectancy from the elimination of disease.

Along with the triumph over disease, a revolution in agriculture enabled population growth. Innovations in the use of mechanization, energy, fertilizers, and pesticides boosted agricultural output. The world's food supply increased even faster than the rapidly growing population. With rising global trade, the incidence of famine declined and the cause of famine became increasingly due to local political strife rather than global food shortage.

## THE POPULATION CONTROL MOVEMENT

The overpopulation fears described by Malthus accelerated after the Second World War, resulting in a worldwide population control movement. Henry Fairfield Osborn, Jr., conservationist and President of the New York Zoological Society, wrote *Our Plundered Planet* in 1948, which called for "world-wide planning" to control population growth.[11] In 1953 he wrote *The Limits of Earth*, arguing that the world could never feed a population of four billion.[12]

In 1958, English author Aldous Huxley published the essay *Brave New World Revisited*, a commentary on the future of humanity and an update of his 1932 *Brave New World* classic. Huxley's central concern was no longer the loss of individual freedom, but was now the looming threat of overpopulation:

> At the present time the annual increase in world population runs to about forty-three millions. This means that every four years mankind adds to its numbers the equivalent of the present population of the United States, every eight and a half years the equivalent of the present population of India.... The problem of rapidly increasing numbers in relation to natural resources, to social stability and to the well-being of individuals—this is now the central problem of mankind .... So far as the masses of mankind are concerned, the coming time will not be the Space Age; it will be the Age of Over-population.[13]

Dr. Paul Ehrlich, a professor at Stanford University, authored *The Population Bomb* in 1968. The book was written at the suggestion of David Brower, Executive Director of the Sierra Club, and used the same title as a pamphlet published by Hugh Moore of the

Population Action Committee in 1954. The prologue of the book began:

> The battle to feed all of humanity is over. In the 1970s and 1980s hundreds of millions of people will starve to death in spite of any crash programs embarked upon now.[14]

Ehrlich warned of the onset of famine, resource shortages, and disease and advocated coercive remedies, including compulsory population control. His book sold more than two million copies and had a major influence on both public opinion and public policy.

A consistent theme of the population control movement was that human society was out of control and that population growth was "unplanned." Ehrlich stated:

> A cancer is an uncontrolled multiplication of cells; the population explosion is an uncontrolled multiplication of people.[15]

**THE POPULATION BOMB**

Pamphlet published in 1954 by Hugh Moore, founder of the Dixie Cup Company, warning that human population growth was unsustainable.[16]

Dr. David Suzuki, Canadian professor and environmental activist, recently compared human population growth to growth of bacteria in a test tube, concluding:

> Our home is the biosphere, it's fixed and finite—it can't grow. And we've got to learn to live within that finite world.[17]

Another theme has been that the fast-growing populations of the developing world must be "educated." James Grant, Undersecretary General for the United Nations, wrote in 1992:

> Family planning could bring more benefits to more people at less cost than any other single "technology" now available to the human race. But it is not appreciated widely enough that this would still be true even if there were a no such thing as a population problem.[18]

According to the UN, people are not intelligent enough to plan the size of their families and require the help of the UN to do so. Further, governments of developing nations must employ programs to bring the uncontrolled multiplication of population of the "uneducated" masses under control.

The population control movement convinced leaders that the world faced a population crisis. Overpopulation became a major concern for government officials and citizens alike. Tragically, the coercive population control policies recommended by Ehrlich and others were put into practice.

## POPULATION CONTROL IN PRACTICE

The tragic outcomes of the population control movement are well-documented in *Merchants of Despair* by Robert Zubrin and other works. In the mid-1960s, the United States Agency for International Development (USAID) began providing population control assistance to developing nations. It became US government policy to grant foreign aid only if population control measures were also implemented. The World Bank and the UN Fund for Population Activities also established policies requiring population control measures in exchange for loans or aid.[19]

In order to receive food aid from the US, the government of India established sterilization and intrauterine device (IUD) insertion quotas in 1966 for administrative districts within each Indian state. Sterilization camps were set up to augment limited hospital facilities. Administrators were paid for each vasectomy or tubectomy to meet birth control quotas. "Creative" measures, such as withholding of land allotments, water, housing, medical care, and pay raises, and even forced seizures of persons, boosted the number of procedures. Accounts tell of teenagers hiding in sugarcane fields in the middle of the night to escape from the sterilization vans. In 1976 alone, eight million Indians were sterilized. By the early 1980s, four million Indians were being sterilized every year, as part of a two-child-per-family policy. Over

The Seeds of
Our Destruction

"... unless the runaway human population is brought under control—and soon—the result will be catastrophe. *What kind* of catastrophe cannot be predicted, but numerous candidates have been discussed in this book: ecological collapses of various kinds, large-scale crop failures due to ecological stress or changes in climate and leading to mass famine; severe resource shortages, which could lead either to crop failures or to social problems or both; epidemic diseases; wars over diminishing resources; perhaps even thermonuclear war."
—*Ecoscience: Population, Resources, Environment* by Paul Ehrlich, Anne Ehrlich, and John Holdren, 1977[20]

40 million people were sterilized between 1965 and 1985, most coercively.[21] Since boys were preferred to support parents in old age and to continue the family line, government control policies induced Indian parents to choose sex-selective abortion and even the killing of girl babies.[22]

But it was in China where the recommended policies of population control reached their full flower. Under the rule of Mao Zedong, contraception and abortion were outlawed, and Chinese families were encouraged to have as many children as possible until the late 1960s.[23] China's population grew from about 540 million in 1949 to 830 million in 1970.[24] But in 1970, the government changed direction. A "long, late, and few" voluntary policy was adopted, calling for later childbearing, greater spacing between children, and fewer children. This policy appeared to be successful, reducing the children born per family by half by 1979.[25]

PEOPLE Are The PROBLEM

"It's terrible to have to say this. World population must be stabilized and to do that we must eliminate 350,000 people per day. This is so horrible to contemplate that we shouldn't even say it. But the general situation in which we are involved is lamentable."
—Oceanographer Jacques Cousteau, *UNESCO Courier*, November 1991[26]

In 1978, Song Jian, a high-level manager in China's guided-missile program, received copies of *Limits to Growth* from the Club of Rome and *A Blueprint for Survival* by environmentalist Edward Goldsmith. Song developed his own analysis, drawing heavily on both documents, calling for radical population control in China. Premier Deng Xiaoping accepted Song's analysis, ultimately resulting in the passage of China's one-child policy in 1979.[27]

China's one-child policy imposed strict controls on reproduction for all citizens. The policy consisted of regulations on family size, late marriage, child bearing, and the spacing of children. The State Family Planning Bureau established overall policy with local family planning committees imposing implementation methods. Many coercive policies still remain in place today.[28]

Married couples were required to obtain government permission, in the form of a "birth permit," before the woman became pregnant. Until recently, abortion and IUDs were used for birth control, with Chinese families forced to accept the control method dictated by the local government. Urban parents were generally limited to one child and rural families were limited to two children. Child-bearing women in many villages were required to report their menstrual cycle to local officials who tracked their fertility, and to

report for quarterly ultrasound exams to check the status of their IUD.[29]

The penalties for non-compliance were ruthlessly administered, including forced abortion, forced sterilization, infanticide, heavy fines for "illegal births," ransacking of homes, and dismissal from employment. Local crackdown efforts could be particularly brutal. In 2007, squads in Bobai County in southwestern Guangxi province rounded up 17,000 women and subjected them to sterilizations, abortions, and fines. The round-up triggered riots that were reported internationally.[31] In March 2013, the China government reported that 336 million abortions and 222 million sterilizations had been carried out since 1971.[32]

Beyond the coercive and sometimes brutal population control, China's one-child policy caused other serious problems. Sex-selective abortion was illegal, but widely practiced. With the societal preference for male children, government programs resulted in a rising sex ratio, now approaching 1.2 males born for each female. China has one of the highest rates of female suicide in the world. Government-run orphanages and illegal operators sold seized infants on the black market.[33]

Population control policies typically impact disadvantaged races or societal classes disproportionately. In India, coercive policies often targeted the people of the lower castes. Beginning in 1966 in the US, sterilization programs were set up at federally funded Indian Health Services hospitals. Thousands of native American women were sterilized between 1966 and 1976, often without informed consent.[34] In Peru, the majority of population control sterilizations targeted rural natives of Incan descent.[35]

In all, more than one-third of the world's people have been impacted by misguided population control measures, many of which continue today. Planet-saving philosophies proposed by Western intellectuals and endorsed by the United Nations were ruthlessly implemented in the form of anti-human policies by the governments of India, China, and dozens of other nations. But demographic trends show that these coercive policies were unnecessary to reduce the growth of population.

## A LESSON IN HUMAN ADAPTATION

By 1970, it appeared to many that the alarmists might be right and that the world was headed for widespread famine. Population had climbed to 3.7 billion and the growth rate exceeded two percent per year. At this same rate of growth, population would reach 6.8 billion by the year 2000. But the predicted famines never happened. Nor was the need for coercive government-mandated population control programs supported by societal trends. Instead, recent population trends teach us a lesson about human adaptation.

First, human ingenuity produced an agricultural revolution in the 1960s. Biologist Norman Borlaug developed disease-resistant, high-yield strains of wheat and rice that revolutionized modern agriculture. Just a few years before Paul Ehrlich warned of global famine, Borlaug's wheat and rice were introduced to Mexico and Asia with astounding results. Mexico's wheat production soared six-fold in 1970 from previous levels. India's wheat production leaped from a huge deficit in 1965 to a surplus only five years later. Borlaug was awarded the Nobel Peace Prize in 1970 and is credited with saving the lives of a billion people.[36] Yet today, the false overpopulation warnings of Ehrlich are better known on college campuses than the successes of Borlaug.

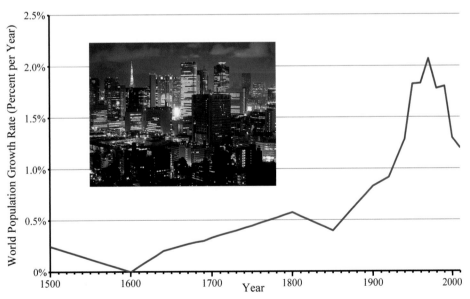

**World Population Growth Rate 1500–2010.** The rise and fall of estimated world population growth rate in percent growth per year. Image of Tokyo at night. (Kremer, 1993; UN Population Division, 2012)[37]

Second, the world population growth rate began to decline in 1975, for the first time in more than 100 years. The growth rate dropped from over 2 percent per year in 1970 to 1.2 percent in 2010.[38] This growth rate decline was not due to famine and environmental collapse, but instead to lower birth rates in both developed and developing nations.

Contrary to predictions by the alarmists, fertility rates throughout the world have plummeted. Total fertility rate is defined as the average number of children born per woman. Demographers tell us that a country's fertility rate must be about 2.1 children born per woman to sustain the current level of national population. In 1950, the average woman would bear 5 children during her lifetime. By 2010, the average woman would bear only 2.5 children. In 60 years, the fertility of women in the less developed regions dropped by more than half, from 6.1 children to 2.7 children. During the same period, the fertility of women in industrialized regions dropped from 2.8 children to 1.7 children, below the 2.1 births-per-woman zero-growth level. By 2010, 74 of the 210 nations in the United Nations Population Division database had moved to negative population growth, including Australia, Brazil, Canada, China, Iran, Japan, Russia, South Korea, the United States, and all nations of Western Europe. Africa remained the only region with high fertility rates, with a modest drop from 6.6 children per woman in 1950 to 4.9 children in 2010.[39] Hania Zlotnik of the UN Population Division puzzles:

> We still don't understand why fertility has gone down so fast in so many societies, so many cultures and religions. It's just mind-boggling.[40]

But wasn't the decline in fertility rates because of government-imposed population control measures? The answer is "no." The drop in fertility rates of China and India is matched by the drop in fertility in other nations that did not mandate population control. The fertility rate in China dropped from 6.1 births per woman to 1.6, a 74 percent drop. Chinese leaders praise their one-child policy and credit it with preventing the births of 400 million people.[41] But the fertility rate in neighboring South Korea dropped from 5.1 to 1.2 births per woman, a 76 percent drop over the same period. From 1962 to 1996, the government of South Korea encouraged smaller families through public information and voluntary birth control programs, including legalization of abortion and free access to contraceptives. But larger factors in the Korean fertility decline appear to be economic development, rising incomes, increased levels of education for women, and growing female participation in the work force. In 1996, because of concerns that their nation's fertility rate had fallen too low, the Korean government ended the nation's family planning program.[42]

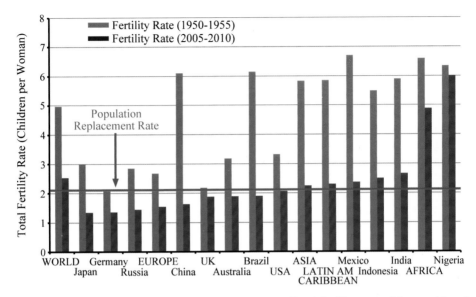

**Declining Fertility Rates of Nations and Regions.** Total fertility rate of the world and selected regions and nations for 1950–1955 and 2005–2010, expressed as the average number of children per woman. The fertility rate required to sustain population levels, 2.1 children per woman, is shown as a green line. (UN Population Division, 2012)[43]

The coercive policies adopted in India helped to drop the fertility rate from 5.9 to 2.7 births per woman, a 54 percent decrease over the 60-year period. But Brazil's rate dropped from 6.2 to 1.9 births, a 69 percent decline, and Mexico's rate dropped from 6.7 to 2.4 births per woman, a 64 percent decline over the same period, without coercive control measures.[44] Both Brazil and Mexico promoted voluntary birth control, but rising incomes, the transition of population from rural to urban living, rising education levels, and rising female participation in the work force again appear to have played larger roles.

The recent rise and fall in population growth rates and the recent decline in global fertility is part of what population experts now call a "demographic transition." For the last 200 years, societies have transitioned from agricultural to industrial to technological economic systems. The demographic transition is driven by trends in reduced premature mortality, rising personal incomes, improved education, an employment shift from agriculture to industry/services, a migration from a rural to an urban population, and a rise in the employment of women in the labor force.

In past societies, and in some remaining underdeveloped nations, most people earned their livelihood in agriculture. Large numbers of children (six or more per family) provided labor on the farm. Children often died in infancy or youth, so parents produced many

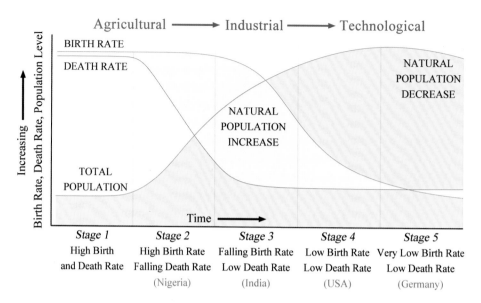

**The Demographic Transition of Population.** The transition of a society from high birth and death rates to low birth and death rates, showing the associated natural burst and eventual stabilization of population. All nations today have reached at least stage two of the transition. (Roser, 2014)[45]

children to support them in their old age. In 1800, about 70 percent of the US labor force worked in agriculture.

The demographic transition of a society begins with a decline in premature deaths and infant mortality from the elimination of infectious disease, improved sanitation, and improved food supplies. In the beginning of the transition, birth rates remain high, so the population soars as death rates decline. As the nation industrializes, income rises. People move to cities and employment shifts from agriculture to industry and services. Rising trade and rising levels of education allow people to succeed in specialized jobs. Women enter the work force in greater numbers, postponing or limiting childbirth. People choose to have smaller families, and fertility then also declines. Finally, population stabilizes at a higher level. It appears that this demographic transition occurs in all nations.

It's clear that human population is stabilizing. The United Nations Population Division projects that world population will rise from 7.2 billion in mid-2013 to 10.9 billion by the year 2100. The UN projects total fertility will drop to under two children per woman by 2100, essentially zero to negative population growth.[46] We will need to feed about 11 billion people, but as we'll discuss later, the trends indicate that human ingenuity will find a way to do so.

*We do not multiply like bacteria.* Rather than being a "species out of control," humans plan their own families and react to changing societal conditions. But population control advocates continue to warn that population growth is out of control with dire consequences for humanity.

## THE BENEFITS OF LARGER POPULATION

As we discussed in Chapter 2, the last 200-year period has been a golden age for mankind, when human population rose from about one billion to seven billion. During this period, lifespan doubled, infant mortality declined by 80 percent, income per person rose by a factor of seven, world trade increased by a factor of 1,800, agricultural output increased faster than population, education levels more than doubled, infectious disease was defeated in industrialized nations, and almost half of the world adopted the freedoms of democratic government. Could it be that the growth in population over the last 200 years has been beneficial to humanity?

Many economists support the idea that population growth is beneficial, at least in the long run. Julian Simon pointed out that history supports this conclusion:

> … demographic history suggests that, contrary to Malthus, constant geometric growth does not characterize human population history. Rather, at each stage a major improvement of economic and health conditions has produced a sudden increase in population, which gradually moderated as the major productive advances and concomitant health improvements were assimilated. Then, after the initial surge, the rate of growth slowed down until the next big surge. In this view, population growth represents economic success and human triumph, rather than social failure.[47]

Economist Michael Kremer of Harvard University concluded that "higher population leads to faster technological change."[48] The more people, the more opportunity for invention that will benefit society. If today's population were only half of the current seven billion, the polio vaccine of Jonas Salk or the high-yield wheat strains of Norman Borlaug might not have been invented. In addition to faster technological change, larger populations provide larger markets for business, increased opportunities for trade, and increased specialization of labor.

But haven't population densities become too high in some nations? Paul Ehrlich used India as an example of a country that had become too crowded. But India's 2010 population density of 367 people per square kilometer was less than South Korea's 487 people per square kilometer and the Netherlands' level of 400 people/sq. km, and on par with Belgium's 358 people/sq. km.[49] Even Bangladesh, with 1,050 people/sq. km had a population density less that the state of New Jersey, at 1,196 people/sq. km.[50] Economic development is the key issue, not population density.

Low fertility rates have become a serious concern in some regions. Countries with very low fertility rates are projected to have population declines this century. Fewer young workers will be available to support growing numbers of elderly citizens. In 2014, the sex education program in Danish school systems changed focus to teach children not only about preventing pregnancy, but also about how to improve fertility.[52] In 2015, the Polish government approved a program of family bonuses to encourage greater fertility.[53] Within the last ten years, Denmark, Iran, Japan, Poland, Russia, Singapore, South Korea, Turkey, and Ukraine initiated active programs to promote population growth. Expect an increasing trend of pro-natal and pro-immigration policies by nations with low fertility rates.

**Maybe...and Maybe Not!**

**Climate-Change Activists Call for Tax Policies to Discourage Childbirth**

"Climate-change activists are mobilizing to cut the birthrate, arguing that richer nations should discourage people having children in order to protect them from the ravages of global warming and reduce emissions."
—*The Washington Times*,
      August 19, 2016[51]

## CONTINUING ENVIRONMENTAL FEARS

Expanding human population remains at the core of environmental fears today. Over-population continues as a false foundation of sustainable development, despite the evidence that population growth is slowing, that people plan the size of their families and adapt to the conditions around them, and even that population growth appears to be good for humanity. Even if we enjoy a golden age of improving health, higher per person income, expanded food availability, and better quality of life, green advocates fear that a big problem still remains: Each additional person increases the level of pollution, climate destruction, and depletion of scarce resources. And the improving lifestyle of billions of poor people adds to the problem.

Proponents of sustainable development say the Earth is suffering an increasing level of environmental destruction from human industry. Deforestation, land and ocean degradation, air and water pollution, and species extinction are underway and all but irreversible, according to many. Increasing population is regarded as a driver of this destruction.

Population growth and the economic growth are regarded to be the cause of climate destruction, the greatest of environmental fears. The larger the population, the more cars, the more meat consumption, the more energy used, and the greater the emissions impact. The United Nations Population Fund discussed the "benefits" of falling birth rates for the climate in 2009:

> Each birth results not only in the emissions attributable to that person in his or her lifetime, but also the emissions of all his or her descendants. Hence, the emissions savings from intended or planned births multiply with time.... No human is genuinely "carbon neutral," especially when all greenhouse gases are figured into the equation. Therefore, everyone is part of the problem, so everyone must be part of the solution in some way.[55]

Finally, most agree that we'll add an additional three billion people to our planet's population by the year 2100. The green movement tells us that we live on a finite world, and that more people will accelerate resource depletion. Doomsayers warm that our finite natural resources will never be able to supply the growing needs of so many.

**Below the Bottom Line**

**Environmentalists Giving Away Earth Day Condoms to Combat Overpopulation**
"We need people across the country to help distribute 44,000 Endangered Species Condoms in time for Earth Day. These colorful, fun condom packages feature six species threatened by our growing human population—already more the seven billion—along with talking points to help get the conversation started."
—The Center for Biological Diversity, *The Daily Caller,* March 21, 2014[54]

**PEOPLE Are The PROBLEM**

"The big threat to the planet is people: there are too many, doing too well economically and burning too much oil."
—James Lovelock, environmentalist and scientist, *The Guardian,* September 16, 2000[56]

## OVERPOPULATION NOT A PROBLEM

Contrary to the forecasts of population catastrophe by Malthus, Ehrlich, and others, history tells us a different story. Rather than famine and population truncation, human population surged from one to seven billion over the last two hundred years. During this same period, the unprecedented population growth was intertwined with revolutionary improvements in human longevity, health, income, agricultural abundance, education, and lifestyle. The expansion of trade, exchange of ideas, and advancement in technology

## Faulty Forecast

"By the year 2000, thirty years from now, the entire world, with the exception of Western Europe, North America, and Australia, will be in famine."
—Professor Pete Gunter, *The Living Wilderness*, Spring, 1970[57]

probably would not have occurred to the same extent without the remarkable increase in numbers of people.

Population trends over the last 60 years provide a lesson in human adaptation. Global fertility rates declined from 5 births per woman to 2.5 births per woman and continue to fall. The demographic transition from an agricultural society to a modern technological society appears to apply to all nations. Contrary to the warnings of the overpopulationists, the evidence shows that people plan their own families and react in a rational way to changing conditions. The "population crisis" appears to be headed for a soft landing.

Nor will population be the cause of a coming environmental catastrophe. As we'll discuss in the next three chapters, trends show that humans are willing and able to control societal pollution, are not measurably affecting the climate, and continue to expand access to global resources. These trends will continue as human population stabilizes over the next century.

# CHAPTER 4

# OUR POLLUTED PLANET?

*"O beautiful for smoggy skies, insecticided grain. For strip-mined mountain's majesty above the asphalt plain. America, America, man sheds his waste on thee. And hides the pines with billboard signs, from sea to oily sea."*
—COMEDIAN GEORGE CARLIN (1972)[1]

Fear of rising pollution is the second of the Four Horsemen of sustainable development. The green movement warns that the growth of human industry, rising energy use, and expanding production and consumption are unsustainable and lead to degraded air and fouled rivers and streams. We are warned that pollution cannot be controlled by improving technology and processes alone, but that it demands radical constraints on the lifestyle of every citizen and business. Overconsumption and overproduction must be eliminated. Unless we move to sustainable development, we are doomed.

## MODERN ALARM ABOUT AIR POLLUTION

Our news media ring daily with alarms about air pollution. A headline from *The Independent* decries air quality in Britain: "Air pollution to blame for 60,000 early deaths per year."[2] A news release from the World Health Organization declares:

> "Air quality deteriorating in many of the world's cities.… In most cities where there is enough data to compare the situation today with previous years, air pollution is getting worse."[3]

The American Lung Association makes this astonishing claim about air in the United States: "More than 147.6 million people—47 percent of the nation—live where pollution levels are too often dangerous to breathe."[4]

All of these headlines were from 2014–2015. Can these statements be true? Are people dying today in Britain and the US from air pollution?

## POLLUTION IN THE GOOD OLD DAYS

Pollution and disposal of waste have been a challenge throughout most of human history. Past societies freely discharged pollution into air, field, and stream. "Control" of pollution and waste was literally to dilute it or move it away from towns and villages. Improved pollution control meant taller smokestacks.

As cities grew, so did the need for improved pollution control and waste disposal. As early as 1300, Londoners began using "sea coal" for residential heating and factories instead of dwindling supplies of wood. Lime kilns burned coal to produce cement, discharging increasing quantities of pollutants into the air. London earned the nickname "The Big Smoke" and became famous for smog.[6]

As in all major cities, water pollution and waste disposal problems became acute in London. The dumping of human refuse from second story windows into the streets below was common practice in the 1700s. Storm sewers were primitive, so heavy rains washed "sweepings from butchers' stalls, dung, guts and blood" and other refuse into the Thames River, which supplied the city's drinking water.[7]

Nelson's Column at mid-day, during The Great Smog of London in December 1952[5]

---

### The Good Old Days of Horse-Drawn Transportation

By the late 1800s, refuse from domesticated animals added to waste problems in the world's large cities. The International Urban Planning Conference in New York City in 1898, the first of its kind, wrestled with what seemed to be an unsolvable issue. It wasn't crime, or poverty, or housing. The big issue of the day was horse manure. Horse-drawn omnibus taxi services within and between cities had grown rapidly during the 1800s. By 1890, each New Yorker took an average of 297 horse-car rides per year, and New York City was home to 200,000 horses. Each horse deposited 15 to 30 pounds of manure per day into streets or stables, for a total of 3 to 6 million pounds of manure daily.[8]

Picture the streets of New York in the late 1800s:

> Urban streets were minefields that needed to be navigated with the greatest care. "Crossing sweepers" stood on street corners; for a fee they would clear a path through the mire for pedestrians. Wet weather turned the streets into swamps and rivers of muck, but dry weather brought little improvement; the manure turned to dust, which was then whipped up by the wind, choking pedestrians and coating buildings.[9]

When the "horseless carriage" began replacing horse and carriage in the early 1900s, some regarded the car as a pollution-reduction invention.

---

Despite efforts to reduce air and water pollution, such as the establishment of London's Coal Smoke Abatement Society in 1899, air and water continued to deteriorate in industrialized nations well into the twentieth century. The Great Smog of London killed between 4,000 and 12,000 residents over a course of five days in December 1952.[10] In October 1948, hydrogen fluoride and sulfur dioxide emissions from steel factories in Donora, Pennsylvania, killed 20 and sickened thousands in one of the worst air pollution incidents in US history.[11] Today, visitors to Cleveland, Ohio, still ask to see the river that caught fire. Oil and chemicals floating on the Cuyahoga River caught fire thirteen times between 1868 to 1969, establishing the river's infamous reputation.[12]

Cuyahoga River fire in Cleveland, Ohio, in 1952 (Cleveland State University)[13]

## THE GREATEST POLLUTION TRIUMPH: CLEAN WATER

Concern about pollution today is focused on the quality of our air and the purity of our lakes and streams, but we often take for granted the miracle of a clean glass of water.

Perhaps the greatest victory in the struggle against pollution has been the attainment of clean drinking water. As discussed in Chapters 2 and 3, infectious disease plagued society for much of human history. Viruses, bacteria, and parasites in drinking water spread diseases such as cholera, typhoid, and dysentery. Infectious diseases from pathogen-infected water were a major cause of past high levels of infant mortality and shorter life spans.

In China, the boiling of drinking water may have begun with Emperor Shennong as early as 2737 B.C. Water was boiled as a personal method of killing pathogens and improving quality. Because boiling removed minerals, water was flavored with tea leaves very early in China's history.[14] Today, boiling of water remains the leading global method of household water treatment.

Clean drinking water: Humanity's greatest victory in the struggle against pollution.[15]

Modern nations use filtration and disinfection to remove not only pathogens, but also heavy metals, trace organic compounds, and suspended solids. Public water supplies and private wells are monitored to safeguard water quality. Water impurities are measured to parts-per-billion levels. Clean water, free of pollutants, is the foundation of health in modern society.

People in poorer countries do not take a glass of clean water for granted. In 2015, 663 million people, or almost ten percent of the world's population, lacked ready access to sources of clean drinking water. Almost 2.4 billion people do not have access to improved sanitation. Hundreds of millions do not have soap and water for handwashing. Water-borne diseases remain a major scourge for these people. Approximately two million people die each year from water-borne or diarrheal diseases.[16]

## THE IPAT EQUATION

A fundamental basis for today's environmental movement is the assertion that growing human population and rising economic activity result in an increasing level of environmental damage. This was captured in the early 1970s by Paul Ehrlich and John Holdren in the form of the IPAT equation:

$$I = P \times A \times T$$

Environmental impact (I) is a product of the size of the population (P), the affluence of society (A), and technology (T). According to Ehrlich and Holdren, growing population, rising levels of amenities (affluence), and increasing levels of technology multiply to result in an increasing level of damage to Earth's environment.[17]

The IPAT equation has been used in many forms to try to capture human impacts on the environment. In a 1974 paper, Ehrlich and Holdren restated the concept, warning that "environmental disruption" was a function of population and human consumption.[18] This supported United Nations efforts to reduce "overconsumption" and "overproduction" in the 1990s.

The "Special Report on Emissions Scenarios" published by the Intergovernmental Panel on Climate Change in 2000 elevated the IPAT equation to truth, calling it an identity. The report explained that greenhouse gas emissions were a function of population, Gross Domestic Product (GDP), and energy use.[19] Other scholars have attributed rising pollution to rising levels of energy use. Environmental groups have waged a war on energy for the last 30 years based on the IPAT equation and the notion that increasing energy consumption increases environmental damage.

The IPAT equation is the theoretical foundation for the concept of sustainable development and for alarm about rising environmental pollution. If we accept the IPAT concept, lifestyles in the US and other industrialized nations are unsustainable. Developing nations can never achieve the standard of living available to advanced societies. Consumers should forego purchases of household conveniences and reduce leisure travel. Businesses should eliminate production increases from the list of company goals. The IPAT equation dictates that we have no choice but to constrain

## Sustainable Sincerity?

"Green protesters are our best passengers. They're always flying off to their demonstrations."
—Michael O'Leary, CEO of Ireland-based Ryanair, *The Times*, August 2, 2008[20]

## The Church of Environmental Destruction

Julian Simon, the late economist, was presenting at an environmental forum and asked, "How many people here believe that the earth is increasingly polluted and that our natural resources are being exhausted?" Naturally, every hand shot up. He continued, "Is there any evidence that could dissuade you?" Nothing. Again he asked, "Is there any evidence I could give you—anything at all—that would lead you to reconsider these assumptions?" Not a stir. Simon then said, "Well excuse me, I'm not dressed for church."[21]

population growth, economic growth, consumption, production, and energy use if we are to avoid environmental destruction. But the good news is that the IPAT equation fails as a predictor of pollution.

## AIR QUALITY, A LITTLE-KNOWN SUCCESS

One of the greatest public success stories of the United States over the last four decades has been the remarkable improvement in air quality. While driving through Gary, Indiana, in the early 1960s, our family station wagon was coated with brown smoke from the steel mills, forcing us to stop for a window cleaning. On another vacation, we observed smog rolling up the valley as our car approached Los Angeles from the east. But today, the air over the US is much cleaner, and these pollution examples are rare.

In 1881, Chicago and Cincinnati passed the first air pollution laws in the US in an effort to control smoke and soot from locomotives and furnaces. County governments began to pass air pollution statues by the early 1900s. Oregon became the first state to pass an air pollution control law in 1952. Other states soon passed laws aimed at controlling smoke and reducing particulate emissions.[22]

During the 1940s and 1950s, coal was a commonly used residential fuel. My grand-

Clark Avenue bridge,
Cleveland, Ohio, July, 1973 (EPA)[23]

father had a coal bin and furnace in the basement of his Chicago home. Within a few days after a snowfall, ground snow became blackened with a layer of soot deposited from the air. Chicago residents washed walls at least once a year to remove accumulated dirt from furnace emissions. But smoke and airborne soot (particulates) over US cities peaked about 1950. State and local laws, and a switch to cleaner-burning natural gas for residential heating, reduced emissions and started the trend toward cleaner air.

The US Clean Air Acts of 1963, 1970, and 1990, authorized the Environmental Protection Agency (EPA) to monitor and set standards for air pollutants considered harmful to public health and the environment. National Ambient Air Quality Standards were established for six principle pollutants, called "criteria

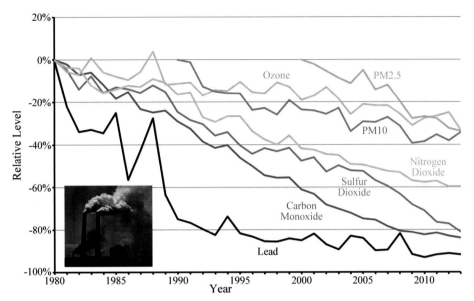

**Air Pollution in the United States 1980–2013.** Declining concentration levels of lead (Pb), carbon monoxide (CO), sulfur dioxide ($SO_2$), nitrogen dioxide ($NO_2$), ozone ($O_3$), and particulates ($PM_{2.5}$ and $PM_{10}$) are shown. (EPA, 2014)[24]

pollutants." These were carbon monoxide, lead, nitrogen dioxide, ozone, particle pollution, and sulfur dioxide. According to EPA data, these six pollutants were down more than a combined 60 percent since 1980 by 2013. Ambient carbon monoxide was down 84 percent, lead down 92 percent, nitrogen dioxide down 60 percent, ozone down 33 percent, and sulfur dioxide down 81 percent.[25]

Particle pollution, a mixture of extremely small particles such as dust, nitrates and sulfates, metals, pollen, and organic chemicals, has been tracked for fewer years, but also showed declines. Particulates are classified as fine particles, with a diameter of 2.5 microns, and coarse particles, with a diameter of between 2.5 and 10 microns. These inhalable particles are much smaller than a human hair, which has a diameter of about 60 microns. Since 2000, 2.5 micron particles ($PM_{2.5}$) are down 34 percent, with 10 micron particles ($PM_{10}$) down 34 percent since 1990.[26]

This remarkable achievement is all but unreported in the press. Headlines are dominated by concerns about carbon pollution, methane pollution, ozone, and chemical pollutants. Students continue to be taught that acid rain from sulfur dioxide ($SO_2$) and nitrogen oxides ($NO_x$) is a serious concern, even though emissions of these gases have been greatly reduced in developed nations. It remains a deeply held belief at colleges and universities

**Faulty Forecast**

"The first great forests will die in the next five years. They are beyond redemption."
—Professor Bernard Ulrich,
   University of Göttingen, on forest dieback in Germany, 1981[27]

that acid rain causes damage to forests and lakes, even though the evidence is weak that acid rain was ever a serious problem.

Pollution reduction efforts have been equally effective in Europe. Emissions of carbon monoxide, lead, nitrogen oxides, and sulfur dioxide are sharply down over the last three decades. Airborne levels of ozone and particulates are down from high levels in the 1950s. The European Environment Agency contends that more work needs to be done to reduce these pollutants.

Note that the declining level of pollutants over the US and Europe does not fit the "increasing environmental damage" hypothesis of the IPAT equation. According to Ehrlich and Holdren, pollution should worsen with economic growth. From 1980 to 2014, US Gross Domestic Product (GDP) more than doubled, driven vehicle miles increased 97 percent, population increased 41 percent, and energy usage was up 26 percent. At the same time, the aggregate level of the EPA's six criteria air pollutants dropped 63 percent.[28] From

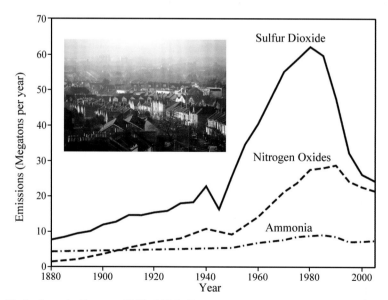

**Emissions in Europe 1880–2005.** European emissions of ammonia ($NH_3$), nitrogen oxides ($NO_x$), and sulfur dioxide ($SO_2$) peaked between 1975 and 1990 and are now trending downward. Image of haze over southeast London in 2008. (Schöpp, 2003)[29]

## Acid Rain: Was It Ever a Serious Problem?

It has long been known that sulfur dioxide ($SO_2$) and nitrogen dioxide ($NO_2$) emitted from natural and human processes react in the atmosphere to form sulfuric and nitric acid. These acids dissolve in water droplets and are returned to Earth by rainfall. Rainfall is normally somewhat acidic, but human emissions of $SO_2$ and $NO_2$ can increase the acidity of rainfall.

In the early 1980s, acid rain became a major environmental concern. Deposition of acid from rain was blamed for acidifying lakes and damaging forests in Eastern Canada, the Northeastern United States, and Northern Europe. Magazines and newspapers showed photographs of dying trees, blaming industrial air pollution. In Germany, the word *Waldsterben* (forest dieback) was coined, and acid rain was said to be destroying Germany's Black Forest.[30]

In the US, The National Acid Precipitation Assessment Program (NAPAP), a $500-million multi-year assessment and research effort, was established in 1982 to study the issue. The Geneva Convention on Long-Range Transboundary Air Pollution initiated efforts in Europe in 1983. Acidification of lakes and destruction of forests from air pollution became a widely held belief taught in schools and universities across the world. Acid rain became a driver of US and European efforts to reduce $SO_2$ and $NO_2$ emissions.

But the actual impact of acid rain has been much less than assumed. The 1990 NAPAP report, titled "Acidic Deposition: State of Science and Technology," found that "acidic deposition has not been shown to be a significant factor contributing to current forest health problems in North America," with the possible exception of the high-elevation red spruce in the northern Appalachian Mountains.[31] A later study found that damage to Appalachian red spruce forests was caused by the conifer swift moth, not acid rain.[32]

The NAPAP study also found that only 4.2 percent of lakes in the Eastern US were acidic, and that acidic conditions for many of these lakes were due to natural factors or surface mining runoff, not acid rain. The NAPAP study also concluded that 1990 levels of pollution-caused acid rain were not harmful to agriculture or human health.[33] In Europe, subsequent analysis showed German forest dieback to be due to disease, weather, and other factors, with acid rain playing only a very small role.[34]

Possibly the greatest evidence against harmful effects of acid rain is the fact that acidic lakes have not "recovered" after most sulfur and nitrogen pollution was removed from the atmosphere. The 2011 NAPAP report to the US Congress stated that $SO_2$ and $NO_2$ emissions were down, that airborne concentrations were down, and that acid deposition from rainfall was down, but could not report that lake acidity was significantly reduced. The report states, "Scientists have observed delays in ecosystem recovery in the eastern United States despite decreases in emissions and deposition over the last 30 years."[35] In other words, pollution was mostly eliminated, but the lakes are still acidic.

Similarly in Europe, there is little evidence of lake acidity recovery after $SO_2$ and $NO_2$ pollution reductions. A 2005 report from the Norwegian Institute for Water Research uses Lake Lille Hovvatn in Norway as an example of improvement, but fails to mention that local officials have added lime to the lake for 20 years to reduce acidity.[36] Natural factors appear to dominate incidences of acid lake and forest dieback, with acid rain only a minor factor.

1970 to 2012, the GDP of Europe more than doubled, yet air quality in all European nations improved. The IPAT equation is a poor predictor of air pollution trends.

## THE ENVIRONMENTAL KUZNETS CURVE

A better predictor of pollution and environmental damage is the Environmental Kuznets Curve. In the 1950s, Simon Kuznets theorized that, as the per capita income of nations rises, the income inequality of citizens increases at first, but then at some point, income inequality begins to decline. Dr. Kuznets won a Nobel Prize in 1971 for his work on the economic growth of nations. In the 1990s, Dr. Gene Grossman and Dr. Alan Kruger of Princeton University expanded the work of Kuznets by noting a relationship between environmental pollutants and the per-person income of nations, which came to be known as an Environmental Kuznets Curve (EKC).[37]

The EKC takes the form of an inverted U-shaped curve. When nations first develop, they give priority to increased output of goods and services and rising wealth at the expense of the environment. During this period, per-person income increases along with environmental damage. Rising incomes provide healthier lifestyles and rising life expectancy. But as conditions improve, people begin to give greater priority to environmental issues. Wealthier societies gain an improved ability to provide clean air and water and to handle industrial waste. At some point, a "turning-point income" is reached when a clean environment becomes a higher priority for citizens than material gain. From this point on, pollution levels decline as income rises.

In economic terms, environmental quality can be considered a luxury good. Today, more than a billion people live in severe poverty. For these people, nutritious food, housing,

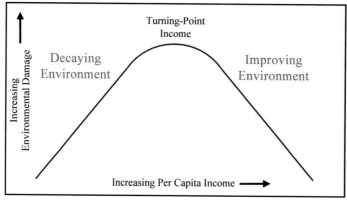

**The Environmental Kuznets Curve.** At some turning-point level of income, increasing per-person income leads to environmental improvement.

clothing, electricity, clean water, modern sanitation, protection from disease, and health care are higher priorities than environmental quality. The environment only becomes a priority in places with higher levels of income.

In addition to income level, reduction in environmental damage also appears to be tied to the development of property rights. Land and resources are typically considered to be commonly shared goods, or "commons," in underdeveloped nations. Individual incentives to preserve commons resources are low, resulting in over-grazing or over-fishing as populations grow. The ban on private ownership of property in Communist states during the twentieth century resulted in severe levels of air and water pollution. As societies mature, land and resources are redefined as public or private property, raising incentives for people to conserve, manage, and protect resources and to pass resource wealth on to future generations. The development of private property rights that accompanies rising national income plays an important role in improving the environment.

Mounting evidence shows that environmental damage is related to societal affluence by the theory of Environmental Kuznets Curves, rather than the IPAT Equation theory. More than 100 peer-reviewed papers since 1991 show that levels of pollution from nations follow the inverted U-shaped curves of EKC theory. British economists, Matthew Cole, Anthony John Raynor, and J. M. Bates, studied more than 20 nations and showed that levels of six different air pollutants first rose and then declined as national incomes increased.[38] A 1995 paper by Grossman and Kruger showed that 11 different water pollutants formed Kuznets Curves in ten different countries.[39]

There is also evidence that deforestation follows a form of Kuznets Curve. People in poor nations do not have access to modern building materials or modern fuels, such as propane and natural gas, for heating and cooking. Instead, they use a high proportion of wood for construction and fuel. A 2006 study by Dr. Pekka Kauppi and others at the University of Helsinki found that as the per-person income of nations increases, deforestation decreases and eventually changes to forest regrowth.[40] We'll discuss this again in Chapter 8.

*The proponents of sustainable development have it exactly wrong.* Historical trends of pollution show that the best way to preserve the environment is not to restrict energy use, constrain national economic growth, or reduce consumption and production. The best way to stop pollution, deforestation, and environmental damage is to boost the income of people. The wealthier societies are, the more people will value clean air and water, and the stronger their efforts will be to reduce pollution and handle industrial waste.

## TODAY'S POLLUTION TRENDS

An objective look at global pollution trends shows that humanity is not only capable of reducing environmental damage, but in many cases is already actively improving the environment. Wealthy nations are monitoring and improving air and water quality and developing nations are beginning to do so. Emissions from power plants, exhaust gases from transportation, waste water and solid waste from industry, water runoff from agriculture and mining, and trash discarded by consumers are increasingly monitored, reduced, and recycled. Air pollutants are declining over the US, Europe, and all major developed nations today. Water quality in rivers and streams has also begun to improve in wealthy nations. Over the last three decades, we've also seen the first examples of improved air quality in major cities in developing nations.

Smoke and soot tend to be the first air pollutants reduced when countries improve air quality. One measure of airborne smoke and soot is the quantity of $PM_{10}$ particles per cubic meter of air. The US and Europe achieved major reductions in smoke and soot in the 1950s and 1960s. Recently, developing nations made great strides to reduce $PM_{10}$ particulate levels. According to data from the World Bank and World Health Organization, from 1995 to 2008 particulate levels in the air over Rio de Janiero, Brazil, dropped 54 percent, levels in Beijing, China, dropped 68 percent, levels in Delhi, India, dropped 52 percent, and levels in Manila, Philippines, dropped 77 percent.[41]

In 1992, the United Nations declared Mexico City the world's most polluted city. Situated at an altitude of 7,300 feet, the city is surrounded by mountains reaching 17,000 feet that tend to trap pollutants in the city valley. Air over Mexico City contained hazardous levels of sulfur dioxide, particulate pollution, ozone, and carbon monoxide in addition to high levels of lead and nitrogen oxides.[42] Over the next two decades, the city removed lead from gasoline, expanded public transportation, increased the use of natural gas fuel for heating and cooking, and relocated industrial facilities.[43] $PM_{10}$ particle pollution in Mexico City dropped by more than 80 percent from 1995 to 2008.[44]

Water pollution is a more complex problem than air pollution, both to assess and to control. The water quality of a stream, lake, or estuary depends on many factors. Human discharges and land use activities, seasonal and watershed changes, chemistry and hydrology, and other natural factors affect the quality of a body of water.

Early water pollution control statutes, such as the US Clean Water Act of 1972, aimed at establishing a sanitary level of water quality in lakes, rivers, and streams. Temperature, salinity, bacteria counts, oxygen levels, and suspended solids were monitored, with measured levels used for setting standards for industrial compliance. Control of point-source pollution was the focus, such as discharge of "end-of-pipe" industrial waste or outflow from large sewers.[45]

**Wonderfully Sustainable!**

**Barrington School Keeps Students— and Parents—In the Dark**
"The lights are off every Tuesday inside Grove Avenue Elementary School in Barrington, Illinois, thanks to the Green Tuesdays program. The school also asks its kindergarten-to-grade-five students to wear an article of green clothing Tuesdays."
—*The Barrington Hills Observer*, September 4, 2013[46]

Over the last 30 years, water pollution efforts in the US, Europe, and other developed nations have expanded their scope to track more pollutants and monitor a wider variety of pollution sources. Levels of synthetic organic compounds, such as pesticides, volatile organic compounds, nutrients, such as nitrogen and phosphorus from agricultural fertilizer, pharmaceutical compounds, microbial and viral contaminants, and natural contaminants, such as arsenic and radon, are now measured down to parts-per-billion levels. Today's control efforts are concerned with distributed pollution sources, such as runoff from agriculture and urban development, forestry, and deposition from the atmosphere. Standards consider not only if water is safe for human activities, but also whether water systems provide good habitats for fish and other aquatic life.

Comprehensive assessments of US surface water quality are only available from the last two decades. These assessments show water quality to be below goals, but improving. A 2009 study of rivers and streams by the EPA sampled over 1,900 river and stream sites, concluding that only 21 percent of the nation's rivers and streams were in good biological condition, 23 percent in fair condition, and 55 percent in poor condition. But the study did find that fish habitat, vegetation cover, and the level of stream disturbance all improved from the 2004 EPA assessment.[47]

The water quality in US lakes and coastlines is better and improving. A National Lakes Assessment conducted by the EPA and state regulators in 2007 found that 56 percent of more than 1,000 US lakes sampled supported healthy biological communities, with 21 percent rated fair and 22 percent rated poor. The study also found that water quality improved in 26 percent and remained stable in 51 percent of lakes sampled since the early 1970s.[48] The EPA's fourth National Coastal Condition Report of 2012 found that US coastlines were much improved from poor conditions found in the early 1990s, but overall rated US coastal water conditions as fair. The report rated 55 percent of US coastal waters as good, with only 6 percent rated as poor.[49]

The European Environment Agency (EEA) assesses surface water quality according to two criteria—ecological status and chemical status. The EEA rates groundwater in underground aquifers in terms of chemical status and quantity criteria. The agency reported that 52 percent of rivers, lakes, and coastal waters (the surface waters) of Europe are "expected to reach good status" in 2015, compared with 42 percent in 2009. They forecasted that by 2015, 89 percent of groundwater sources would be in good status. These quality levels are below goals set by the European Community (EC), but significantly improved over past levels.[50]

The Great Lakes of North America are the largest group of freshwater lakes in the world, containing about 21 percent of Earth's surface fresh water.[51] As population and industry grew in Chicago, Cleveland, Detroit, Milwaukee, Toronto, and other cities situated on the lakes during the nineteenth and twentieth centuries, water quality deteriorated severely. Untreated municipal and industrial waste entered the lakes in growing volume until the mid-1900s. Rising levels of mercury, chemicals such as polychlorinated biphenols (PCBs) and dichlorodiphenyltricloroethane (DDT), and other contaminants were measured in fish, waterbirds, and water samples, raising public health concerns.

Great Lakes clean-up efforts began as early as 1857, when Chicago built the first major sewage system in the United States to treat waste water.[52] In 1909, the US and Canada established an international joint commission to prevent and resolve disputes regarding the use and quality of boundary waters, including the Great Lakes. In 1978, the Great Lakes Water Quality Agreement was signed by the US and Canada to begin focused efforts to clean up the Great Lakes. Since 1978, steady achievements have been made to reduce pollution and improve Great Lakes water quality.

The "State of the Great Lakes 2011" report from Environment Canada and the EPA rated the lake status for water quality, aquatic life, and landscapes and natural processes as only "fair." But the report also stated that water was clearer than 30 years ago in "all offshore areas of the lakes," that levels of chemical pollution such as PCBs and mercury were down from 1970 levels, and that nutrients such as phosphorus were down from levels in the 1980s. The report warned about recent increases in levels of algae in some areas and problems with invasive species.[53]

The Rhine and Danube Rivers are the primary rivers in central Europe. For more than a thousand years, rising levels of pollution, first from growing cities and later industrialization, have fouled the waters of these great rivers. Salmon once teemed in the Rhine but completely disappeared from the river in the 1950s.[54] In the early 1970s, the river annually carried an estimated 400 tons of arsenic, 130 tons of cadmium, 1,600 tons of lead, 1,500 tons of copper, 1,200 tons of zinc, 2,600 tons of chromium, and 12 million tons of chlorides into the Netherlands on route to the North Sea.[55] The Danube River basin is the world's most international river basin, today crossing 19 nations. Urbanization, agriculture, mining, and other human activities created serious pollution and ecosystem problems along the length of the Danube. By the 1980s, nitrates and phosphates from farming, carried by the river, created eutrophication (oxygen depletion) and a severely degraded ecosystem in tens of square kilometers of the western Black Sea.[56]

Political conflict slowed efforts to improve Rhine and Danube water quality for much of the twentieth century. Two world wars raged across both rivers in the first half of the century. The Cold War conflict delayed improvements for the Danube in the second half of the century.

The International Commission for Protection of the Rhine was established in 1950, and the Rhine is making a comeback. Cooperative efforts between nations and investment of over €80 billion in wastewater treatment plants reduced discharge of pollution and significantly improved river flow and ecology.[57] By 2005, levels of zinc and cadmium had been reduced to less than ten percent of 1980 levels.[58] The Atlantic Salmon was reintroduced into the Rhine in 1990 and today's small population of salmon is growing.[59]

Clean-up of the Danube River is still in its infancy, with most serious efforts started after the breakup of the Soviet Union in 1990. Programs for waste-water treatment, reduction of industrial point-source pollution, and reduction of nutrient pollution from agriculture are still under development. But results of recent cooperative clean-up efforts are already showing improvements in water quality. Possibly the greatest visible success is the improving condition in the Black Sea. Levels of nitrogen and phosphorus pollution discharged from the river are down, algae blooms are down, and oxygen levels are up in northwest Black Sea waters.[60]

Headlines We Expect to See?

Post-Herald

"The World Ended Decades Ago," Scientists Report[61]

Similar to successes in reduction in air pollution, the surface waters of both the US and Europe show improving water quality and reductions in pollution. Focused efforts by governments and businesses have achieved not only cleaner water for human activities but also improving habitats for aquatic life, even in heavily-populated areas such as the Great Lakes and the Rhine and Danube River basins. Treatment of municipal and industrial waste water is probably the biggest factor in improved water quality in lakes and rivers over the last 40 years. Much work still remains to reach regional goals, but the trends are positive for water systems and the environment.

Metals, such as arsenic, cadmium, chromium, lead, mercury, nickel, and zinc have long been exhausted into the environment from human activity, such as mining and smelting. Lead and copper mining began about 4,000 BC, and both metals were used extensively in Roman society 2,000 years ago.[62] Mercury was used to extract gold during the California Gold Rush of the 1850s, releasing mercury vapor as part of the process.[63] Combustion of coal releases trace amounts of mercury and other metals into the atmosphere. Metals find their way into air and water from industrial processes, vehicle emissions, and the use of everyday products, such as batteries and paint.

Small quantities of metals are essential for human health, but metals can be toxic in higher concentrations. Lead and mercury are neurotoxins that can damage the human nervous system. Metals released into air and water persist in the environment, tending to accumulate in the tissues of humans and animals. Many studies point to high levels of mercury and other metals in the tissues of top marine predators, such as sharks and salmon.

Today, programs are in place to reduce metal pollution. By 2013, almost all countries had phased out leaded gasoline. Lead paint was banned in the US in 1978 and is banned in many other nations. Modern factories, mines, and power plants track and control the level of metal emissions.

Metal vapor emitted by industry is transported through the atmosphere and deposited in glacial ice. Ice depositions over many centuries capture a record of airborne metal pollution that can be recovered by scientists. Like the reductions in levels of metal contaminants measured in US and European surface waters, recovered ice core records show that airborne levels of metal pollutants have also declined.

**Destroying The Environment To Save It?**

**Six Flags Great Adventure to Cut 18,000 Trees to Go Solar**

"The theme park plans to cut down more than 18,000 trees for the construction of what it says will be the largest solar farm in New Jersey."

—*CBSNewYork/AP*, March 27, 2015[6]

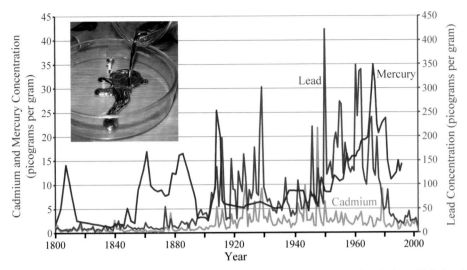

**Metal Pollution in Ice Cores (1800–2003).** Concentration levels of cadmium (Cd), lead (Pb), and mercury (Hg) deposited in glacial ice from airborne transport over the last 200 years are shown. Cadmium and lead levels are from Greenland ice cores. Mercury levels are from Wyoming glacial cores. Concentration is measured in picograms per gram of water. The years of peak atmospheric levels were cadmium (1947), lead (1951), and mercury (1978). All are now trending downward. Image of liquid mercury. (Krabbenhoft and Schuster, 2002; McConnell and Edwards, 2008)[65, 66]

Ice cores from Greenland show rising levels of cadmium and lead from the early years of the Industrial Revolution, but also recently declining levels, reflecting control efforts. Cadmium levels peaked in 1947, and lead peaked in 1951. Deposited levels of both metals in 2000 were down about 90 percent from twentieth century peaks.[67] Ice cores from glaciers in Wyoming show that airborne mercury peaked in 1978 and dropped more than 50 percent by 1993.[68] Metal depositions in Greenland and Wyoming reflect declining metal emissions from the US and Europe, while emissions from Asia or other regions may still be on the rise. Note that airborne levels of cadmium, lead, and mercury as measured in Greenland and Wyoming ice cores roughly follow the inverted U-shape of an Environmental Kuznets Curve.

Concerns about synthetic pesticide and chemical pollution in the environment and consumer goods are common today. Rachel Carson warned in 1962:

> For the first time in the history of the world, every human being is now subjected to contact with dangerous chemicals from the moment of conception until death.[69]

Chemicals are indeed an integral part of modern society, used in pharmaceuticals, foods, cosmetics, apparel, agriculture, and a wide range of materials and industrial processes. Use of fertilizer and pesticides played a major role in the doubling of global grain production during the last 40 years. Between 1960 and 1995, global use of nitrogen fertilizer grew sevenfold, and pesticide production tripled.[70] Today's chemical industry converts petroleum, natural gas, metals, and minerals into synthetic products, about 80 percent of which are plastics, comprising over five trillion dollars in sales in 2013.[71] But despite fears about health issues from rising chemical use, human lifespan, nutrition, and quality of life continue to improve for most of society. Age- and smoking-adjusted cancer rates are flat or falling. We'll discuss pesticides again in Chapter 8 and chemicals in Chapter 9.

In 1974, Dr. Mario Molina and Dr. Sherwood Rowland of the University of California asserted that chlorofluorocarbon (CFC) pollution from industry was destroying the ozone layer in Earth's stratosphere.[72] CFCs include Freon gases that were used in refrigerators, insulating foams, and hair spray. Molina and Rowland received a Noble Prize in Chemistry in 1995 for their work. In 1983, three researchers at the British Antarctic Survey discovered a thinning of the ozone layer over Antarctica, which became known as the ozone hole. They published a paper in 1985, reporting that ozone concentrations over Antarctica had been declining since 1957.[73] Their observations appeared to confirm the work of Molina and Rowland. Scientists feared that a depleted ozone layer would increase rates of cataracts, skin cancer, and immune system problems in humans.[74]

In September 1987, 29 nations and the EC signed the Montreal Protocol on Substances that Deplete the Ozone Layer, agreeing to ban use of CFCs. Over the next decade, the Protocol was universally signed by 197 parties, and global consumption of ozone depleting substances (ODS) dropped more than 80 percent. The Montreal Protocol was hailed by many as an international success in resolving a major environmental issue. But despite the global elimination of CFCs, the ozone hole has been slow to disappear.

The rising wealth of developed nations stimulated investment toward improving the environment. According to Organization for Economic Cooperation and Development data, developed nations spend between 0.4 and 2.1 percent of GDP on pollution abatement and control. Pollution control spending levels

# Maybe...and Maybe Not!

"A thinner ozone layer allows more ultraviolet radiation to strike the earth's surface and all living things on or near the surface.... In Patagonia, hunters now report finding blind rabbits; fishermen catch blind salmon."
—Al Gore, *Earth in the Balance*, 1992[75]

## Did We Really Save the Ozone Layer?

The ozone layer, which contains 90 percent of the ozone in the atmosphere, is located in the stratosphere, between 10 and 40 kilometers (6 and 25 miles) above Earth's surface. The ozone layer is known to block ultraviolet rays, shielding the surface of the Earth from high-energy radiation.

The theory of Molina and Rowland asserts that, over a period of years, human-produced CFCs migrate upward through the atmosphere to the stratosphere, where ultraviolet radiation breaks down CFC molecules, releasing chlorine atoms. Chlorine then reacts with ozone as a catalyst, breaking down ozone molecules into oxygen and reducing the ozone concentration.[76] According to the theory, the more CFCs used, the greater the destruction to stratospheric ozone.

The World Meteorological Organization, the EPA, and other groups warn of dangers from a thinner ozone layer and higher levels of ultraviolet radiation. But no harmful effects on human or biological populations have appeared. There is no evidence of blind rabbits or blind salmon, as some have claimed.

Since 1986, world consumption of ozone depleting substances (ODS) is down more than 99 percent, but the ozone hole area over Antarctica has not disappeared.[77] Scientists assert that the levels of free chlorine atoms in the stratosphere remain high, and that it will take until after year 2040 for the hole to disappear.[78] But it remains an open question whether the ozone hole is dominated by human CFC emissions or natural factors.

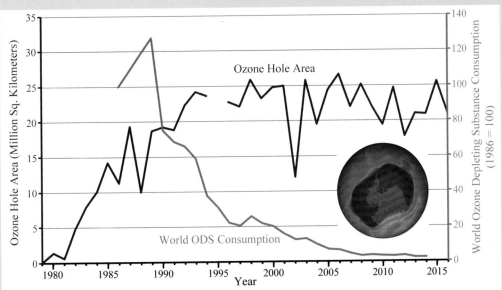

**Ozone Hole Area and World Ozone Depleting Substance Consumption 1979–2016.** Ozone hole mean area between September 7 and October 13 shown from 1979 to 2016, excepting year 1995. Estimated world consumption of ozone depleting substances shown from 1986 to 2014 compared to the 1986 base year (1986=100). False-color image of the record hole above Antarctica on September 24, 2006. (NASA, 2016; EEA 2016)[79]

for the latest year in the 2002-2005 period were Australia ($1.5 billion, 0.4 percent of GDP), Canada ($8.9 billion, 1.2 percent of GDP), Germany ($38.5 billion, 1.6 percent of GDP), United Kingdom ($28.8 billion, 0.6 percent of GDP), and the United States ($45.8 billion, 0.4 percent of GDP).[80] As GDP rises, both national and per person expenditures on pollution control rise as well. Developing nations are behind, but catching up fast. Scrubbers for power plant exhaust, automobile catalytic converters, water treatment plants, and other modern control technologies are being adopted by emerging nations at an earlier point in their economic growth than occurred in the developed nations.

The discussion so far this chapter has been about real pollution. Real pollutants include exhaust, effluents, and waste from processes that can be harmful to humans or that can damage the environment. But what about carbon dioxide, the gas blamed for causing dangerous global warming?

## THE DEMONIZATION OF CARBON DIOXIDE

One of the most absurd aspects of sustainable development and the modern environmental movement is the assertion that carbon dioxide ($CO_2$) is "dirty" and a pollutant. The city of Evanston, Illinois, promotes its annual Bike to Work Week, and warns that "dirty carbon dioxide emissions come out of the tailpipe" of your automobile.[81] A website at University College London promotes using hydrogen fuel cells in cars "rather than using 'dirty' carbon dioxide-emitting petrol in engines."[82] HOK, a global architectural design firm, promotes an algae bioreactor that can "process dirty carbon dioxide on the site and turn it into clean oxygen and energy."[83]

Because carbon dioxide has been declared dirty, fuels that emit $CO_2$ when burned, such as coal, oil, and natural gas, are deemed to be dirty. Former Vice President Al Gore's website advises:

**How To Use $CO_2$
When Growing Marijuana**
"Plant growth can be accelerated by increasing the $CO_2$ levels in your growing area."
—Dr. Who, *The Weed Blog*,
February 29, 2012[84]

"The answer to our climate, energy and economic challenges does not lie in burning more dirty fossil fuels—instead, we must continue to press for much more rapid development of renewable energy and energy efficient technologies and cuts in the pollution that causes global warming."[85]

Senator Harry Reid from Nevada agrees:

The future of energy in Nevada lies with our ability to develop our solar, wind and geothermal resources and rid ourselves of our dependence on dirty fossil fuels.[86]

On December 7, 2009, the EPA declared carbon dioxide emitted from industry to be a pollutant under the Clean Air Act. The United Nations and the European Community also describe carbon dioxide emissions as pollution. But what makes $CO_2$ a pollutant? Carbon dioxide is not toxic and is harmless to humans at low concentrations. Humans inhale only a trace of $CO_2$, but since we produce $CO_2$ as our bodies burn sugars, we exhale one hundred times the atmospheric level of $CO_2$ with each breath. Levels of $CO_2$ in crowded business conference rooms typically rise 2–3 times above the 400 parts per million (ppm) in today's atmosphere, without any negative health effects. Geologists tell us that atmospheric levels of $CO_2$ were more than 2,000 ppm during an ice age in Earth's distant past.[87]

In fact, the "dirty" and "pollutant" labels for carbon dioxide are very much undeserved. Carbon dioxide is a harmless, odorless, invisible gas that, along with water and oxygen, is one of the three essential building blocks for life on Earth. Carbon dioxide is plant food, a primary ingredient in photosynthesis. Plants use energy from sunlight to convert water and $CO_2$ to produce carbohydrates and biomass. Hundreds of peer-reviewed studies show that increased levels of atmospheric carbon dioxide produce increased rates of plant

**Pine Tree Growth and $CO_2$.** Dr. Sherwood Idso next to pine trees grown with different levels of atmospheric carbon dioxide, from 385 to 835 parts per million. (Idso, 1989)[88]

growth. With more $CO_2$ in the air, plants grow taller, get larger leaves, grow bigger root systems, and produce larger fruits and vegetables. Carbon dioxide is green and great for the biosphere.

In 2011, Dr. Craig Idso of the Center for the Study of Carbon Dioxide and Global Change, compiled the results of more than 1,000 scientific papers reporting on $CO_2$ enrichment experiments. He developed estimates of the mean crop rate growth in response to a 300-ppm increase in atmospheric $CO_2$. All 92 of the world's top food crops grew larger with increased levels of $CO_2$. The seven largest food crops, sugar cane, maize, rice, wheat, potatoes, sugar beets, and soybeans, showed average biomass increases of between 21 and 66 percent in controlled experiments.[89]

In 2013, a team of scientists, led by Dr. Randall Donahue at Australia's Commonwealth Scientific and Industrial Research Organization, analyzed plant growth in warm arid regions using satellite data. After accounting for changes in precipitation, the team found an eleven percent increase in green foliage from 1982–2010 across the world that they attributed to rising levels of atmospheric $CO_2$.[90] Increased atmospheric levels of $CO_2$ have been a significant contributor to rising levels of world agricultural output over the last 50 years. Yet today, every company and university measures its carbon footprint and foolishly strives to reduce greenhouse gas emissions.

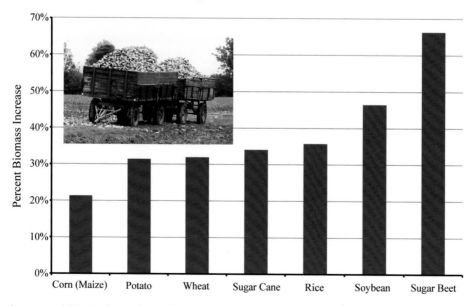

**Increased Food Crop Growth from Increased $CO_2$.** Average percentage biomass increase from an additional 300 parts per million of atmospheric $CO_2$ concentration for seven top world food crops. Image of a sugar beet harvest in Germany. (Idso, 2011)[91]

But what about global warming? Isn't carbon dioxide a pollutant because it causes dangerous warming of Earth's climate? Next chapter is devoted to the failing theory of human-caused climate change, but another comment on the silly logic of "carbon dioxide pollution" is needed here. Water vapor, not $CO_2$, is Earth's dominant greenhouse gas. Combustion of fuel by industrial processes releases not only carbon dioxide, but also water vapor. For example, burning methane, or natural gas, releases two water vapor molecules for each molecule of $CO_2$. Since water produced by human industry adds to Earth's greenhouse effect, by the absurd logic of the EPA we should also label water a pollutant. Companies who believe in man-made warming should also be measuring their dirty water vapor footprint.

**LOGIC FOR CHILDREN?**

Wash Your Hands!
Brush Your Teeth!
Never Emit Dirty $CO_2$!

## WASTE NOT, WANT NOT

In August 1955, *Life Magazine* published an article titled "Throwaway Living," first using the term "throw-away society" to describe consumerism in our modern age.[92] CBS News Correspondent Andy Rooney lamented in 2002 that Americans generate too much trash:

> We're running out of places to dump things. We spent all that money getting to the moon, and we aren't doing anything with that. Maybe we could ship our junk up there. We can end up throwing away the whole Earth.[93]

Achim Steiner, Executive Director of the United Nations Environment Programme, has talked about the urgent need "to move from a throw-away society and towards a resource-efficient society."[94] Many people today have the impression that accumulating solid waste is a major problem.

We generate large amounts of solid waste, in the following amounts. About half of all solid waste is agricultural waste, such as crop residues and animal manure, which is generally recycled on farms where produced. About one-third of all waste is industrial waste, produced by mining, manufacturing and construction.

Monsters University
*"Fame and Fortune Through Scaring"*

"I think the odds are no better than fifty-fifty that our present civilisation on Earth will survive to the end of the present century."
—Sir Martin Rees, Professor, University of Cambridge, 2003[95]

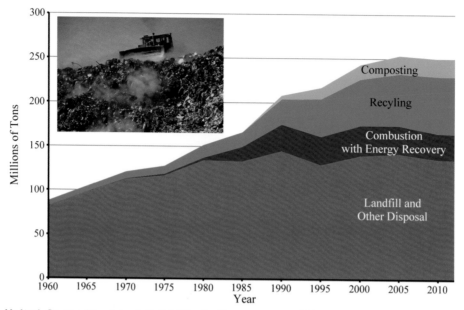

**United States Municipal Solid Waste Management, 1960–2012.** Flattening waste management trends by landfill, combustion with energy recovery, recycling, and composting. Landfill includes incineration without energy recovery. Composting does not include backyard compost. Image of Fresh Kills landfill in New York City, 1973. (EPA, 2014)[96]

Advanced nations generally require industrial waste to be recycled, destroyed, or disposed of in private landfills or deep-injection wells. The final one-sixth is the "throw-away" waste from households, municipal solid waste, which is processed by recycling, composting, incineration, and landfill.

According to the EPA, municipal solid waste generated in the United States increased from about 88 million tons in 1960 to 251 million tons in 2012. Trash generated each day increased from about 2.7 pounds per person in 1960 to 4.4 pounds per person in 2012.[97] At first glance this looks like a mounting problem. But waste handling in the US and other advanced nations is actually a good-news story.

The amount of municipal waste recovered is rising faster than waste is being generated. US recycling increased from 6.4 percent of waste in 1960 to 26.0 percent in 2012. Composting and combustion with energy recovery increased from negligible amounts in 1960 to 8.5 percent and 11.7 percent in 2012, respectively. Total US waste recovered by recycling, composting, and combustion with energy recovery has risen from 6.4 percent in 1960 to 46.2 percent in 2012. As a result, the amount of waste deposited in landfills peaked in 1990 and has been slowly declining for more than 20 years. Total US solid waste generated also peaked in 2005 and has entered a slow decline. The amount of solid waste generated per US resident also peaked in 2000 and has begun to decline.[98]

Europe's waste management efforts are improving as well. The 501 million people in Europe (EU-27 countries) in 2012 produced 245 million metric tons (270 million US tons) of municipal solid waste. Europe's total generated waste per person peaked in 2002. Recycling handled 26.8 percent of Europe's waste in 2012, about the same percentage as the US.[99] More than 60 percent of municipal waste is now recycled in Austria and the Netherlands.[100] Each European resident generates only two-thirds of the waste of a US resident. In the logic of sustainable development, Americans are guilty of the sin of profligate overconsumption.

As we learn to capture and reuse materials of all kinds, recycling has become a growth industry. In 2012, 65 percent of US paper was recycled, up from just 17 percent in 1960. Twenty-eight percent of glass, 34 percent of metal, and 9 percent of plastic were recycled in 2012, all increased by more than a factor of ten since 1960.[101] The trend of increasing recycling is likely to continue.

Many environmentalists are concerned about landfill trash, but modern landfills are designed to accept waste with a minimum of environmental impact. Sanitary landfills include a waterproof lining to prevent leaching of chemicals into underground water aquifers. Trash and garbage are crushed each day and covered with earth to reduce smell and litter and prevent the growth of vermin and insect populations.

Are we running out of landfill space? It may be in short supply in some municipal locations or small nations, but overall we have no shortage. It has been estimated that, at current rates, all US municipal waste for the next 1,000 years could fit in a landfill 300 feet tall and 30 miles on a side. Compaction could reduce this volume by more than half.[102]

With technological advances, today's landfills may even become resource caches in the future. Today, methane (natural gas) is recovered from landfills and used as fuel for industry. The day may come when catalysts are injected into old landfills to recover usable industrial materials.

Plastic waste accumulating in the ocean is a growing problem. The inert quality that makes plastic an excellent material for packaging also causes plastic litter to persist in the environment. Society needs technological solutions to this problem. We'll discuss this in Chapter 9.

In summary, trends show that modern methods for handling urban solid waste are effective and safe for people, without polluting the environment. Landfills in developed nations are environmentally safe depositories and, in most cases, landfill space is not limited. Recycling rates are rising, and total urban waste generation appears to have plateaued and is falling in the US, Europe, and other developed nations. Waste handling in developing nations can be expected to improve as income levels rise and modern methods are adopted.

## GOVERNMENT ALARM ABOUT AIR POLLUTION

Public health is serious business. Many people fear that unseen pollutants cause harm. It's important that government officials carefully consider risks from pollution and implement sound policies to limit health risks without imposing needless economic hardships upon citizens and businesses.

Earlier in the chapter, we cited a few of many headlines claiming that thousands of people are dying from air pollution in developed nations. The Environmental Protection Agency, the American Heart Association, the American Lung Association, the British Heart Foundation, the World Health Organization, the European Environment Agency, and other organizations warn that air pollution causes premature death. But the medical evidence for air pollution-caused premature death in modern nations is highly questionable.

The blamed culprit is small-particle pollution, $PM_{2.5}$. The EPA and other organizations assert that *any* level of small particles can cause premature death. The EPA claims that death from particle pollution may be short term, occurring within a few hours of inhalation, or caused by long-term inhalation of $PM_{2.5}$ over several years.[103] Amanda Brown, EPA policy analyst, stated that between 130,000 and 320,000 Americans died prematurely in 2005 due to small-particle pollution, or an incredible 6 to 15 percent of total US deaths.[104]

The EPA claims that particle pollution triggers heart failure, respiratory failure, and other causes of death. For example, suppose Bill is a senior citizen with a weak heart. He dies a few days before his 66th birthday, and the coroner determines the cause of death to be heart failure. But according to the EPA, Bill's death may have been "premature" and caused by small-particle air pollution. It's clear that very high concentrations of airborne smoke and soot can cause health problems and death. The 1952 Great Smog of

"Particulate matter causes premature death. It doesn't make you sick. It's directly causal to dying sooner than you should."
—Lisa Jackson,
EPA Administrator, 2011
Congressional testimony[105]

London killed thousands. But smoke and high particulate levels have been eliminated from outdoor air over today's developed nations.

In contrast, indoor air pollution remains a serious problem in many parts of the developing world. According to the World Health Organization (WHO), three billion people cook and heat homes with open fire, burning wood, charcoal, animal dung, crop waste, and coal. These people do not have access to electricity and modern cooking fuels. WHO estimates that 4.3 million people die prematurely each year from illnesses due to household air pollution from open indoor fires.[106]

But these killer indoor pollution levels are much higher than levels in ambient air over developed nations. Dr. Christopher Olopade of the University of Chicago measured air quality in 100 homes in Nigeria that used indoor fires. He found average airborne $PM_{2.5}$ levels of 1,800 micrograms per cubic meter during cooking. This is more than 100 times higher than the EPA outdoor average $PM_{2.5}$ limit of 15 micrograms per cubic meter ($\mu g/m^3$).[107]

Nigerian woman cooking indoors using biomass. (Olopade, 2014)[108]

Fifteen micrograms of particles per cubic meter of air isn't very much. Dr. James Enstrom, retired professor of the UCLA School of Public Health estimates that, at this level, the average person would inhale less than one teaspoon of microscopic small particles over an 80-year lifetime.[109] How does the EPA conclude that these low levels of particle pollution annually cause tens of thousands of premature US deaths? Further, how does the EPA conclude that inhalation of small particles can cause death within hours of inhalation? Few coroner reports attribute death to air pollution and none assign the cause of death to particle pollution. Instead, the EPA uses statistical associations from epidemiological studies to conclude that small-particle pollution is killing Americans.

A number of epidemiological observational studies have concluded that an association exists between $PM_{2.5}$ particulate pollution and premature death. Most often cited are the Harvard Six Cities study of 1993 and the American Cancer Society (ACS) study of 1995. The Six Cities research was a study of 8,111 adults in six US cities between 1979 and 1991.[110] The ACS research was a nationwide study of 552,138 adults in 151 US metropolitan areas between 1980 and 1989.[111] These studies looked at death rates from heart disease, lung disease, and other mortality associated with measured levels of airborne particles for the analyzed populations.

From the Six Cities study, Dr. Douglas Dockery and others concluded:

Although the effects of other unmeasured risk factors cannot be excluded with certainty, these results suggest that fine-particulate air pollution, or a more complex pollution mixture associated with fine particulate matter, contributes to excess mortality in certain US cities.[112]

The ACS study conducted by Dr. Arden Pope and others found that "particulate air pollution was associated with cardiopulmonary and lung cancer mortality."[113]

The EPA uses results from epidemiological studies to justify the benefits of new air pollution regulations compared to economic costs, as required by law. They take a small level of increased risk of mortality, assign a multi-million-dollar cost to each premature death, and multiply by the large US population. The 2012 EPA Regulatory Impact Analysis estimated that reducing ambient particulate concentrations from the current annual standard of 15 $\mu g/m^3$ to 11 $\mu g/m^3$ would deliver health benefits of $11 billion to $29 billion by 2020. Ninety-eight percent of the benefit was due to avoidance of early death.[114]

At first glance, the Six Cities, ACS, and other studies provide evidence that particle pollution causes premature death. But a closer look calls such conclusions into question. Epidemiological studies often find associations that are not causes. Confounding factors such as age, sex, personal health status, metropolitan or geographic location, and other factors can produce the apparent association, rather than particle pollution. Some studies have tried to adjust for as many as 44 confounding factors.[115] People older than 60 years of age account for most deaths. Hard-to-measure factors, such as incidents of stressful exercise or failure to take daily medicine, can skew results for senior citizen deaths.

Small levels of relative risk characterize studies that find premature death from $PM_{2.5}$. The Six Cities study found a relative risk of 1.26 and the ACS study found a relative risk of 1.15–1.17 for each 10 micrograms per cubic meter increase in $PM_{2.5}$.[116] This means about a 20 percent increase in risk for populations exposed to particle pollution compared to populations that are not exposed. A relative risk of 1.2 is so small that it can easily be caused by confounding factors or even by random chance. This is far below the relative risk level of 2.0, a doubling of risk, that is the limit for accepting an association as causal in federal court. No epidemiological studies show a doubling of relative risk from particle pollution at ambient levels in developed nations.

## Epidemiological Studies

Epidemiology is the field of public health that examines the cause of disease in human populations. The purpose of epidemiology is to understand causation in groups of individuals in order to better prevent or cure disease. Epidemiology assumes that disease is not distributed randomly in populations, but that individuals exposed to certain agents are at increased risk of contracting particular diseases.[117]

Epidemiological studies analyze statistical associations between exposure to an agent and appearance of a disease in a population. They are observational studies, not experimental studies. Experimental studies typically use randomized clinical trials between exposed and control groups to determine the relationship between an agent and a health outcome. But when an agent's effects may be harmful, researchers cannot knowingly expose people to the agent. In this case, epidemiological studies are used to observe populations to determine if exposure to the agent is associated with the disease.[118]

A measure of association between an agent and a disease is the relative risk (RR), which is the ratio of the disease incidence rate in exposed individuals to the rate in unexposed individuals. For example, Richard Doll and Bradford Hill observed a population of 41,000 British medical doctors in the 1950s and analyzed the association between smoking and deaths from lung cancer. They found that physicians that smoked 10 to 20 cigarettes per day suffered a lung cancer mortality rate that was about 10 times higher than non-smoking physicians, or a RR=10.[119] A RR of 1.0 would indicate no association. A relative risk of 2.0 implies a doubling of deaths for those exposed to the agent.

An identified association is not necessarily evidence of causation. Estimation of whether a study has found an association that is causal depends on the strength of the association (the size of the RR), the limitations of the study (bias and possible errors), confounding factors that might be an alternative cause for the result, evidence of a dose-response effect, whether the study can be duplicated, and a physiological theory that supports the association.

All epidemiological studies have flaws. The Achilles' heel of observational studies is the effect of confounding factors other than the agent that might produce the apparent association. In the case of premature mortality from particle air pollution, smoking, employment status, age, race, sex, size of community, geographic location, and many other confounding factors may be the cause of the results, rather than pollution. Researchers use statistical techniques to try to remove the effects of confounding factors.

The size of the relative risk measures the strength of the association and is often a key measure of whether an association is causal. The RR of 10 in the case of cigarette smoking was large enough to make it unlikely that other factors could cause the association. For a relative risk as low as 1.2, confounding factors and even random occurrences could produce an association, rather than the agent under test. The Reference Manual on Scientific Evidence, published by the Federal Judicial Center, points out that the legal standard for causation should be at least a doubling of risk, or an RR of 2.0:

> ... when there is group-based evidence finding that exposure to an agent causes an incidence of disease in the exposed group that is more than twice the incidence in the unexposed group, the evidence is sufficient to satisfy the plaintiff's burden of production and permit submission of specific causation to a jury.[120]

Other studies show no increased risk from particle pollution. A 2009 reanalysis of the ACS data by the Health Effects Institute lowered the all-cause relative risk to only 1.03, an all but negligible 3 percent increase in relative risk.[121] In 2005, James Enstrom published a study on mortality and particle pollution for 49,975 elderly citizens in California, a state with higher levels of $PM_{2.5}$ than most other states. The study found a relative risk of 1.04 from 1973-1982 and a risk of 1.00 (no association) from 1983-2002.[122] The EPA tends to ignore studies that do not find a particle association with death.

Short-term premature death should be apparent, not something that is purely statistical. Medical investigations showing that individuals died from inhalation of today's levels of particle pollution *do not exist*. Statistical studies do not connect individual mortality to the level of airborne particles that each person actually inhaled.

Nor do statistical studies account for indoor air. $PM_{2.5}$ levels inside buildings or vehicles may be higher or lower than outdoor levels. One person may spend more time indoors or in his car compared to another person. People typically live in one location and drive to work at another location. Epidemiological studies are unable to account for these factors.

In addition to the thinness of the association, there are two major issues that call into question the validity of research that has found premature death from particle pollution. First, most of this research has been paid for by the EPA or other government environmental organizations in the US or Europe. The EPA funds small-particle pollution studies either directly, or provides funding to the American Heart Association, the American Lung Association (ALA), or other organizations, which then sponsor such research. Over the last decade, the EPA provided more than $20 million in grants to the ALA.[123] Funded studies of the ALA and other groups find associations between particle pollution and mortality, thereby providing evidence to support tighter EPA pollution regulations.

**Senators Vote to Block EPA's Use of "Secret Science"**

"EPA has a long history of relying on science that was not created by the agency itself. This often means that the science is not available to the public, and therefore cannot be reproduced and verified."
—Senator John Barrasso, *The Hill*, April 28, 2015[124]

Second, data from many of the key studies that the EPA relies on have not been publicly released. Data from the Harvard Six Cities and the American Cancer Society studies have not been made public. Both studies are controversial for a number of methodological reasons. But the EPA refuses to release or to compel the release of data so that the studies can be checked by other researchers, in effect asking Americans to "trust us" on the assertion that $PM_{2.5}$ causes premature death.

Does inhalation of small-particle pollution cause premature death? In the case of very high levels of indoor pollution from open fires in poor nations, the answer may be yes. But it is doubtful that tens of thousands are dying in the US and Europe from today's outdoor low particle pollution levels, despite claims by the EPA and environmental organizations.

## PROGRESS BY BUSINESS

In a 2007 survey of 2,687 Chief Executive Officers by consulting firm McKinsey & Company, 65 percent thought that large corporations were "polluting, damaging the environment."[125] But over the last century, businesses have made remarkable strides to reduce pollution and improve waste recycling. Impressive environmental gains in transportation, automobiles, electronics, steel, and petroleum are worthy of discussion.

The Stockton and Darlington railway, the world's first steam-powered railroad, began operations in Britain in 1825. Early coal-burning steam locomotives were notorious for belching large quantities of smoke and soot onto rail passengers and local communities alike. A local resident complained to the *Leads Intelligencer* in 1831:

On the very line of this railway, I have built a comfortable house; it enjoys a pleasing view of the country. Now judge, my friend, of my mortification, whilst I am sitting comfortably at breakfast with my family, enjoying the purity of the summer air, in moment my dwelling, once consecrated to peace and retirement, is filled with dense smoke and foetid gas; my homely, though cleanly, table covered with dirt; and the features of my wife and family almost obscured by a polluted atmosphere.[126]

Postcard image of the San Juan Express, a narrow-guage passenger train operating in Colorado between 1937 and 1951.[128]

The good news is that emissions from today's diesel railway engines are down more than 90 percent since 1970 according to the EPA, and probably down 99.9 percent since the first steam locomotives of the 1800s.[127]

Emissions from today's highway vehicles exhaust a tiny fraction of past emissions. The adoption of unleaded gasoline, catalytic converters, and clean-burning engines have all but eliminated emissions of real pollutants (not carbon dioxide) from today's vehicles. The EPA reports that 2015 vehicles emit 99 percent less common pollutants (hydrocarbons, carbon monoxide, nitrogen oxides, and particles) than vehicles manufactured in 1970. Volatile organic compound (VOC) emissions, which react with sunlight to produce ozone, are down more than 90 percent from 1970 vehicles.[129]

Business today is heavily committed to product recycling, with the automobile and electronics industries two notable examples. In the 1960s, automobile shredders were invented, leading to a robust car recycling industry. About 86 percent of the materials are recycled from today's end-of-life vehicles.[130] Complex electronics products are also increasingly recycled. Hewlett-Packard operates company-owned recycling factories and has take-back programs in more than 70 countries.[131] Dell operates global recycling programs and takes back its old computers at no charge in most locations.[132]

The making of smoke was once an integral part of the making of iron and steel. In the early twentieth century, steel mills in Pittsburgh in the US, Birmingham in England, and Essen in Germany exhausted large amounts of combustion products from furnaces. But the addition of dust catchers, equipment to capture exhaust gases, and use of advanced furnaces has reduced emitted pollutants to a tiny fraction of past levels.

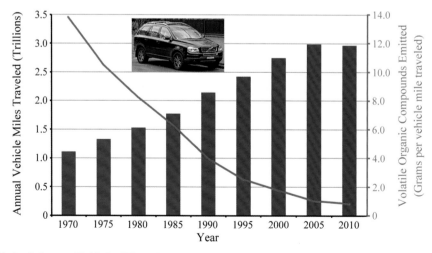

**United States Vehicle Miles Traveled and VOC Emissions 1970–2010.** Growing annual highway vehicle miles traveled (blue bars) and declining volatile organic compounds emitted from highway vehicles in grams per vehicle mile (red curve). (EPA, Federal Highway Administration, 2014)[133]

Of course, business success in pollution reduction and recycling has been driven by government actions and pressure from environmental groups. Clean air and water and waste recycling regulations enacted by state, provincial, and nation governments mandated many of the improvements by businesses over the last 50 years. Nevertheless, the pollution-reduction achievements by business have been remarkable.

The 2010 Deepwater Horizon oil spill from the BP platform in the Gulf of Mexico was the largest accidental marine oil spill in history. The 4.9 million barrels of crude oil released into the ocean rivalled the 1991 deliberate release of oil into the Persian Gulf from Kuwait during the 1991 Gulf War.[134] The Deepwater Horizon blowout produced a public relations "black eye" for BP and the petroleum industry.

But the oil industry has also made tremendous strides to reduce environmental damage from operations. Both the number of petroleum spills and the volume of oil discharged from offshore extraction and petroleum transport have been declining since the 1970s due to improved technologies and operational procedures. During the last five years, there have been less than 2 major tanker oil spills per year, down from 24 spills per year during the decade of the 1970s.[135] Today's natural resource extraction companies restore mined lands after operations are completed, as required by law in developed nations. Air and water pollution from refineries is also well controlled, a vast improvement from past practices.

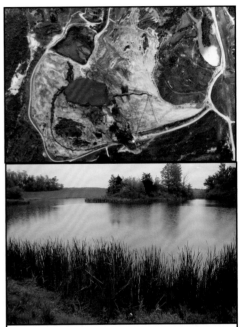

Beever Mine reclamation in Missouri 1988–2006. Top aerial image shows mine area in 1988 with red acidic pond. Bottom image shows restored area in 2006. (Missouri Dept. of Natural Resources, 2016)[136]

## POSITIVE POLLUTION TRENDS

The doctrine of sustainable development warns that humans are increasingly polluting our planet. But the evidence and trends show something else. Instead, humanity is making steady progress to reduce environmental damage, control pollution, and contain waste.

> **CAUTION: FAULTY LOGIC AHEAD**
>
> **Center for Biological Diversity Petitions EPA to List CO2 as a "Toxic Substance"**
> —*WattsUpWithThat*, June 30, 2015[137]

The air over developed nations is vastly cleaner, with airborne pollutants today only a small fraction of conditions 40 years ago. Concentrations of nitrogen and sulfur oxides, particulates, carbon monoxide, ozone, and heavy metals are declining. Ninety percent of the world's people today have access to clean drinking water, free of bacteria, viruses, and parasites that caused infectious diseases in the past. Water quality in the Great Lakes, the Rhine and Danube rivers, and other bodies of water in Europe and the US is slowly improving. Modern landfills safely contain discarded waste and recycling rates are rising.

Pollution remains a serious issue in the developing world, but we should have every expectation that environmental conditions will improve. Trends show that the Environmental Kuznets Curve, rather than the IPAT Equation, best describes environmental damage and the growth of nations. Nations handle their pollution problems as a normal course of societal development. The best way to reduce environmental damage is to boost the income of people, not to force a reduction in energy use or retard economic growth.

The claims of the EPA and environmental groups that thousands are dying in developed nations from small particle air pollution are shaky at best. Cited epidemiological studies produce associations at very low risk levels that should not be declared causal. Funding links and the practice of withholding of data call into question the validity of cited studies.

Carbon dioxide is not a pollutant. More than 1,000 empirical studies show that higher levels of atmospheric carbon dioxide produce significant increases in plant growth and better agricultural crop yields. But don't industrial emissions of $CO_2$ cause dangerous global warming? Let's examine this question in the next chapter.

# CHAPTER 5

# CLIMATE DELUSION

*"Scientists are saying this. Glaciers are falling down. Ecosystems are suffering. You can see the world's climate change because of two factors: one) man-made pollution, and number two) a huge, huge reliance that the world has on petroleum and fossil fuels."*

—NEW MEXICO GOVERNOR BILL RICHARDSON (2007)[1]

Fear of climate destruction is the third of the four Horsemen of sustainable development. Climatism, the belief that humans are causing dangerous global warming, has become the heart of today's environmental movement. Even if humanity is making steady progress controlling traditional air and water pollutants as we talked about last chapter, environmentalists point out that emissions of greenhouse gases continue to rise. With carbon dioxide branded a pollutant, green advocates argue that industry is destroying the planet. Unless we change our carbon-emitting ways, melting ice caps, flooding coastal cities, stronger hurricanes and storms, droughts and floods, killer heat waves, and dying polar bears will plague our future. But mounting evidence shows that climate change is dominated by natural forces, and that the effects of man-made emissions are probably insignificant.

## THE WORLD IN THE GRIP OF A MADNESS

Climatism is the greatest societal delusion in modern history. The United Nations established the Intergovernmental Panel on Climate Change (IPCC) in 1988, with the stated mission:

> …to provide the world with a clear scientific view on the current state of knowledge in climate change and its potential environmental and socio-economic impacts.[2]

In less than 20 years the world was captured by the fear that humans were destroying the climate.

By 2010, more than 190 heads of state said they believed that humanity was causing dangerous global warming. All of the world's major scientific organizations accepted the theory of human-caused climate change and recommend reductions in greenhouse gas emissions. Mayors of more than 80 of the world's largest cities, including Buenos Aires, Cairo, Houston, Paris, and Shanghai, joined the C40 Cities group, pledging to "address" climate change.[3] Leading universities bought in, including the presidents of 685 US colleges and universities who signed the Presidents' Climate Commitment, declaring, "We recognize the scientific consensus that global warming is real and is largely being caused by humans."[4] Leading faith-based organizations, such as the Catholic Church and many Protestant groups, concluded that God no longer controls Earth's climate, but that the descendents of Adam and Eve now determine global temperatures. Also, under pressure from our misguided society, business swallowed global warming ideology—hook, line, and sinker.

Carbon dioxide is produced by almost all human activity. Our agriculture, industry, transportation, lighting, heating, cooking, and even mowing the lawn produces greenhouse

**Monsters University**
*"Fame and Fortune Through Scaring"*

"When we consider the fate of the planet as a whole, we must be under no illusions as to what is at stake. Earth's average temperature is around 59°F, and whether we allow it to rise by a single degree or 5°F will decide the fate of hundreds of thousands of species, and most probably billions of people."
—Tim Flannery, Professor, Macquarie University, 2001[5]

gases. In the demand to move to a "low-carbon society," the Climatism movement seeks nothing less than the total transformation of modern civilization.

Leaders of developed nations call for an 80 percent reduction in greenhouse gas emissions by the year 2050. The goal of the Obama administration was an 83 percent emissions reduction by 2050 from 2005 levels.[7] This equates to a return to US emissions levels of 1870, before electricity, aircraft, automobiles, computers, air conditioning, washing machines, cell phones, and all other energy-using inventions common today. But this goal to return to a horse-and-buggy society is just the beginning. The G7 industrial nations now call for zero emissions by the year 2100, including the complete halt to the use of hydrocarbon fuels.[8]

Green crusaders have convinced governments to pass thousands of laws to reduce greenhouse gas emissions from agriculture, industry, transportation, and everyday living. In addition to mandates and subsidies to promote biofuel, solar, and wind energy, and to impair the use of coal, natural gas, and petroleum, countless other regulations now impact our daily lives. Bans on incandescent light

**ECO-INSIGHT?**

**Manicured Lawns Contribute to Global Warming by Producing Greenhouse Gases**
—*Tribune India*, January 18, 2015[6]

**Drinking The Green Cool-Ade**

**Ben & Jerry's "Save Our Swirled": Company Seeks To Raise Global Warming Awareness with New Flavor**
"Ahead of the United Nations climate change talks in Paris in December, Ben & Jerry has released its newest flavor that should help spark climate change interest from consumers.... 'We created a flavor to bring attention to this historic issue and to send out our own SOS for our planet,' company reps said....'"
—*HNGN*, June 1, 2015[9]

**ECO-INSIGHT?**

**Tepid Coffee Anyone? Europe Rules Percolators Must Shut Off After Five Minutes**
—*The Telegraph*, January 11, 2015[10]

bulbs, regulations promoting high-efficiency refrigerators, laundry, and other appliances, green building standards, fuel economy requirements for vehicles, mandates for smart electric meters, markets for carbon trading, and punitive carbon taxes have been enacted to fight climate change. Even your coffee percolator is now regulated. Vegetarianism, insect diets, bicycle riding, "buying locally," one-child families, electric cars, and mass transit are praised by Climatism as part of the solution to the alleged crisis.

Given the overwhelming public support for efforts to save the world from climate catastrophe, powerful science must support concerns that humanity is destroying Earth's climate. Let's briefly discuss the theory of human-caused global warming.

## THE THEORY OF GLOBAL WARMING

The theory of human-caused global warming is based on four principles. These are: 1) rising global surface temperature, 2) rising atmospheric carbon dioxide concentration, 3) the physics of Earth's greenhouse effect, and 4) projections of climate models.

Most scientists agree Earth warmed over the last century. The Climatic Research Unit at the University of East Anglia in the UK, regarded as the leading authority on global surface temperatures, shows a one degree temperature rise over the last 130 years, quantitatively about 0.8 degrees Celsius (°C) or 1.4 degrees Fahrenheit (°F).[11] In historical terms, this is a period of gentle warming, as we will discuss. But the IPCC asserts that this one degree rise is both abnormal and alarming. In its 2001 Third Assessment Report, the IPCC stated:

> … the increase in temperature in the 20th century is likely to have been the largest of any century during the past 1,000 years.[12]

Most scientists agree that atmospheric carbon dioxide levels have also been rising over the last century. Modern measurements of atmospheric $CO_2$ were first made in 1958 at the Mauna Loa Observatory on the island of Hawaii. At that time, scientists measured atmospheric $CO_2$ at 315 parts per million (ppm). By 2015, atmospheric carbon dioxide levels had reached 400 ppm at several global measuring stations.[13] Proponents of the theory of man-made warming say that carbon dioxide emissions from industry are causing this rise, enhancing Earth's greenhouse effect and causing global warming. Industry has certainly contributed to the rise in atmospheric $CO_2$, but the portion of the rise due to humans, and the warming affect of the rise, are disputed by many scientists.

The greenhouse effect is the theoretical basis for the hypothesis of man-made warming. Sunlight, which is high-energy radiation, enters Earth's atmosphere. Most of the sunlight not reflected by clouds passes through the atmosphere and is absorbed by Earth's surface. Like any warm body, Earth then emits lower energy infrared radiation not visible to our eyes. A small amount of the infrared radiation passes directly out to space, but most is absorbed by greenhouse gases in our atmosphere. These gases then re-radiate the infrared energy, causing Earth to warm. This warming is called the greenhouse effect. Scientists generally agree that absorption of infrared radiation by Earth's atmosphere raises global surface temperatures by over 30°C, compared to what temperatures would be if the atmosphere was not present.[14] Most scientists also agree that industrial emissions of greenhouse gases add to the greenhouse effect.

The fourth basis for the theory of man-made warming is projections by computer models. For the last 40 years, increasingly complex models, called General Circulation Models, have been run on supercomputers and used to model Earth's climate. These models use the laws of physics, past temperature and climate history, and lots of computing power

"... the death penalty is an appropriate punishment for influential GW deniers."
—Professor Richard Parncutt,
University of Graz, October, 25, 2012[15]

to estimate the future of global temperatures and weather. The models warn of a faster rise in temperatures during the twenty-first century, accelerating from the one degree rise during the twentieth century. In the IPCC's Fourth Assessment Report of 2007, the models predicted a rise of about 3°C (5.4°F) in global temperatures by 2100.[16]

The theory of human-caused global warming was plausible when originally developed in the 1980s. It was promoted from the start by the IPCC and the UN, environmental groups, well-meaning government officials, and favored industries, inducing world opinion to jump to acceptance in the early 1990s. But little empirical evidence actually supports the theory. Twenty-eight years after the establishment of the IPCC, it's now clear that nature is not cooperating with the warnings of Climatism.

## CLIMATE AND TEMPERATURE HISTORY

Climate and global temperatures have been changing for all of history. According to geologists, four ice ages dominated Earth's history over the last 400,000 years, each about 90,000 years in length. During these ice ages, much of the Northern Hemisphere was covered by a sheet of thick ice, including areas now occupied by London, New York, and Chicago. Each ice age was followed by a warm period about 15,000 years long. Surface temperature swings of 7–12 °C (12–22 °F) characterized the transition from ice ages to intervening warm periods and back again.[17] Our society today enjoys a warm period that began about 11,000 years ago.

**Swallowed By Smart People**

"Everyone understands climate change is occurring, and the people who oppose it are really hurting our children and our grandchildren and making the world a much worse place."
—Google Chairman Eric Schmidt, Sepember 22, 2014[18]

Earth's climate is dominated by long, medium, and short temperature cycles. Scientists believe that long-term cycles, called the Milankovich Cycles, caused the ice ages. The Milankovich Cycles are 20,000 to 100,000 years in length, thought to be driven by changes in the angle and precession of Earth's axis and the shape and inclination of Earth's orbit around the Sun.[19] Medium-length cycles about 1,500 years long are well-documented in Earth's temperature record since the last ice age. These medium-length cycles are characterized by warm ages such as the Roman Warm Period, when Roman soldiers conquered civilizations around the Mediterranean Sea. During the Medieval Warm Period from 900 to 1300 AD, Viking explorers settled southwest Greenland and founded a colony at Hvalsey, 600 years before the Jamestown colony. These warm periods are separated by cooler periods, such as the Little Ice Age, a naturally cooler age from about 1300 to 1850 AD. Medium-length temperature cycles show temperature changes of 1–2°C and are probably caused by variations in the radiation and magnetic field of the Sun.[20]

Since thermometer records only date back to the late 1800s, scientists instead use temperature proxies to estimate historic temperatures. Temperature proxies are physical or chemical processes that change along with temperature. Variation in the atomic composition of oxygen atoms in glacial ice and the changing width of tree rings are two proxies used to estimate past temperatures.

Our planet also experiences short-term temperature cycles, which are associated with Earth's oceans. The El Niño Southern Oscillation (ENSO) is an irregular cycle three to seven years in length in the Central Pacific Ocean that affects weather all over the world.[21] The ENSO contributes to the Pacific Decadal Oscillation (PDO), a powerful temperature cycle in the North Pacific Ocean that varies 1–2°C over a period of about

**LOGIC FOR CHILDREN?**

Climate Change is Real!

50 years.[22] Weather in Europe and the United States is shaped by the Atlantic Multidecadal Oscillation (AMO), a natural temperature cycle of the Atlantic Ocean.[23] Scientists understand that the ENSO, the PDO, the AMO, and other natural cycles have been operating

for thousands of years. The long-term, medium-term, and short-term cycles of Earth are natural factors, not caused by humans, and have little to do with greenhouse gas emissions.

The IPCC ignores the large body of evidence that documents past global temperature variation and past periods of warm temperatures. For one example, temperature reconstructions from ice cores in Greenland show that past temperatures were warmer than today during the Minoan Warm Period 3,300 years ago, the Roman Warm Period 2,000 years ago, and the Medieval Warm Period 1,000 years ago. Surface temperatures have risen over the last 300 years as we emerged from the Little Ice Age into our Modern Warm Period, but global temperatures have actually gradually declined for most of the last 8,000 years.[24]

Hundreds of peer-reviewed studies using temperature proxies from all over the world are collected on Craig Idso's excellent website, *CO2Science*.[25] Most of these studies show that temperatures during the Medieval Warm Period from 900-1300 AD were warmer than those of today.

The historic record shows many past periods of warm temperatures and many examples of large temperature rises. The rise and variation of twentieth century global temperatures can be fully explained by a natural rise in temperatures as we moved from the Little Ice Age to our current Modern Warm Period, combined with natural variation caused by

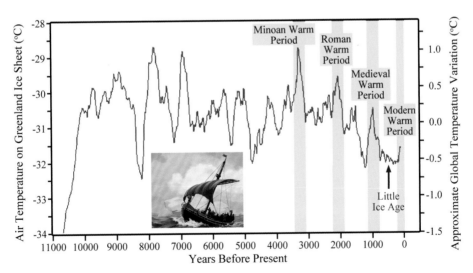

**Global Temperature Variation Over the Last 10,000 Years.** Surface air temperature variations estimated from changes in oxygen isotope ratios in Greenland ice cores. This record shows past warm periods including the Minoan Warm Period, the Roman Warm Period, the Medieval Warm Period, and our current Modern Warm Period, and also cooler periods such as the Little Ice Age. Image of Viking ship. (Alley, 2000; Climate4you, 2015)[26]

short-term temperature cycles such as the Pacific Decadal Oscillation, without any need for man-made warming causes.

## THE NATURAL GREENHOUSE EFFECT

Climate scientists today are *obsessed* with the level of carbon dioxide in the atmosphere. The Goddard Space Center of the National Aeronautic and Space Administration (NASA) states:

> Previously published research shows that a dangerous level of global warming will occur if carbon dioxide in the atmosphere exceeds a concentration of about 450 parts per million. That's equivalent to about a 61-percent increase from the pre-industrial level of 280 parts per million …[27]

The environmental group 350.org adds:

> We're taking millions of years worth of carbon, once stored beneath the earth as fossil fuels, and releasing it into the atmosphere.[28]

The theory of human-caused global warming is based on the simple idea that greenhouse gases emitted by industry are warming our planet dangerously. Rising atmospheric carbon dioxide levels are regarded as the primary indicator of a coming thermal apocalypse. But there are many holes in this theory.

There is little historical evidence that rising atmospheric $CO_2$ has ever caused global temperatures to rise. Ice core evidence shows that, over the last four ice ages, global temperatures rose first, followed by a rise in atmospheric $CO_2$ levels centuries later.[29] Scientists estimate that global temperature rise triggered a rise in atmospheric $CO_2$, probably released from the oceans. Geologists point out that, for much of Earth's history, atmospheric $CO_2$ levels were more than 2,000 ppm, more than five times today's atmospheric concentration, even during glacial periods.[30]

Carbon dioxide is a trace gas. Only four of every ten thousand molecules in our atmosphere are carbon dioxide. The amount of $CO_2$ that humans could have added in all of history totals only a fraction of one of those four molecules. The idea that one molecule in 10,000 can have more impact on changing global temperatures than the Sun, ocean cycles, and the effects of clouds and weather is doubtful.

Earth's most important greenhouse gas is not carbon dioxide. It's not methane. Earth's dominant greenhouse gas is water vapor. Scientists estimate that between 75 and 90 percent of Earth's greenhouse effect is caused by water vapor and clouds. Emissions of carbon dioxide from nature cause most of the remaining portion of Earth's greenhouse effect.[31] Human effects are yet smaller.

According to the IPCC's own carbon cycle model, oceans hold 50 times as much dissolved carbon dioxide as the atmosphere. Oceans continuously release $CO_2$ to the atmosphere and absorb $CO_2$ from the atmosphere. When plants die, they release $CO_2$. When plants grow, they absorb $CO_2$ as part of photosynthesis. Volcanoes above the surface of the ocean, and about ten times that number of volcanoes under the surface of the ocean, continuously release $CO_2$ and other gases into the environment. Every day, nature puts about 20 times as much carbon dioxide into the atmosphere as all of the industries of man.[32]

After accounting for the contributions of water vapor and emissions of carbon dioxide from nature, humans are responsible for only about one or two parts in one hundred of Earth's greenhouse effect. *Less than two percent.* If we shut down our industry and completely eliminate all emissions of greenhouse gases, the change in global temperatures would be too small to measure. The greenhouse effect is overwhelmingly dominated by natural factors.[33]

Scientists also generally agree that carbon dioxide, by itself, cannot cause dangerous global warming. The absorption of infrared radiation by carbon dioxide in our atmosphere, which causes the $CO_2$ portion of the greenhouse effect, is nonlinear. This means that the first 100 ppm of natural atmospheric $CO_2$ causes most of the warming effect. As more and more carbon dioxide is added, less warming occurs. Doubling of atmospheric $CO_2$ from the 280 ppm pre-industrial level to 560 ppm, from either human emissions or natural causes, will only increase global temperatures by about one degree Celsius. It would take another doubling of $CO_2$ concentration to increase temperatures by another degree.[34] So how do climate models reach their alarming conclusions? They assume additional warming from water vapor.

Dr. Syukuro Manabe, working at the Geophysical Fluid Dynamics Laboratory at the Environmental Science Services Administration, developed one of the early climate models in the 1960s. Since his early work, all major models assume a "positive feedback" from water vapor.[35] The idea is that, since warmer air can hold more moisture, atmospheric water vapor will increase as temperatures rise. Climate models assume that rising carbon dioxide enhances the greenhouse effect, causing a small rise in global surface temperatures, but triggering a rise in atmospheric water vapor. Since water vapor is a greenhouse gas, increasing water vapor is assumed to add additional greenhouse heating to that of $CO_2$.

Climate scientists use the term "climate sensitivity" to estimate how much global temperatures will rise from increasing atmospheric carbon dioxide. The IPCC defines climate sensitivity as the rise in mean global temperature for a doubling in atmospheric $CO_2$ concentration.[36] Of the 3°C average rise by 2100 projected by the IPCC's ensemble of climate models, 1.8°C, or 60 percent of the rise, is due to positive feedback from increased levels of atmospheric water vapor.

So is Earth's climate sensitive to a rise in carbon dioxide? Are rising atmospheric $CO_2$ levels causing a large water vapor feedback, boosting global temperatures? Mounting evidence shows that Earth's climate is not sensitive to rises in atmospheric carbon dioxide, and that the feared warming is not happening.

## THE FAILURE OF THE CLIMATE MODELS

For almost 20 years, the juggernaut of Climatism swept all in its path. From the formation of the IPCC in 1988, to the award of the Nobel Peace Prize jointly to the IPCC and Al Gore in December 2007, the theory of human-caused global warming grew to be almost universally accepted by scientists, political leaders, universities, businesses, and the public at large. But then a funny thing happened. The Earth stopped warming.

According to satellite and weather balloon data, there has been no statistically significant warming of Earth's lower atmosphere for the last 18 years, since 1997. Scientists are at a loss to explain the pause in global temperatures. Dr. Kevin Trenberth, IPCC Lead Author, commented in a disclosed 2009 e-mail:

> Well I have my own article on where the heck is global warming?… The fact is that we can't account for the lack of warming at the moment and it is a travesty that we can't.[37]

In its First Assessment Report in 1990, the IPCC forecasted a rise in global temperatures of 0.3°C per decade, based on model projections.[38] But that was about the time when the current warming trend stopped. According to Dr. John Christy of the University of Alabama, Huntsville, observations from four weather balloon data sets and two satellite data sets show recent flat global temperatures, in sharp contrast to the average projections of 102 climate models used by the IPCC. During the period of flat global temperatures from 1997 to 2014, atmospheric carbon dioxide levels rose about 10 percent, which should have forced higher global surface temperatures.[39] It's now clear that the climate models have exaggerated the effects of rising $CO_2$, and that we are not seeing catastrophic warming.

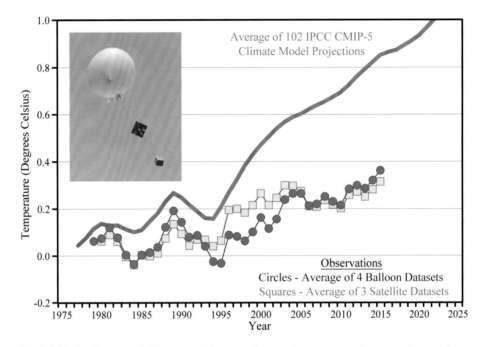

**Model Projections and Measured Temperatures.** An average of temperature projections of 102 CMIP-5 climate model runs used by the IPCC (red line) compared to actual lower atmosphere temperature measurements from weather balloons (blue circles) and satellites (green squares). Image of weather balloon. (Christy, 2016)[40]

So why are the climate models wrong? It appears that the error is the assumption of positive feedback from water vapor. Analyses of satellite data by Lindzen and Choi in 2011[41] and other studies conclude that climate system feedbacks are likely to be low or even negative, rather than positive. This means that changes to water vapor and clouds may act to *reduce* the warming effect from rising atmospheric carbon dioxide. The reason may be that rising temperatures create more clouds in tropical latitudes, boosting the reflection of sunlight and causing a cooling of Earth's surface, countering the effect of rising $CO_2$.

It seems that the models have made a "flea wagging the dog" assumption. Water vapor is part of Earth's water cycle, which encompasses all weather, the oceans, and Earth's ice caps. The forces involved in the water cycle are orders of magnitude greater than the smaller carbon cycle and carbon dioxide. The idea that changes in atmospheric levels of the trace gas carbon dioxide are controlling the weather and the water cycle is improbable. The assertion that mankind's relatively tiny $CO_2$ emissions measurably change the water cycle is even less likely.

Nevertheless, warnings from climate alarmists about coming melting ice caps, rapidly rising oceans, stronger hurricanes and storms, more severe droughts and floods, killer heat waves, vanishing snow, extinction of polar bears and other species, ocean acidification, and other calamities fill academic textbooks and frequent news headlines. But like the failure of the climate models to account for recent flat global temperatures, these predictions of climate-driven disaster have not come to pass. Let's review the evidence.

## SEA LEVEL, ICE CAPS, AND GLACIERS

In his 2006 best-selling book *An Inconvenient Truth*, former Vice President Al Gore states:

> We are melting the North Polar ice cap and virtually all of the mountain glaciers in the world. We are destabilizing the massive mound of ice on Greenland and the equally enormous mass of ice propped on top of islands in West Antarctica, threatening a worldwide increase in sea levels of as much as 20 feet.[42]

Dr. James Hansen, climate computer modeler and former head of the National Aeronautic and Space Administration (NASA) Goddard Institute for Space Studies, warned in 2015:

> Humanity faces near certainty of eventual sea level rise of…5–9 meters, if fossil fuel emissions continue on a business-as-usual course…[43]

Sea level rise is the greatest calamity projected by Climatism. According to Gore, Hansen, and others, rising global temperatures, driven by human emissions of greenhouse gases, threaten to melt Earth's ice caps, raise ocean levels, and flood coastal cities. A 20-foot rise in sea levels, should it occur, would indeed be a disaster, flooding major cities, such as Buenos Aires, Calcutta, Hong Kong, Karachi, Miami, New York, Shanghai, and Tokyo.

According to satellite data, arctic sea ice has been declining since 1979. North Pole sea ice reached 30-year minimums in 2007 and 2012. Dr. Guy Williams of the University of Tasmania calls Arctic sea ice around Greenland the "canary in the coal mine" and has declared the canary to be dead.[44] Williams and other scientists conclude that melting Arctic sea ice is an early indicator of the effects of man-made global warming.

Three things are important to know about Arctic sea ice. First, ice at Earth's North Pole floats entirely on the Arctic Ocean. Should the sea ice in the Arctic Ocean melt entirely, no significant rise in the world's ocean levels would be measured. Floating ice that melts does not raise water levels. You can do the experiment at home by measuring the water level in a glass of ice water before and after ice melt. Melting of ice sheets on the land masses of

Greenland and Antarctica would be necessary to raise global ocean levels.

Second, the volume of Arctic sea ice has varied in the past. Historical accounts of low North Pole sea ice are available from 1907, 1922, 1935, and other past periods. Arctic sea ice has expanded and receded throughout history. Third, Arctic ice is only 1–2 percent of Earth's ice. Climate scientists wring hands about shrinking Arctic sea ice, but conveniently forget to discuss Antarctic sea and land ice.

Antarctic ice, which is 90 percent of Earth's

"The slow thawing of the Arctic is given as a partial explanation for the record voyages of Soviet ice-breakers to northern latitudes, which have never before been reached by navigating vessels. The Sadko in 1935, in ice-free water of the North Kara Sea, steamed to 82 degrees, 42 minutes of northern latitude—an all-time record."
—*Launceston Examiner*, April 25, 1939[45]

ice, is growing. The same satellite data that shows shrinking North Pole sea ice shows that South Pole sea ice has been expanding for 30 years, reaching a 30-year maximum in 2015.[46] A look at a graph of combined Arctic and Antarctic sea ice shows large annual variation, but little change in total sea ice area.

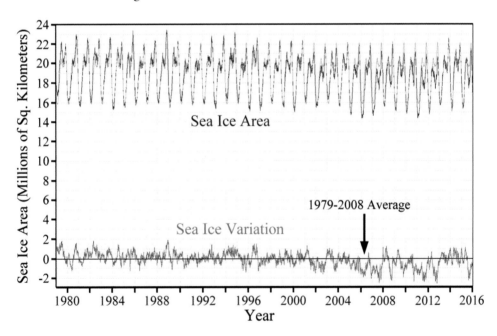

**Global Sea Ice Area 1979–2015.** Satellite data shows large annual variation in sea ice around the North and South Poles, but little change in total ice area. Total global sea ice area at the end of 2015 was near the 1979–2008 average. (University of Illinois, 2016)[47]

Antarctic temperatures in the lower atmosphere have been flat since 1979, as measured by satellites.[48] The Antarctic Peninsula has experienced some warming, but temperatures in most of Antarctica have been flat to cooling. The climate models cannot explain the failure of Antarctic temperatures to warm. The World Meteorological Organization points out that annual mean Antarctic surface temperatures are projected by models to increase by 0.2°C to 0.3°C per decade over the twenty-first century.[50] But it isn't happening.

Geodesic dome at the Amundsen-Scott South Pole Station. When built in 1975, the level of the snow was at the bottom of the open door. (National Science Foundation, 2010)[49]

**This Isn't the Warming You're Looking For**

**Global Warming Expedition to Prove Antarctic Ice is Melting Trapped by Ice**
Expedition leader Chris Turney: "One of the purposes of the expedition was to 'determine the extent to which human activity and pollution has directly impacted on this remote region of Antarctica.'"
—*FrontPageMag*, December 29, 2013; Image of icebreaker Polar Star, sent to rescue the trapped expedition.[51]

The United States has maintained a continuous scientific presence at the South Pole since the 1950s. Scientists today are housed in the Amundsen-Scott Scientific Station that was completed in 2008. The previous station, a black geodesic dome built in 1975, is half-buried in snow.

The South Pole is effectively a desert and gets little precipitation. But snow has accumulated for many years at the average rate of eight inches per year.[52] Temperatures are always below freezing, so the snow never melts. South Pole ice is getting thicker.

Are global ice caps shrinking? Earth's ice caps have become smaller over the last century as our planet emerged from the cold temperatures of the Little Ice Age. Greenland is an example. Greenland contains most of the last 8–9 percent of Earth's ice, with the very small remainder in mountain glaciers. Greenland ice has been thickening in the central plateau and shrinking on the edges of the continent, with a small net loss of ice in total. But there is little evidence that melting ice is due to emission of greenhouse gases, rather than natural temperature cycles.

Shrinking glaciers are frequently cited as evidence for man-made climate change. The environmental group Union of Concerned Scientists attributes melting glaciers to "early warning signs of global warming":

> There is widespread evidence that glaciers are retreating in many mountain areas of the world. Since 1850 the glaciers of the European Alps have lost about 30 to 40% of their surface area and about half of their volume … glaciers in the New Zealand Southern Alps have lost 25% of their area over the last 100 years …. Glaciers on Mt. Kenyan and Kilimanjaro have lost over 60% of their area in the last century …[53]

But the link to human emissions is weak at best. As Dr. Fred Singer, emeritus professor of George Mason University, points out, melting is evidence of warming, but not evidence that the warming is human-caused.[54] Global temperatures have increased 1–2°C since the depth of the Little Ice Age in year 1600, so glaciers should be receding.

The Mendenhall Glacier east of Juneau, Alaska, has been retreating since the 1800s. Global warming advocacy groups had long blamed human emissions for the glacier's retreat. In 2011, the activist group Del Mar Global Trust placed a large billboard in the Reagan International Airport that contrasted an 1894 image of a robust Mendenhall Glacier with an image of the much shrunken glacier in 2008.[55] The apparent message was that the world's glaciers were disappearing because of human-caused global warming.

The receding Mendenhall Glacier in Alaska has uncovered ancient forests from warmer eras. (Lowell, 2013)[56]

**STOP** **FALSCH**

## Not Just Wrong, Spectacularly Wrong!

**Grim Forecast**

"A senior environmental official at the United Nations, Noel Brown, says entire nations could be wiped off the face of the earth by rising sea levels if global warming is not reversed by the year 2000."
—*San Jose Mercury News,*
June 30, 1989[58]

But in 2013, researchers from the University of Alaska Southeast entered an ice cave under the Mendenhall Glacier and took some amazing photographs. They found logs and tree stumps under the glacier, with some of the stumps still standing in an upright position. The trees were carbon-dated to be about 1,000 years old.[57] One thousand years ago, during the Medieval Warm Period, a forest stood where the Mendenhall Glacier stands today, evidence of past warmer temperatures.

So what does all this mean for sea level rise? NASA points out that oceans have risen about 120 meters (390 feet) since the last ice age, 20,000 years ago.[59] Over the last 150 years, seas have risen at the rate of about seven to eight inches per century, according to tidal gauge observations.[60] No scientist can tell us when natural sea level rise stopped and man-made sea level rise began. But there is no empirical evidence for the coming 20-foot sea level rise that some have predicted.

## STORMS, FLOODS, AND DROUGHTS—OH MY!

One of the most absurd claims of Climatism is that storms, tornados, floods, and droughts are growing more numerous or extreme because of greenhouse gas emissions. In May 2014, the US Global Change Research Program released the report, "Climate Change Impacts in the United States." The report concludes that "evidence of human-caused climate change continues to strengthen and that impacts are increasing across the country." The 841-page report uses the word "extreme" more than 600 times to create an alarming picture of the future. It predicts that Americans are in for "extreme droughts," "extreme floods," "extreme rainfall," "extreme snowfall," "extreme winds," and other extremes, all caused from emissions. But the report is based largely on predictions from climate models and contains a remarkable lack of actual empirical data.[61]

At 11:30 PM on October 29, 2012, Hurricane Sandy struck the East Coast with Category 1 hurricane-force winds of 81 mph. It struck New Jersey and nearby New York City at high tide, causing extensive flooding. Sandy was a large hurricane, with tropical-force winds across a diameter of 1,000 miles when it came ashore, impacting 24 states. The storm resulted in 147 deaths in eight countries and over $50 billion in assessed damage.[62] Sandy was the costliest hurricane to hit the US since Hurricane Katrina hit New Orleans in 2005 and the deadliest hurricane to hit the US since Hurricane Agnes struck Florida in 1972.

A number of factors combined to make Sandy a special storm. Sandy's path had turned northeast, away from the US coast, as Atlantic hurricanes tend to do. But the combination of a high pressure area over the North Atlantic Ocean and an unusual path of the jet stream redirected the storm back toward the US, resulting in a direct hit on New Jersey. Sandy collided with a cold front coming from the west, which added energy to the storm, and made landfall at high tide, creating a major flooding event in nearby New York City.

The storm was christened "Superstorm Sandy" by the media and attributed to man-made climate change. Two days after the storm struck, Senator Bernie Sanders stated,

"Hurricane Sandy is a wake-up call for all Americans that we must act to reverse global warming."[63] President Barack Obama has said, "Climate change didn't cause Hurricane Sandy, but may have made it stronger."[64]

But this has happened before. In September 1821, the Norfolk and Long Island Hurricane came rampaging up the Eastern Seaboard. It hit New Jersey with Category 3 force winds, much stronger than the Category 1 winds of Sandy. Even though it struck New York City at low tide, when the ocean level was five feet lower than when Sandy hit, the 1821 storm flooded one-third of Manhattan Island up to Canal Street.[65] More than 80 tropical or sub-tropical storms have struck New York state during the last 300 years.

According to the National Hurricane Center, 170 hurricanes made US landfall during the twentieth century. Fifty-nine of these storms generated Category 3 or stronger wind speeds, much stronger than Category 1 Sandy.[66] How is it, when a single storm makes a direct hit on New York City, we have evidence of human-caused climate change?

In fact, during the last 50 years, a period when US temperatures were gently warming, hurricanes have grown less extreme. The number of hurricanes making landfall over the last century has been flat to declining. In 2015, the US completed a decade-long period without landfall of a single Category 3 or stronger hurricane, a hiatus not previously recorded in the hurricane record.[67]

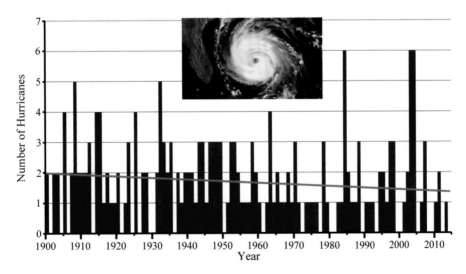

**United States Hurricanes 1900–2015.** The number of hurricanes making landfall in the United States each year over the last 115 years. The red line indicates the trend in the number of landfalls each year. Image of Hurricane Fran, 1996. (NOAA, 2015)[68]

Tornados are sometimes cited as evidence of human-caused global warming. In May 2013, US Senator Sheldon Whitehouse scolded Republicans:

> How wise is it for the Republican Party to wed itself to the deniers and proclaim that climate change is a hoax?… When cyclones tear up Oklahoma and hurricanes swamp Alabama, and wildfires scorch Texas, you come to us, for billions of dollars to recover.[69]

The US is home to about 90 percent of the world's tornados. According to the National Climatic Data Center (NCDC), an average of 1,253 tornados occur each year in the US. Most of the world's remaining tornados occur in Canada, about 100 each year. On average, the US is impacted by about 37 strong tornados annually, twisters that are measured at EF-3 or stronger on the Enhanced Fujita Scale.[70] In 1974, more than 130 EF-3 or stronger tornados were counted, the peak year in recent US history.[71] But according to NCDC data, the number of strong tornados has been declining since the 1970s.[73] Tornado strength has been declining during a period of gently rising temperatures and steadily rising levels of atmospheric carbon dioxide.

Leading scientists point out that the formation of hurricanes and tornados depends on differences in temperature between the tropics and the high latitudes. According to Dr. Richard Lindzen of the Massachusetts Institute of Technology, this temperature difference is expected to decrease in a warmer world.[75] Dr. Roy Spencer of the University of Alabama at Huntsville agrees, stating, "more violent tornados, if anything, would be a sign of global cooling, not global warming."[76]

Global tropical cyclone data from 1971 to present shows no trend of an increasing number of tropical storms. If tropical storms were getting stronger, more storms would grow to hurricane strength, increasing the number of hurricanes. But the number of hurricanes

**Fear Uncertainty Doubt**

**Is Air Conditioning Killing the Planet?**
"… the solution to staying cool by cranking up the air conditioning has a dark side; the energy it uses also happens to be a big contributor to climate change."
—*Discovery News*, July 28, 2015[72]

**Aiming at Your Corporate Foot**

**Oil Giants Call for Global Carbon Pollution Fees**
"Six major European oil companies are asking the United Nations to help impose carbon dioxide emissions pricing in all countries…. The letter was signed by representatives of the United Kingdom's BG Group and BP, Italy's Eni, the UK-Netherlands's Royal Dutch Shell, Norway's Statoil and France's Total."
—*The Hill*, June 1, 2015[74]

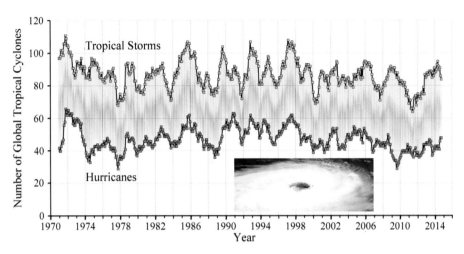

**Global Tropical Cyclones, 1971–2014.** The number of tropical storms (top line) and stronger hurricanes (bottom line) observed worldwide over the last 43 years. No trend of increasing tropical storm frequency or strength can be seen. Image of Cyclone Catarina, 2004. (Maue, 2015)[77]

observed globally is not increasing either. There is no empirical evidence that storms are either more frequent or more extreme.

Drought is the disaster that causes the greatest financial damage, a natural event now blamed on man-made climate change. The summer of 2012 brought the most severe drought in decades to US Midwestern states, including Arkansas, Colorado, Illinois, Indiana, and Missouri. The US Department of Agriculture designated more than 2,000 counties in 32 states as natural disaster areas. The US corn harvest totaled 10.7 million bushels, down 13 percent from 2011. The soybean crop totaled 2.9 billion bushels, down 8 percent.[78] Dr. James Overpeck of the University of Arizona told the Associated Press:

> This is what global warming looks like at the regional or personal level.… This is certainly what I and many other climate scientists have been warning about.[79]

But the National Oceanic and Atmospheric Administration (NOAA) records detailed

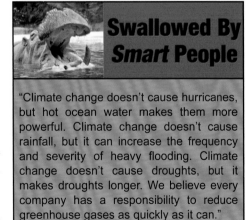

**Swallowed By Smart People**

"Climate change doesn't cause hurricanes, but hot ocean water makes them more powerful. Climate change doesn't cause rainfall, but it can increase the frequency and severity of heavy flooding. Climate change doesn't cause droughts, but it makes droughts longer. We believe every company has a responsibility to reduce greenhouse gases as quickly as it can."
—Walmart Chairman Lee Scott,
   October 23, 2005[80]

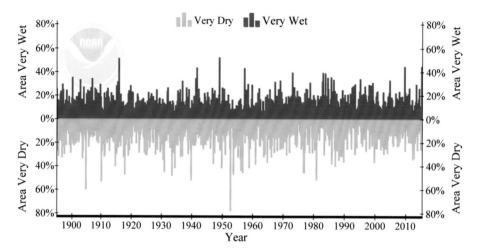

**United States Very Wet/Very Dry Area, 1895–2015.** Percentage of area in the continental United States very wet or very dry over the last 120 years. No trend of increasing drought or flood can be seen. (NOAA, 2015)[81]

historical data on the portion of the US that is very dry or very wet, based on the Palmer Drought Index. A graph of the data over the last 120 years shows no trend in either wetter or dryer conditions for the continental US. The 2012 drought blamed on man-made warming is unremarkable and only one of many periods of drought over the last century.

Of course, not only droughts but also floods are blamed on human-caused climate change. The autumn of 2000 was one of the wettest on record in England and Wales. About 10,000 homes and businesses were flooded at 700 locations. Peak flows on the Thames and other major rivers were the highest in 60 years.[82] In February 2011, Pardell Pall and other scientists published a paper claiming that anthropogenic (man-made) greenhouse gases were a factor in the autumn 2000 flooding:

> The precise magnitude of the anthropogenic contribution remains uncertain, but in nine out of ten cases our model results indicate that twentieth-century anthropogenic greenhouse gas emissions increased the risk of floods occurring in England and Wales in autumn 2000 by more than 20%, and in two out of three cases by more than 90%.[83]

This paper is of typical global warming alarm science, using computer models to try to blame natural events on people. But data from the UK Meteorological Office does not show a measurable change in long-term rainfall trends for England or Wales.[84]

The 2007 Fourth Assessment Report of the IPCC stated, "Africa is likely to be the continent most vulnerable to climate change."[85] In 2010, a severe drought hit the Sahel region in Africa, a semi-arid band of grass-land stretching across north central Africa just south of the Sahara Desert. The drought produced a famine affecting more than 10 million people in Cameroon, Chad, Mali, Niger, and Nigeria.[86] A 2013 paper by Yen-ting Hwang and others used climate models to analyze the decrease in rainfall in the Sahel since the 1950s. The study concluded that a combination of sulfate aerosol pollution from

human industries and variations in ocean circulation from either natural or man-made causes was responsible for the rainfall decline.[88]

But data shows much longer periods of African drought in past centuries. A 2009 study by Dr. Timothy Shanahan and others at the University of Arizona used evidence from sediments at the bottom of Lake Bosumtwi in Ghana to reconstruct the rainfall his-tory in West Africa. The study found that droughts during the Little Ice Age were severe and persisted for decades to centuries, driven by Atlantic Ocean circulation currents.[89] During those long dry periods, the water of Lake Bosumtwi was much lower than today's level. Stumps stand in the lake today from huge trees that grew during the drought periods. The Sahel droughts of recent decades are shorter than past droughts and well within the bounds of normal climate variation. There is also conflicting evidence that the Sahel, like other regions, is greening from a combination of higher recent rainfall and increased levels of atmospheric $CO_2$.[90] Alarm about a human-caused drought disaster in Africa is unfounded.

Earth naturally experiences a wide varia-tion in weather and temperature. On almost any day of the year, a storm, drought, flood, heat wave, or cold snap can be found at some location that appears to be a once-in-a-century event. A decade ago, when it was clear that global temperatures were no longer rising, Climatists adopted the label "climate change" and retired the phrase "global warming."

Apparently "climate change" can be better connected with fears of extreme weather events. Dr. Lindzen concludes:

> The failure of the public to get unduly alarmed over a degree or two of warming has led the environmental alarmists to turn to the bogey man of extreme weather.[92]

Throughout most of history, people believed that human actions could change the climate and cause extreme weather. The Aztecs of the 1500s practiced human sacrifice in an attempt to control the weather and keep the Sun moving across the sky.[93] After King Henry VIII divorced his wife, Catherine, in 1533, Englanders believed that nine months of unusually heavy rainfall were a result of the divorce.[94] During the cool climate of the Little Ice Age between the fourteenth and nineteenth centuries, hundreds of thousands of people in Europe were executed for the crime of witchcraft, blamed for short growing seasons and crop failures.[95] Today, Climatists warn that rising oceans and storms are caused by coal-fired power plants and your neighbor's SUV.

## POLAR BEARS, HUMAN HEALTH, AND ACID OCEANS

The polar bear is the poster animal for alarmism. Countless images of bears stranded on ice floes, emaciated bears, and dying bears, both real and those created by image manipulation, accompany stories of polar bear demise due to global warming. Greenpeace members protest climate change dressed in white fluffy polar bear costumes.

The IPCC Fifth Assessment Report of 2014 states:

> Models that account for population dynamics indicate that some species populations, such as those of polar bears, will decline precipitously over the course of the next century due to climate change.[96]

Dr. Michael Mann of the University of Pennsylvania adds to the alarm from the Fifth Report:

> What the latest report shows is that climate change is adversely impacting us now, wherever we live. It isn't just the Arctic and the polar bear anymore. We are now the polar bear.[97]

But rather than a global warming disaster, the polar bear is an example of conservation success. During the mid-1900s, polar bears were almost hunted to extinction. By 1960, only about 5,000 polar bears remained. In November 1973, Canada, Denmark, Norway, the USSR, and the US signed the Agreement on Conservation of Polar Bears.

The agreement prohibited the hunting, killing, or capturing of polar bears except in specific cases.[98] During the next 40 years, polar bear populations doubled and doubled again, to an estimated 25,000 bears today. This growth in bear populations occurred during a period of gently rising global temperatures and declining Arctic ice. Polar bears survived through the

**Climate Change is Causing Polar Bears to Eat Dolphins** —*The Week*, June 12, 2015[99]

Roman Warm Period, the Medieval Warm Period, and other warm eras of the last 10,000 years when temperatures were warmer than today and when Arctic ice extent was smaller. Fear of bear demise is only based on climate model projections.

Despite the fact that the polar bear population is large and stable, World Wildlife Fund (WWF) and Coca-Cola use polar bear fear for fund raising and public relations. At the WWF website, you can adopt a bear for $25, $50, $75, $100, or $250 and receive a "polar bear adoption kit." The kit may include a fuzzy polar bear toy, a photo, an adoption certificate, and a species card. WWF states:

> As a result of climate change, sea ice is melting earlier and forming later each year, leaving polar bears less time to hunt. As their ice habitat shrinks, skinnier and hungrier bears face a grave challenge to their survival.[100]

Coke introduced its polar bear mascot in a French print advertisement in 1922. But marketing efforts using the bear have increased over the last 20 years. In 2011, Coke announced its Arctic Home campaign, joining with WWF on a three-year effort "to raise money and awareness to help protect and conserve the polar bears' habitat."[101] In addition to raising millions for WWF, the Arctic Home campaign tugged at the hearts of consumers, boosting Coca-Cola consumption in northern nations during winter months, typically a slow sales period.[102] Global warming concerns are great for saving the planet *and* boosting sales.

But alarm about extreme weather and dying polar bears hasn't been enough to convince a skeptical public about the coming dire consequences of climate change. A 2013 national survey of Americans by Yale University and George Mason University found that only 47 percent of those surveyed believed that global warming was mostly caused by human activities. This was down 7 percent since 2012. Americans who thought that global warming was mostly due to natural changes rose to 37 percent, the highest percentage in five years.[103] Trends appear to show that acceptance of climate change alarm is declining. So

Edward Maibach, professor at George Mason, and others recommended that climate fighters "reframe" the climate message:

> Successfully reframing the climate debate in the United States from one based on environmental values to one based on health values, which are more widely held and cut across ideology and partisanship holds great promise to help American society better understand and appreciate the risks of climate change …[104]

In other words, scare people about the health risks of global warming to convince them.

In 2010, the EPA published a "fact sheet" titled "Climate Change and Health Effects" that was long on propaganda and short on facts:

> The Earth's climate is changing in ways that could have serious consequences for public health. In addition to the direct effects of higher temperatures, climate change will likely increase the number of people suffering from illness and injury due to floods, storms, droughts, and fires, as well as allergies and infectious diseases.[105]

The fact sheet warns of respiratory problems from increasing ground-level ozone, transmission of cholera and salmonella due to increased flooding, and an increase in ticks, mosquitoes, allergy problems, and heat-related deaths due to higher temperatures.

But these EPA warnings are about as valid as a North Korean election. As we discussed, strong tornado activity and hurricane landfalls in the US are down over the last 40 years. NCDC data shows no increase in droughts or floods over the last century. The EPA's own data shows that US ground-level ozone levels have been declining since at least 1980. Nor is there any evidence that ticks, mosquitoes, and allergy problems are rising because of higher temperatures.

Why do US senior citizens retire to Florida, Texas, and Arizona? Don't they know the EPA says warm climates are dangerous?[106]

In fact, there is much evidence that warm weather is good for people. In a 2000 study, Dr. William Keating at Queen Mary and Westfield College studied temperature-related deaths for people aged 65 to 74. He found that deaths related to cold temperatures were nine times greater than deaths related to hot temperatures in six European countries.[107] Dr. Matthew Falagas of the Alfa Institute of Medical Sciences in Greece studied seasonal mortality in eleven countries. He and his team found that the average number of deaths was highest in the coldest months of the year in all cases.[108] According to the World Health Organization, influenza (flu) season occurs during the winter months in both the Northern and Southern Hemisphere. Moderately warmer temperatures will likely be better for human health.

If warnings about extreme weather and dying polar bears aren't enough to convince you that we have a climate crisis, how about acid oceans? According to the theory, carbon dioxide exhausted into the atmosphere from industry is absorbed by the oceans, where it is converted to carbonic acid, thereby changing the chemical balance of the oceans. Dr. Jane Lubchenco, administrator for NOAA, labeled ocean acidification climate change's "equally evil twin." She compared ocean acidification to osteoporosis, a bone-thinning disease, and raised concern about possible negative effects on coral reefs.[109] Actress Sigourney Weaver testified before the US Senate in 2010, stating:

> … the oceans are 30 percent more acidic today than they were during pre-industrial times and, if we continue burning fossil fuels as we are now, we will *double* the ocean's acidity by the end of the century.[110]

But studies show that minor changes to the chemical balance of the oceans from human-emitted $CO_2$ are dwarfed by natural variability.

The acidity or alkalinity of a solution is measured on a 14-point logarithmic scale, called the pH scale. Battery acid has a pH of about one. In contrast, lye, a base or alkaline solution, has a pH of as high as 13. Seven on the pH scale is neutral. Rainwater, milk, and most of our foods are slightly acidic.

Sea water in the ocean is basic, with a pH of about 8.2. Computer models based on global warming theory predict a decline in ocean pH to about 7.9 by the year 2100, still alkaline, but less so.[111] It's unlikely that the oceans will ever be acidic.

Human activity certainly has an impact on our oceans. Overfishing and chemical pollution are problems that need continuous improvement. Carbon dioxide absorbed by the oceans does form carbonic acid. But fears of ocean acidification are grossly exaggerated.

Peer-reviewed papers show that the natural short-term pH variation in the oceans is huge. A 2014 study by Dr. Hannes Baumann and

**ECO-INSIGHT?**

**Stern: Rich Nations Will Have to Forget About Growth to Stop Climate Change**
"At some point we would have to think about whether we want future growth."
—Lord Nicholas Stern, *Guardian*, September 11, 2009[112]

**Next Great Deluge Forecast by Science**
"Melting Polar Ice Caps to Raise the Level of Seas and Flood the Continents"
—*The New York Times*, May 15, 1932[113]

others showed that pH naturally varied from 8.2 at the end of winter to 7.6 in late summer in tidal pools in Long Island Sound, pools which teamed with aquatic life.[114] A 2011 study by scientists at the Scripps Institution of Oceanography measured pH levels at 15 locations in the Atlantic, Pacific, and Antarctic Oceans. They found that pH levels vary as much as 0.35 units *in a single day*, more than the change projected by computer models over the next 100 years.[115]

With such large natural variations in ocean pH chemistry, sea creatures have learned to adapt to pH variations. Recent studies show that bacteria, plankton, coral, fish, crustaceans, and other organisms can adapt to and even thrive in lower pH ocean environments.[116] Higher atmospheric $CO_2$ levels may even boost the growth of ocean organisms.

Internationally famous diver Bob Halsted provides real-world evidence that high ocean carbon dioxide levels are not harmful to coral reefs. In the Coral Sea north of Australia, numerous vents in the ocean floor exhaust $CO_2$ into the sea at temperatures too hot for a diver's hand. But the coral reefs, sea grasses, and fish above the vents are doing just fine!

**Healthy Coral Reef and $CO_2$ Vents.** A healthy coral reef in the north Coral Sea. Note the carbon dioxide bubbling all around from vents in the ocean floor. (Image by Halsted, 2010)[117]

# THE CORRUPTION OF CLIMATE SCIENCE

A huge flow of money has corrupted climate science. Over the last 20 years, governments of the world collectively poured tens of billions of dollars into climate research at scientific laboratories and universities. Numerous government grants were awarded to monitor global temperatures, forecast coming extreme weather, and predict sea level rise. Countless studies were funded to determine every conceivable impact of man-made climate change on human population, health, poverty, disease, agriculture, industry, and society. The carbon footprint of every possible human activity was estimated and projected. Money was plentiful for "essential" studies on human-caused climate impacts to the size of birds, the size of humans, kidney stones, the frequency of earthquakes, poison ivy growth, lizard extinction, the growth of flesh-eating bacteria and toxic ocean algae, cougar attacks, shark attacks, and even human hair color. Allegiance to the theory of human-caused warming was required for award of a scientific grant.

Each year the US government provides about $10 billion in climate funding to major government agencies, such as the Department of Energy, the Department of Agriculture, the EPA, NOAA, NASA, and the National Academy of Sciences. These agencies then provide multi-million-dollar research grants to colleges and universities to study the impacts of man-made climate change. Is it any wonder that universities are "all in" for the theory of climate destruction?

It costs about $50 million to set up a state-of-the-art climate-modeling team using a supercomputer and $20 million per year to operate.[118] Dozens of large-scale modeling teams are continuously funded by the US, the UK, and other countries. If any of these modeling teams concludes that natural factors, rather than human factors, dominate climate change, their reason for existence disappears.

**Follow The Money**

"When I joined the American Physical Society sixty-seven years ago it was much smaller, much gentler, and as yet uncorrupted by the money flood .... the choice of physics as a profession was then a guarantor of a life of poverty and abstinence .... How different it is now.... the money flood has become the raison d'être of much physics research, the vital sustenance of much more, and it provides the support for untold numbers of professional jobs.... It is of course, the global warming scam, with the (literally) trillions of dollars driving it, that has corrupted so many scientists, and has carried APS before it like a rogue wave. It is the greatest and most successful pseudoscientific fraud I have seen in my long life as a physicist."
—Dr. Harold Lewis, resignation letter to the American Physical Society, October 6, 2010.[119]

**Does Climate Change Impact National Security? ASU Gets $20M to Find Out**

"The National Geospatial Intelligence Agency (NGA) has awarded Arizona State University a five-year, $20 million agreement to research the effects of climate change and its propensity to cause civil and political unrest."
—*The Republic*, July 3, 2014[120]

The most visible evidence of the corruption of was Climategate, the release of private e-mails from scientists at the Climatic Research Unit (CRU) at the University of East Anglia in the United Kingdom. In November 2009 and November 2011, thousands of e-mails sent by CRU scientists were publicly released by an unidentified hacker or internal whistleblower. The e-mails were private communications between top climate scientists in the US and the UK, the same scientists who developed the global surface temperature data sets and who wrote and edited the IPCC assessment reports. The disclosed e-mails showed bias, manipulation of data, efforts to subvert the peer-review process, avoidance of freedom of information requests, and brazen efforts to promote the theory of human-caused warming. The e-mail release was branded "Climategate" by the press and climate skeptics.

Why the bias at the CRU? Many in climate science today owe their careers to the theory of man-made warming and the IPCC. Dr. Judith Curry, atmospheric scientist at the Georgia Institute of Technology, comments:

> … at the heart of the IPCC is a cadre of scientists whose careers have been made by the IPCC. These scientists have used the IPCC to jump the normal meritocracy process by which scientists achieve influence over the politics of science and policy. Not only has this brought some relatively unknown, inexperienced and possibly dubious people into positions of influence, but these people become vested in protecting the IPCC, which has become central to their own career and legitimizes playing power politics with their expertise.[121]

## SOME COMMON SENSE ABOUT GLOBAL WARMING

Should individuals and businesses question the conclusions of climate scientists? By analogy, do you check the navigational calculations of the pilot when boarding a commercial jet? Of course not. But suppose your flight arrives in London when it was scheduled to go to in Paris. After such a trip, you'd conclude that the pilot didn't know his business. The failure of the climate models to predict flat global temperatures over the last 18 years shows that today's climate scientists are wrong in their claim that humans drive global

## Some Disclosed Climategate E-mails

Below are a few of the disclosed Climategate e-mails from the Climatic Research Unit of the University of East Anglia in the United Kingdom.[122]

E-mails showing bias toward the theory of human-caused warming:

"I know there is pressure to present a nice tidy story as regards 'apparent unprecedented warming in a thousand years or more in the proxy data' but in reality the situation is not quite so simple."
—Dr. Keith Briffa, Climatic Research Unit, disclosed e-mail, Sep. 22, 1999

"… it would be nice to try to 'contain' the putative 'MWP' [Medieval Warm Period] …"
—Dr. Michael Mann, IPCC Lead Author, disclosed e-mail, June 4, 2003

"Well, I have my own article on where the heck is global warming…. The fact is that we can't account for the lack of warming at the moment and it is a travesty that we can't."
—Dr. Kevin Trenberth, IPCC Lead Author, disclosed e-mail, Oct. 12, 2009

E-mails showing manipulation of temperature data:

"I've just completed Mike's [Mann] Nature trick of adding in the real temps to each series for the last 20 years (i.e. from 1981 onwards) and from 1961 for Keith's [Briffa] to hide the decline."
—Dr. Phil Jones, Director, Climatic Research Unit, disclosed e-mail, Nov. 16, 1999

"Also we have applied a completely artificial adjustment to the data after 1960, so they look closer to observed temperatures than the tree-ring data actually were …"
—Dr. Tim Osborn, Climatic Research Unit, disclosed e-mail, Dec. 20, 2006

E-mails showing data suppression and Freedom of Information avoidance:

"I'm getting hassled by a couple of people to release the CRU station temperature data. Don't any of you three tell anybody that the UK has a Freedom of Information Act."
—Dr. Phil Jones, Director, Climatic Research Unit, disclosed e-mail, Feb. 21, 2005

"Mike [Mann], can you delete any e-mails you may have had with Keith [Trenberth] re AR4? Keith will do likewise…. Can you also e-mail Gene and get him to do the same? I don't have his e-mail address…. We will be getting Caspar to do likewise."
—Dr. Phil Jones, Director, Climatic Research Unit, disclosed e-mail, May 29, 2008

E-mail showing efforts to subvert the peer-review literature process:

"… I can't see either of these papers being in the next IPCC report. Kevin [Trenberth] and I will keep them out somehow, even if we have to redefine what the peer-review literature is!"
—Dr. Phil Jones, Director, Climatic Research Unit, disclosed e-mail, July 8, 2004

**California Targets Dairy Cows to Combat Global Warming**

"'If we can reduce emissions of methane, we can really help slow global warming,' ... California Air Resources Board."
—*Fox News*, November 29, 2016[123]

temperatures. Because climate change is dominated by natural factors, all decarbonization efforts will be fruitless.

The theory of human-caused climate change is at the center of today's environmental movement. It's the foundation for the doctrine of sustainable development and the efforts of businesses to be environmentally sustainable. The United Nations, environmental groups, and thousands of other special interests will fight tooth and nail to preserve the ideology of Climatism. It will take decades for society to recover from this delusion.

The failing science of human-caused climate change and the thousands of remedies proposed and implemented by our misled humanity is too large a subject to be covered in a single chapter. I recommend that you read other works listed in the Further Reading section to gain a deeper understanding of this remarkable subject.

# CHAPTER 6

# RESOURCE SHORTAGE?

*"We live in a world of finite resources. Although it may sometimes seem quite big, Earth is really very small—a tiny blue and green oasis of life in a cold universe."*—ENVIRONMENTALIST DAVID SUZUKI (2004)[1]

Fear of resource depletion is the fourth of the Horsemen of sustainable development. Proponents of the ideology warn that Earth's natural resources are finite, that rich nations produce and consume too much, and that society has already exceeded the "carrying capacity" of our planet. Resources, we are told, are rapidly being exhausted. Sustainable development demands that people forgo consumption and that businesses and governments replace economic growth goals with green alternatives. Without a drastic change in direction, resources will soon run out and humanity will be heading for a fall.

But like the other foundations of sustainable development, the fear of resource depletion is unfounded. Today we have the greatest access to resources in history, and trends indicate that the availability of resources will continue to grow.

## FINITE OR ABUNDANT NATURAL RESOURCES?

The fear of resource shortage has been with us for decades. Back in the early 1900s, American cowboy and entertainer Will Rodgers reportedly said:

> We Americans think we are pretty good! We want to build a house, we cut down some trees. We want to build a fire, we dig a little coal. But when we run out of these things, then we will find out just how good we really are.[2]

Margaret Beckett, UK Environment Secretary, pointed out in 2006:

> It is a stark and arresting fact that, since the middle of the 20th century, humankind has consumed more natural resources than in all previous human history.[3]

Proponents of sustainable development believe that society grows only by depleting Earth's finite resources, such as physicist Joseph Romm:

> We have created a way of raising standards of living that we can't possibly pass on to our children. We have been getting rich by depleting all our natural stocks—water, hydrocarbons, forests, rivers, fish and arable land—and not by generating renewable flows.[4]

It seems intuitive doesn't it? Almost eight billion people live on our planet today, and this number increases daily. Earth is large, but still a fixed size, with a mean diameter of almost 8,000 miles (12,742 kilometers).[5] How can we not be running out of land, water, food, minerals, and energy?

Although counter-intuitive to the simple concept of a finite planet, and even with rising world population, trends show that human access to resources continues to grow. We'll examine the evidence about resource availability for food, land, commodity resources, energy, and water in this chapter and in Chapter 8 on agriculture.

**Food production.** World food production has risen faster than population over the last century. As we discussed in Chapter 2, the portion of world population that is malnourished has been steadily declining. The average middle-class person in a developed nation today has better quality and variety of food than the kings of old.

**Agricultural land.** Where needed, more land is put to use for agriculture each year, through clearing, irrigation, and advanced farming techniques. As a counter trend, in the US and other countries with high agricultural productivity, the amount of land under cultivation has actually declined. In many locations, it is economical to harvest high-yield crops from smaller acreages.

**Commodity resources.** Long-term prices for food and raw materials have declined, indicating greater availability. Stable prices and expanding reserves for metal resources do not show that these materials are being exhausted.

## The Seeds of Our Destruction

"We face today a problem which no previous generation has had to face. In 1982, nations have two choices: to carry on as they are and face, by the turn of the century, an environmental catastrophe which will witness devastation as complete and as irreversible as any nuclear holocaust, or to begin now in earnest a cooperative effort to use the world's resources rationally and fairly."

—Mostafa Tolba, Executive Director of the United Nations Environment Programme, May 3, 1982[6]

**Energy.** Energy tops concerns for resource depletion, but trends do not show that traditional hydrocarbon energy is nearing shortage. On the contrary, reserves of coal, oil, and natural gas continue to grow faster than consumption.

**Water.** Human consumption of water resources continues to rise. While local shortages of fresh water exist, many solutions are available to modern nations.

## RESOURCES ARE CREATED BY HUMANS

"Natural resources" is a misleading phrase. The term natural resources conveys the naive idea that food, water, energy, or materials can merely be plucked from a tree or gathered from a field or stream. Nature is a given, but in almost all cases, resources must be created by people. Nature does not provide a free lunch.

Native Americans disagreed, but the first European settlers perceived that land was available for the taking when they arrived on the shores of North America in the 1600s. But the land was not useful for agriculture without large amounts of human effort. Prior to farming, marshes needed to be drained and trees felled. Fields required clearing of stumps and stones. Dry areas needed irrigation canals. Raising livestock required construction of fences. Arable land is created only with much hard work.

Land is the resource of the farmer, but nature is his foe. Droughts, floods, and early frosts can destroy the year's harvest. Wild animals, such as wolves and snakes, threaten livestock. Locust swarms destroyed crops throughout history. Bacteria, fungi, and molds, such as the potato blight that caused the Great Irish Famine of the 1840s, can bring starvation to millions.

Even producing fruit from trees requires large amounts of labor, as any fruit-grower knows. After arable land is created, orchards require planting and pruning. Fruit crops must be defended from birds, deer, and insect pests. Commercial fruit producers typically spray their trees with pesticides every three weeks to kill insect attackers. Fruit may be naturally available from tropical palms, but throughout most of the world, commercial fruit can only be harvested from orchards planted and tended by people.

Nature purifies water in underground aquifers, but much of the natural water in lakes and streams requires purification by humans. Many years ago I kayaked the Arkansas River in Colorado, at a high altitude in the Rocky Mountains. The water was cold, so my fellow paddlers and I wore pogies to cover our hands on the kayak paddle. I used my teeth to pull on the pogies and ingested a small amount of water in the process. Two weeks after I returned home, I developed such bad stomach pain that I feared I had intestinal cancer. A visit to the doctor revealed that I had contracted a case of giardia, a parasitic protozoan, on my Colorado trip. North American rivers are naturally filled with giardia, even at altitudes

**Aluminum Ore and Aluminum.** The raw material bauxite, aluminum ore, (left) is of little value until it is processed into aluminum (right), using energy and human skill. (Saphon, 2007; Images of Elements)[7]

above 10,000 feet, far above towns and cities. "Natural" water often requires purification to remove salt, minerals, bacteria, and parasites.

Likewise, most of our raw materials are not usable in their natural state. Metal production requires mining, refining, and chemical processing. The average ore of copper contains only about 0.6% elemental copper. To produce copper metal, large quantities of copper ore must be crushed, heated with silica to 1400°C to liquify, converted in a series of furnaces into copper-oxide, and then deposited as pure copper using electrolysis.[8] Aluminum, cadmium, gold, lead, mercury, nickel, silver, and other metals must be similarly refined.

Raw materials come from nature, but today's resources are created by our modern society. But are we running out of the raw materials?

## RAW MATERIAL SHORTAGE?

Most people don't realize the vast quantity of raw materials available on our planet. Canadian geologist David Brooks estimates that a single average cubic mile of rock from Earth's crust contains a billion tons of aluminum (from bauxite), over 500 million tons of iron, a million tons of zinc, and 600 thousand tons of copper.[9] Of course, only a tiny fraction of metals in Earth's crust is economically viable to recover with current technology. So how can we tell if we are nearing depletion of key raw materials?

According to economists, price is the best indicator of raw material scarcity. As history shows, when a shortage occurs, the price of food, metal, or fuel climbs. Current prices also reflect expectations of future supply conditions. According to sustainable development proponents, the prices of non-renewable resources, such as copper, iron ore, and petroleum, should rise continuously as these resources are depleted. Pessimists tell us that every year the world's growing population uses more and more raw materials, which are taken out of the ground, gone forever. Industry must mine or drill in more difficult locations. As the easy-to-recover materials disappear, prices must be forced upward. But despite that fact that world production of almost all resources continues to grow rapidly, long-term trends show that inflation-adjusted prices for most resources are flat to falling.

In 2008, Dr. David Harvey of the University of Nottingham and others published results of a reconstruction of inflation-adjusted (real) world commodity prices spanning the seventeenth through the twentieth centuries. They examined 25 food, metal, energy, and raw material commodities and found that eleven of the commodities showed long-term downward price trends, namely aluminum, coffee, hides, jute, silver, sugar, tea, tobacco, wheat, wool, and zinc. Coffee prices, for example, were found to have declined an inflation-adjusted 0.77 percent per year for about 300 years. None of the 25 commodities showed rising prices. The authors concluded that, "*in the very long run there is simply no statistical evidence that relative commodity prices have ever trended upwards* [our emphasis]."[10]

The Economist industrial commodity-price index is the world's oldest public commodity-price index, first published in 1864. The index has been inflation-adjusted using the US consumer price index since 1871. The index contains 25 commodities, including foods, non-food agricultural commodities (such as timber and cotton), and industrial metals, but does not include petroleum or energy commodities. The index shows an average *decline* in real commodity prices of one-half percent per year over the last 140 years.[11]

The World Bank maintains a world commodity price database of 41 commodities from 1960 to present. Four inflation-adjusted price indices from 1960–2015 show that food commodities have declined, agricultural raw materials and industrial metals have been flat, and energy prices, dominated by the price of crude oil, have risen.[12] Commodity prices

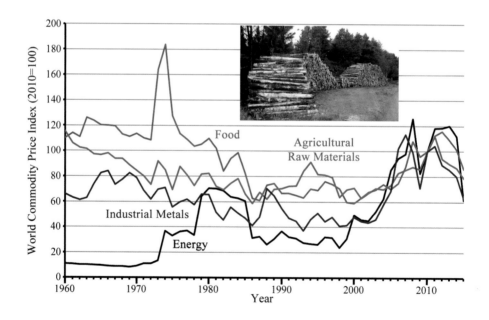

**World Commodity Prices 1960–2015.** Commodity price indices from the World Bank commodity price database. Food includes cereals, vegetable oils and meals, meat and other. Agricultural raw materials include timber, cotton, rubber, and tobacco. Industrial metals include aluminum, copper, iron ore, lead, nickel, tin, and zinc. Energy includes coal, natural gas, and petroleum, with petroleum comprising 84 percent of the index. Indicies are deflated using 2005 US dollars and 2010=100 for each index. (World Bank, 2016)[13]

fluctuate widely from decade to decade, but we don't see a rising price trend indicating resource exhaustion. Even with strengthening commodity prices over the last decade, and with the exception of energy, global resource prices have been generally flat despite huge increases in world production.

Global production of industrial metals soared from 1960–2014. Annual world production levels were up: aluminum (996 percent), copper (417 percent), iron ore (531 percent), lead (343 percent), nickel (455 percent), tin (66 percent), and zinc (348 percent).[14] The relatively small increase in annual tin production is due to the large-scale substitution of aluminum and plastic for tin across many products and processes. At the same time, the World Bank industrial metal real price index of these seven metals was flat, down a little more than one percent by 2015.[15] Industrial metal production is up many-fold, but prices are not rising as predicted by the resource-depletion pessimists.

The two major exceptions to flat resource prices over the last half century are precious metals and energy. From 1960 to 2015, the World Bank inflation-adjusted precious metal index, consisting of gold, platinum, and silver, increased by a factor of five. The World Bank

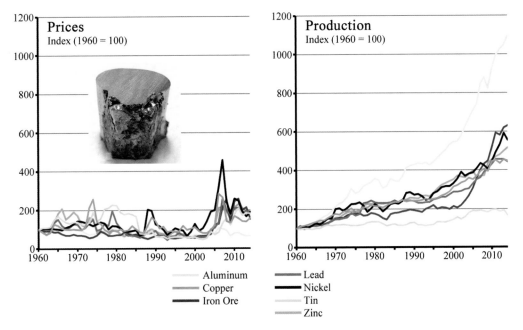

**Industrial Metal Prices and Production 1960–2014.** The left chart shows prices for seven metals over the 54-year period in constant 2005 US dollars. The right chart shows annual world production for each metal over the same period. World production of all metals except tin has at least quadrupled with little increase in real prices. Image of elemental nickel. (British Geological Survey 1960-2013; US Geological Survey, 2015; World Bank, 1960–2014)[16]

energy index, dominated by the price of petroleum, increased by a factor of 5.5. Petroleum real prices have increased by six times since 1960, with almost all of the inflation-adjusted increase occurring before 1980, in large part because of the formation of the Organization of Petroleum Exporting Countries (OPEC) cartel in the 1960s.[17] Prices for gold, platinum, silver, and petroleum have also risen due to the development of global trading of commodity futures. Investment banks, pension funds, and other financial organizations now hold large portfolios of precious metal and petroleum futures as a hedge against inflation and currency fluctuation. Medlock and Jaffe of Rice University pointed out that increased oil future trading by financial organizations appears to be a large factor in oil price increases over the last 15 years.[18]

Another way to gauge whether we are nearing depletion of resources is to look at trends in estimated world reserves of key materials. Raw material reserve numbers are difficult to estimate and can change significantly each year. They depend on estimates of 1) the physical and chemical characteristics of known material deposits, and 2) estimates of the economics of extracting and marketing the resource. Information on material deposits from many regions can be sketchy. Nevertheless, reserve estimates should be shrinking if society is depleting our key raw materials.

But data on key metals, which are labeled "non-renewable," generally shows that world reserves are expanding. The US Geological Survey has been providing estimates of world

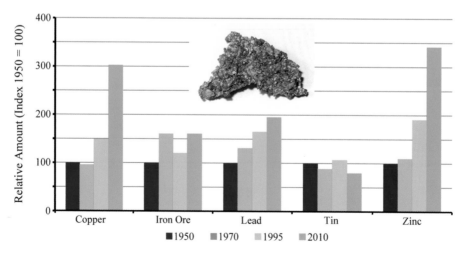

**World Reserves for Five Metals 1950–2010.** World reserves for copper, iron ore, lead, and zinc have increased since 1950, while reserves of tin have decreased, during a period of rapidly rising global metal production. Image of copper mineral. (President's Materials Policy Commission, 1952; Erickson, 1973; US Geological Survey, 1996–2011)[19]

reserves of metals since 1995. Of the 26 metals that have reserve estimates, world reserves have increased for 20 of the metals since 1995, including copper, gold, iron ore, lead, nickel, silver, tungsten and zinc. Reserves of antimony, boron, manganese, and tin are down, with reserves of rhenium and strontium remaining about the same.[20] Estimates of reserves prior to 1995 are sparse, but data shows that global metal reserves have generally been increasing during decades of rising production since 1950.

**Destroying The Environment To Save It?**

**The $2.2 Billion Bird-Scorching Solar Project at California's Ivanpah Plant, Mirrors Produce Heat and Electricity— And Kill Wildlife**

"... the BrightSource system appears to be scorching birds that fly through the intense heat surrounding the towers, which can reach 1,000 degrees Fahrenheit."
—*The Wall Street Journal*, Feb. 13, 2014[21]

Recycling plays a growing role in production of metals. Producers use recycled scrap to reduce energy requirements and deliver metals at lower cost. Iron and steel are the world's most commonly used metals and among the most recycled. Since 1970, US steel recycling rates have increased from near zero to 55 percent of production.[22] For key metals produced in the US in 2014, the portions from scrap were sizable: aluminum (33 percent), copper (32 percent), lead (70 percent), nickel (41 percent), and zinc (52 percent).[23]

As traders know, commodities experience rapid price swings in the short-term. The world price of a commodity can double in a year, driven by increased demand or a fall in supply. But trends show that over the long run, the price and supplies of food, agricultural raw materials, and even non-renewable metals show trends of greater availability, not looming scarcity. Long-term inflation-adjusted prices are flat to down not only for renewables, such as food and timber, but even for non-renewables such as industrial metals. As production of metals multiplied over the last 60 years, world reserves increased. How can it be that prices and supplies of even finite, non-renewable metals, show trends of greater availability?

The answer is that *the price and availability of a resource is mainly determined by the level of human skill available to produce the resource.* Throughout history to the present, people invented better ways to recover our planet's materials. As Julian Simon said:

> In the short run, all resources are limited.... The longer run, however, is a different story.... Greater consumption due to an increase in population and growth of income heightens scarcity and induces price run-ups. A higher price represents an opportunity that leads investors and business-people to seek new ways to satisfy the shortages. Some fail, at cost to themselves. A few succeed, and the final result is that we end up better off than if the original shortage problems had never arisen.[24]

But what about energy? Hydrocarbon energy can't be recycled or re-grown each year, like other commodities. Inflation-adjusted energy prices increased over the last half-century as global demand has risen.  Are we running out of coal, natural gas, and petroleum?

## A MODERN ENERGY MIRACLE

More than any other commodity, oil dominated global politics for much of the last century. Access to petroleum resources in Southeast Asia was a key part of Japan's decision to attack Pearl Harbor in 1941. The oil wells in the Caucasus Mountains factored in Germany's decision to invade the Soviet Union the same year. The OPEC oil embargo of 1973 began a 50-year rise in world oil prices to over $100 per barrel in 2008. To reduce dependence on crude oil, Europe, the United States, and other nations promoted a huge biofuel industry, thereby raising world food prices.

Today, one-third of total energy consumption continues to be supplied by petroleum.[25] Refined petroleum fuels power more than 90 percent of automobiles, trucks, trains, ships, and planes. Over one billion vehicles in today's world are expected to grow to more than two billion by 2050, powered by fuel refined from crude oil.

Over the last 50 years, the concept of "peak oil" stoked fears of a coming depletion of energy resources. The theory of peak oil proposed that oil resources were finite, and as easy oil deposits were exhausted, society would soon reach a point where the oil industry could not produce enough to meet growing world demand. In support of peak oil theory, environmentalists pointed to the rise in world oil prices and the decline in US oil production since 1970. Geologists added that fewer giant oil fields had been discovered in recent years, that output from old fields was declining, and that the cost of oil extraction continued to rise. Many predicted that world petroleum production would peak about 2006.

But instead of depletion, the early twenty-first century brought us a modern energy miracle. Geologists and hydrocarbon engineers in the US developed techniques to profitably extract oil and natural gas from shale rock, a common geologic formation. In the past, oil and gas prospectors searched for pockets of gas and oil in porous sandstone or limestone rock layers. But by using hydraulic fracturing (fracking) and horizontal drilling, today's hydrocarbon engineers are able to access oil and gas tightly held in shale rock.

We'll provide additional comments about fracking in the next chapter, but the bottom line is that the fracking revolution fundamentally changed the world energy picture. As a result of new techniques, US oil production almost doubled from 2008 to 2015, reversing a 38-year decline.[26] US production drove a fall in world oil prices from $100 per barrel in 2014 to under $30 per barrel in 2016.[27] US natural gas import terminals that had been planned to meet a forecasted gas shortage have been instead converted to export terminals to ship a rising gas surplus to other nations. Fracking technologies are now being deployed

## Hubbert Was Right—And Wrong

In 1956, Marion King Hubbert, geologist for the Shell Oil Company, used mathematical models to predict that US oil production would peak in 1970 and decline thereafter. In the same paper, he predicted that world petroleum production would peak by 2000 and then decline.[28] Hubbert's analysis became the basis for the theory of peak oil and the resource-depletion fears of sustainable development.

In the short-term, Hubbert was exactly right. US crude production peaked in 1970 at 9.6 million barrels per day. For the next 38 years, production from the multi-hundred-billion-dollar US petroleum industry declined steadily to 5.0 million barrels per day in 2008.[29] Pessimists warned that a fall in global production could not be far behind.

But Hubbert was wrong in the long run. Spurred by rising crude oil prices, US geologists perfected hydraulic fracturing and horizontal drilling, techniques to profitably extract oil from shale. US crude production soared, again reaching 9.6 million barrels per day in 2015 and erasing a 38-year decline in just seven years.[30] World oil prices plunged from over $100 per barrel in 2014 to under $30 per barrel in 2016.[31] Thanks to the ingenuity of US producers, fracking technology is spreading to shale basins worldwide, assuring low oil prices and plentiful supplies of petroleum for the next generation.

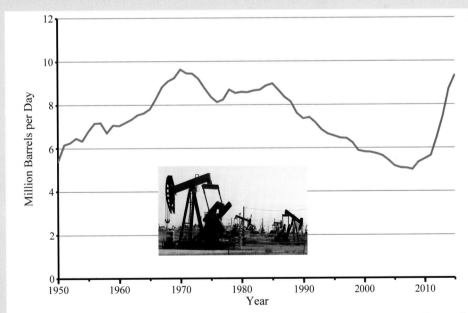

**US Petroleum Production 1950–2015.** US annual petroleum production decline and resurgence in millions of barrels per day. (Energy Information Administration, 2015)[32]

in shale basins in Argentina, China, and the UK, and soon will be used in the vast shale basins throughout the rest of the world.

Despite rising oil and natural gas prices over much of the last four decades, energy reserves show no signs of a shortage. Global production of petroleum increased 45 percent from 1980 to 2014.[34] But petroleum reserves increased even faster. In 1980, the world had an estimated 28 years of oil reserves at the 1980 annual production level. But by 2014, reserves had increased to over 1.6 trillion barrels, or more than 49 years of supply at the higher 2014 usage rates.[35] How can reserves continue to rise faster than production?

Some advocates of sustainability compare non-renewable resources to the volume of water in a bathtub. They warn that society draws water, or resources, out of the tub each year and that the level of non-renewable resources must shrink each year, eventually to be exhausted. But paradoxically, after the last three decades of increasing petroleum production, there are more reserves of oil "in the tub" than in 1980. The reason is that improving

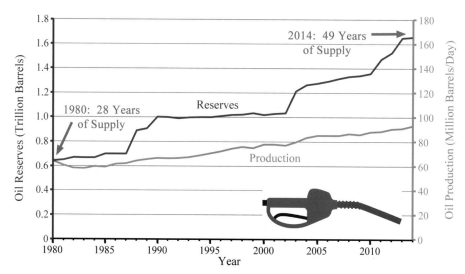

**World Petroleum Production and Reserves 1980–2014.** Over the last 34 years, world oil production increased from 64 million barrels per day to over 93 million barrels per day. At the same time, oil reserves increased from 28 years of supply to 49 years of supply at higher production rates. (Energy Information Administration, 2015)[36]

technology and operational skills of petroleum geologists and engineers allow cost-effective recovery of oil that was not accessible in previous years.

**Drinking The Green Cool-Ade**

"We've embarked on the beginning of the last days of the age of oil."
—Mike Bowlin, CEO of Atlantic Richfield Company, ARCO, February 9, 1999[37]

The ramp in natural gas production and reserves is equally impressive. World gas production more than doubled from 1980 to 2014. Clean-burning natural gas replaced coal for electricity generation, for industrial process energy, and for residential heating. But even during this huge ramp in natural gas production, world natural gas reserves increased from 49 years of supply in 1980 to over 57 years of supply in 2014.[38]

The consequences of the death of peak oil now impact both society and green ideology. The European Climate Change Programme (ECCP) was established by the European Community in 2000 to force Europe's energy systems toward renewable energy and away from hydrocarbons. Key to the program was the belief that oil and natural gas were nearing exhaustion, that hydrocarbon energy prices would rise, and that renewables would become cost effective. As we'll discuss next chapter, ECCP policies have degraded the

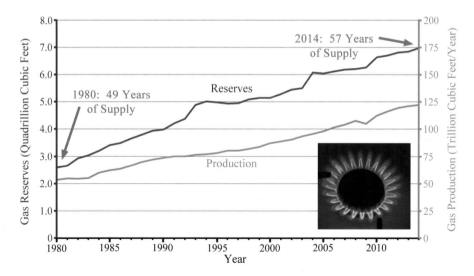

**World Natural Gas Production and Reserves 1980–2014.** Over the last 34 years, gas production more than doubled from 53 trillion cubic feet per day to over 122 trillion cubic feet per day. Gas reserves increased from 49 years of supply to 57 years of supply at higher production rates. (Energy Information Administration, 2015; BP, 2015)[39]

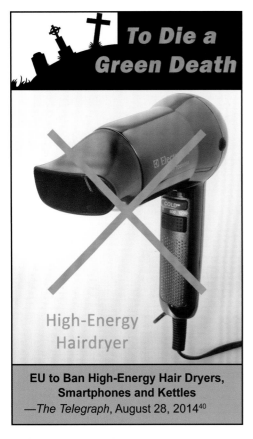

High-Energy
Hairdryer

**EU to Ban High-Energy Hair Dryers,
Smartphones and Kettles**
—*The Telegraph*, August 28, 2014[40]

**We Were Wrong on Peak Oil.
There's Enough to Fry Us All.**
"The automatic correction—resource depletion destroying the machine that was driving it—that many environmentalists foresaw is not going to happen. The problem is not that there is too little oil, but that there is too much."
—George Monbiot, *The Guardian*,
    July 2, 2012[41]

electrical power systems of Europe, damaging the competitive position of European companies compared to US competitors.

Environmental groups are in despair. The fracking revolution has plunged world oil prices and the price of US natural gas. Fracking technology promises low-cost hydrocarbons for centuries. Low-cost hydrocarbon energy threatens to boost the economic growth of developing nations, a benefit to millions of the world's poor, but a benefit also considered "unsustainable" by environmental disciples.

So how much oil and natural gas is really available? No one knows, but the supply continuously expands because of human ingenuity. In all of history through 2014, the world consumed approximately 1.2 trillion barrels of petroleum and about 3.6 quadrillion cubic feet of natural gas. Today, proven reserves of oil are estimated at 49 years and reserves of gas at 57 years at 2014 consumption rates. Technically recoverable global resources for oil and gas are estimated at 99 years and 187 years of consumption, respectively.[42]

But these numbers will continue to expand. Oil sands in Colorado, while not yet economically recoverable, are estimated to contain more oil than reserves in Saudi Arabia. Methane hydrates in undersea coastal areas potentially offer an order of magnitude increase in natural gas reserves when cost-effective recovery technology is invented. It's likely that the world has centuries of oil and gas remaining.

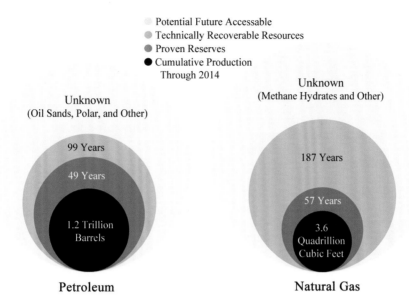

**World Oil and Natural Gas Reserves and Historical Consumption.** Cumulative historical world oil consumption of 1.2 trillion barrels (169 billion tons) and natural gas consumption of 3.6 quadrillion cubic feet (91.5 billion tons of oil equivalent) through 2014, compared to proven reserves, technically recoverable resources, and potential future accessible resources. Years of reserves in terms of 2014 world production. (EIA 2015; BP 2015; Smil, 2010)[43]

Coal remains the lowest-cost fuel for world electricity production. From 1973 to 2014, coal usage climbed from 24.6 percent to 30.0 percent of world energy consumption.[44] Like other hydrocarbons, coal reserves continue to expand. Proven world coal reserves are estimated at 227 years at 2014 production rates, about four times the reserves of oil and gas.[45]

## FINITE BUT VAST

Earth's raw material resources are technically finite, but also are vast like the Pacific Ocean is vast. For all practical purposes, our planet's resources appear to be practically limitless. Trends show that the sustainable fears of resource depletion are unfounded.

Resources aren't natural, but instead are created by humans. The availability of resources is primarily determined by the capability of human technology, not the amount of fruit on the tree or the quantity of rocks on the ground. Commodity prices may rise over years or decades, but decline over the long-term. Businesses and governments should operate with these observations in mind.

*Wonderfully Sustainable!*

**Pig Urine Plates**

"A Denmark company called Agroplast can take urea compounds—a key component of urine—and use it to produce bioplastics that can be made into biodegradable plates and utensils. Other companies use less cringe-inducing starters like vegetable oil, but the Danish company says pig urine, fraught with health hazards and high disposal costs unless processed, is a better environmental solution."

—*Time*, March 3, 2009[46]

There is little evidence that supplies of traditional hydrocarbon fuels, coal, natural gas, and oil are running out or will be exhausted in the near future. Proved reserves of hydrocarbons continue a long-term trend of increasing faster than global production. The hydrofracturing revolution means accessible supplies of oil and natural gas for decades and even centuries to come.

None of the four Horsemen of sustainable development—overpopulation, rising pollution, climate destruction, or resource depletion—are supported by trends or scientific evidence. World fertility rates have dropped by half over the last 50 years and population growth appears headed for a soft landing by mid-century. Environmental damage, as measured by air and water pollution levels, is dropping in developed nations. Developing nations will soon reach the turning point income of their environmental Kuznets Curve and also begin improving their environment. Earth's climate is dominated by natural, not human-caused factors. Eighteen years of flat global temperatures show that the climate models are fundamentally in error. There is no empirical evidence that shows that humans are destroying the climate. And resource prices and reserves show no evidence of a coming resource depletion.

Despite the evidence that the foundations of sustainable development are wrong, governments and businesses strive to be environmentally sustainable. Let's look at the impact of sustainable policies in energy, agriculture, and other industries.

CHAPTER 7

# RENEWABLE ENERGY MYTHS

*"We forget just how painfully dim the world was before electricity. A candle—a good candle—provides barely a hundredth of the illumination of a single 100 watt light bulb."* —AUTHOR BILL BRYSON (2010)[1]

Energy is the foundation of modern society. Since 1800, global energy use has increased by 26 times. Energy powers transportation, communications, health care, agriculture, industry, heating and cooling, and home appliances. Our cell phones, computers, televisions, microwave ovens, and other devices require electricity, energy in its most refined form. Energy powers the washer and dryer, replacing clothes washing by hand and providing a major reduction in housework. Homes and businesses are cooled by air conditioners, an important invention for boosting productivity in hot latitudes. In ages past, when only primitive forms of energy were available, life was cold (or hot), brutal, and short.

But for the last 30 years, proponents of sustainable development warned that energy use, and especially hydrocarbon use, was destroying the planet. Despite the evidence of the last three chapters, which shows such fears to be unfounded, most of the world now pursues policies to reduce energy usage and force the use of renewable energy. But it's increasingly clear that renewable sources can't carry the load.

## MORE ENERGY THAN MY NEIGHBOR

About once a quarter, I receive a notice from Commonwealth Edison, my electricity provider, called a "Home Energy Report." The report says something like, "You used 41 percent more energy than your most efficient neighbor." My wife and I are fairly stingy with electricity use. For years I drove my family batty turning off lights in empty rooms. In the summer, my wife often dries clothes outside in the sunshine, rather than using the dryer. Many of our light bulbs are fluorescent. We do these things to save money on our electric bill, not for other reasons.

But isn't it odd that Commonwealth Edison, a company that markets electricity, urges customers to use less electricity? Suppose Apple sent you a notice once a quarter stating that you're using too many iPhones and iPads? Or suppose Coca-Cola informed you that you were drinking 41 percent more soft drinks than your most efficient neighbor?

The answer to this foolishness is both regulatory and ideological. ComEd is required by Illinois state law to send out notices to try to reduce electricity demand. But it appears that the firm also thinks that reducing energy use can save the environment. In 2013, the ComEd website displayed a colorful cartoon image of the "Power Bandit," with the advice:

> Saving Energy was never so much fun! Beat the Power Bandit and learn lots of ways to save energy, save money, and help save the planet![2]

Media reports indicate that green advocate and former US Vice President Al Gore uses more than 10 times the electricity of the average Nashville household in his Tennessee mansion.[3] What kind of Home Energy Report does Mr. Gore receive?

## ARE RENEWABLES THE ANSWER?

Many claim that renewable energy, especially wind and solar, is the answer to today's energy needs. Sustainability advocates demand that we replace coal- and gas-fired power plants with wind farms and solar fields. As of the end of 2014, more than 250,000 wind turbines were installed across the world.[4] Germany claims more than one million rooftop solar installations. For the last two decades, Europe, Australia, Canada, the US and other nations spent hundreds of billions of dollars in subsidies and deployed a wide array of regulatory mandates to spur the use of wind, solar, and other renewables. Apple, Google, Intel, Total S. A., Walgreens, Walmart, and dozens of other multinational companies crow about their investments in solar energy. But despite 30 years of fanfare, wind and solar still provide only an insignificant amount of the world's energy.

**Sustainable Sincerity?**

**Gore Defends Mansion's Power Consumption**

"Last August alone, Gore burned through 22,619 kWhr .... That is more than an average American family uses in an entire year." —*CBS News*, February 28, 2007[5]

Energy expert Robert Bryce calls it the problem of scale.[6] Global energy consumption is huge. Each day, the world uses the energy equivalent of the oil carried in 177 oil tankers, each with a 200,000-ton capacity, or the equivalent energy output of 360,000 Hoover Dams.[7] The world consumed just short of 13 billion tons of oil equivalent in 2014. Wind and solar provided only 1.6 percent of the total.[8]

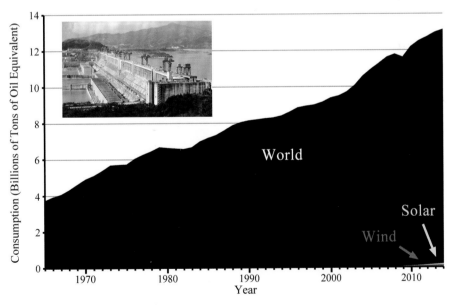

**Total World, Wind, and Solar Energy Consumption, 1965–2014.** Rising total world energy consumption along with the share of wind and solar is shown, measured in billions of tons of oil equivalent. The solar consumption line is enhanced so it can be seen. Image of Three Gorges Dam in China. (BP, 2015)[9]

*Renewables Are Fashionable!*

"Solar power is cool. When you put panels on your roof, people notice, and they'll be nicer to you."
—*Solar Power Your Home for Dummies*, (2010)[10]

Renewable proponents argue that, even though renewables are small, they're growing rapidly. While it's true that renewables are growing quickly, they remain far from replacing hydrocarbons and nuclear fuels. From 2013 to 2014, global energy consumption grew by about 121 million tons of oil equivalent, while total wind and solar growth was only 27 million tons of oil equivalent.[11] Wind and solar cannot even provide for the annual growth in world energy use, let alone replace conventional fuels. Even if global subsidies for wind and solar continue, these technologies may never capture a significant share of global energy consumption.

## WIND AND SOLAR SHORTFALLS

So why haven't wind and solar energy caught on? Wind and solar suffer from three significant deficiencies compared to traditional hydrocarbon and nuclear methods of electricity generation. Wind and solar are dilute, intermittent, and expensive.

At the Equator on a clear day, only about 1,000 watts of sunlight reaches each square meter of Earth's surface after absorption and scattering by the atmosphere. At the latitudes of Southern Europe and the US, this is reduced to about 800 watts per square meter, because the incident sunlight is not vertical. Only about 15 percent of sunlight is converted into electricity. After transmission line losses, only a single 100-watt bulb can be powered from a card-table-sized surface, and only on a clear day with the sun directly overhead.

California Valley Solar Ranch[12]

As a result, huge tracts of land are required for a solar energy field to try to match the output of a conventional coal, natural gas, or nuclear power station. The California Valley Solar Ranch began operation in early 2014 in the Carrizo Plain, about 100 miles northwest of Los Angeles. The ranch covers a whopping 1,500 acres, an area about 100 times the footprint of a typical gas-fired power plant. But the output of the ranch is only an average of

55 megawatts, only about 10 percent of the output of a medium-size gas-fired plant.[13]

Wind farms also need huge amounts of land to utilize the dilute energy in the wind. Wind turbine output is constrained by Betz's Law, which limits the maximum amount of energy that can be captured from the wind.[14] Turbines must be spaced about 140 meters apart, so vast fields of turbines must be deployed to capture a useful amount of energy.[15] The first phase of the London Array, the world's largest offshore wind farm, covers an area of about 100 square kilometers (38.6 square miles) in the North

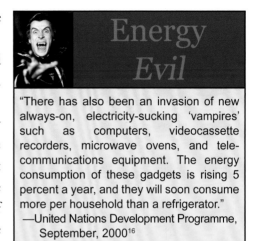

Energy Evil

"There has also been an invasion of new always-on, electricity-sucking 'vampires' such as computers, videocassette recorders, microwave ovens, and telecommunications equipment. The energy consumption of these gadgets is rising 5 percent a year, and they will soon consume more per household than a refrigerator."
—United Nations Development Programme, September, 2000[16]

Sea off the eastern coast of England. This is a footprint about 100 times larger than that of a conventional power plant. The 175 turbines of phase one of the system produce an average output of 233 megawatts, less than half of the output of a typical power plant.[17] To deliver the same average energy output, solar fields require about 75–100 times the area and wind farms require about 200–250 times the area of coal, gas, or nuclear plants.[18]

Second, the output from wind and solar facilities is intermittent. Solar energy is available for only about six hours per day, when the sun is high in the sky. Some locations, such as Massachusetts and much of England, are plagued by cloudy conditions, limiting solar output. Northern latitudes suffer from a low sunlight angle of incidence for much of the year and a scourge of white, fluffy, sunlight-blocking stuff during winter months.

Wind energy is notoriously undependable. At the end of 2014, over 48,000 wind turbines were operating in the US. These turbines achieved at a capacity factor of only 31.5 percent during the year.[19] The capacity factor is the percentage of actual output of an electricity generating system, compared to the rated output. The intermittent nature of wind and solar systems means that they have inherently low capacity factors. Wind output can change from zero to full output and back to zero again over the course of a single day, as the weather changes.

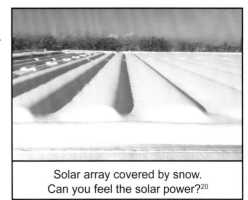

Solar array covered by snow.
Can you feel the solar power?[20]

Electricity systems must deliver a continuous flow of power to match changing customer demand. Electricity is not stored on a large scale like energy is stored in your smart phone battery. When consumers return home at the end of the day and switch on their lights and air conditioners, the system must be able to ramp quickly to meet demand. Wind and solar systems do not provide that reliable output.

Intermittent sources can also deliver too much electricity. When the sun shines and the wind blows, renewable sources can cause electricity supply to exceed demand, raising the frequency of grid electricity. Other generating systems must then be scaled back or shut down to again balance supply with demand.

An intermittency example is the output of wind turbines in the UK. The UK National Grid keeps continuous historical records of electricity generation by technology.[21] A look at wind production during a typical month of operation shows erratic, unpredictable output, with many days of near zero electricity output.

Another important issue relates to peak demand. Today's power systems are sized based on peak consumer demand, which usually occurs during evening hours and seasonally during hot summer months or the coldest days in winter. At the end of a day, solar output

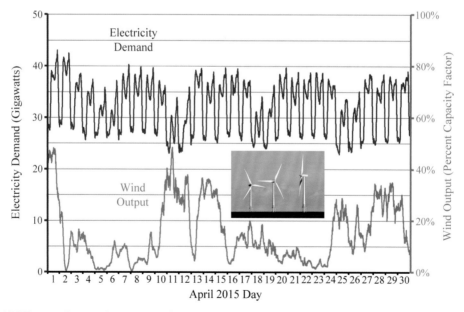

**UK Energy Demand and Wind Output, April 2015.** The blue graph shows United Kingdom electricity demand for April 2015, a month of low wind output. The red graph shows the ratio of actual output to rated capacity for the nation's 6,000 installed wind turbines. Note the days with output less than 10 percent of capacity. (UK National Grid, 2016)[22]

ramps down when electricity demand peaks in many locations. Wind output is typically low during frigid high-pressure days of winter and the hottest days of summer. Grid operators can count on only about ten percent of the rated capacity of a wind system toward meeting times of peak demand.[23]

Because of intermittency, *wind and solar systems can't replace hydrocarbon and nuclear power stations if continuity of electricity supply is to be maintained.* Wind and solar can only replace a part of the output of conventional power plants, which must still provide power when the wind doesn't blow and the sun doesn't shine.

## Sustainable Subsidies?

"I will do anything that is basically covered by the law to reduce Berkshire's tax rate. For example, on wind energy, we get a tax credit if we build a lot of wind farms. That's the only reason to build them. They don't make sense without the tax credit."
—Warren Buffet, CEO Berkshire Hathaway, annual investors meeting, May 2, 2015[24]

## THE LEVELIZED COST OF ELECTRICITY

The third shortfall of wind and solar systems is that their electricity is expensive. The US Energy Information Administration (EIA) annually publishes an estimate of the "levelized cost" of generating electricity for different technologies in the US. The levelized cost is the estimated cost in inflation-adjusted dollars per megawatt-hour of electricity for new facilities, including all capital costs, fuel costs, operation and maintenance costs, and the plant utilization rate for a given technology. The EIA estimates the levelized cost for a new plant starting operations in a future year, for coal, natural gas, nuclear, hydroelectric, geothermal, biomass, wind and solar technologies.

The EIA recognizes the problem of intermittent generation for wind and solar. It divides electricity generation systems into dispatchable technologies, including coal, gas, and nuclear, and non-dispatchable technologies, including wind and solar. The EIA states:

> The duty cycle for intermittent renewable resources, wind and solar, is not operator controlled, but dependent on the weather or solar cycle …[25]

EIA goes on to say that the levelized costs of wind and solar are "not directly comparable to those of other technologies."[26] Nevertheless, the sustainability movement demands the substitution of wind and solar for hydrocarbon power plants.

At first glance, EIA numbers show that the generated cost of electricity from new wind farms matches the cost from new hydrocarbon and nuclear facilities. The 2014 EIA analysis for facilities beginning operations in 2019 places the costs at: conventional coal ($95.6 per megawatt-hour), natural gas ($66.3/MWh), nuclear ($96.1/MWh), wind ($80.3/MWh). EIA estimates solar photovoltaic (PV) costs at $130.0/MWh and offshore wind at the very expensive cost of $204.1/MWh.[27]

But the EIA numbers are heavily biased in favor of wind and solar, as discussed in an excellent 2015 analysis by Thomas Stacy and George Taylor.[28] First, the EIA uses optimistic capacity factors, which comparatively lower the cost estimates for wind and solar. The EIA uses a capacity factor of 35 percent for wind and 25 percent for solar photovoltaic.[29] With the exception of wind farms in Hawaii, few US wind farms can achieve an output of 35 percent of rated output. Photovoltaic solar systems cannot achieve 25 percent without a natural gas back-up system.

Second, wind and solar systems can only be operated in conjunction with other conventional power stations and cannot replace such stations. The addition of wind farms and solar fields to the grid imposes costs on existing hydrocarbon and nuclear facilities, which must then run at lower utilization rates, raising their cost of generated electricity. Proponents of wind and solar do not consider these costs.

Third, the EIA analysis assumes a useful life of 30 years for all facilities. Most US wind farms are new, with an average age of only about four years. Worldwide, there are virtually no examples of 30-year wind turbine life spans. In Denmark, partially due to government incentives, installed turbines are replaced after fewer than 20 years of operation.[30] Nor do solar systems last 30 years. Solar cell output decays at a rate of about 0.5–1.0 percent per year, reaching a 20 percent output loss by year 25, the usual indication of end-of-life.[31]

For conventional power plants, the EIA's application of a 30-year useful life conflicts with actual industry experience. According to data from the Federal Energy Regulatory Commission, the average age of a US coal plant is about 35 years, and coal plants can operate for 50 years or more. The average age of a current US nuclear plant is over 30 years, and with proper renewals, nuclear facilities appear to have a life of 60–80 years. The average age of a US hydroelectric facility is over 50 years.[32] The EIA's assumption of a 30-year useful life is a strong bias that distorts estimated costs in favor of wind and solar to the detriment of conventional technologies.

Fourth, EIA adds 46 percent to the cost of capital for a coal plant, simulating the effects of a carbon tax, which does not exist at the national level in the US.[33] EIA also underestimates transmission costs for wind and solar systems, which typically must be located hundreds of miles from urban centers. US state and federal governments are

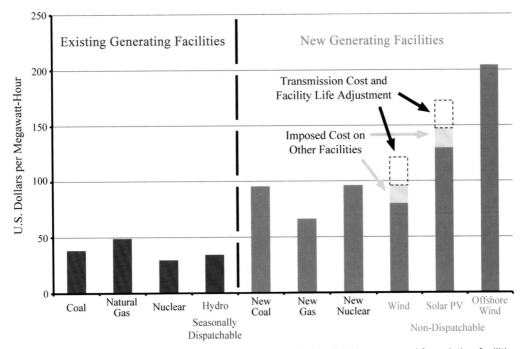

**US Electricity Costs By Technology**. Levelized cost of electricity is compared for existing facilities (blue) and for new facilities to be placed into operation in 2019 (red). Costs are measured in US dollars per megawatt-hour (divide by 100 for cost in cents per kW-hr). Red bars are EIA 2014 estimates with upward adjustments for EIA shortfalls in facility life, transmission costs, and costs imposed by non-dispatchable technologies on existing facilities. (EIA, 2014, Stacy and Taylor, 2015)[34]

constructing new transmission systems especially for wind and solar, amounting to a hidden subsidy.

When adjustments for capacity factor, imposed costs, useful life, and other factors are included, the cost of constructing new wind and solar systems remains significantly higher than that of constructing new conventional generating facilities. But these comparisons miss an even larger consideration. Generating facilities are paid the wholesale price of electricity, only a fraction of the retail electricity price, which includes distribution, marketing, and customer service costs. The 2015 US wholesale price is among the lowest in the world at 3.5 cents per kilowatt-hour ($35/MW-hr).[35] This low price is achievable from existing conventional power plants, many of which have already paid down their capital costs after long years of operation. The ongoing delivered electricity costs from these coal, gas, nuclear, and hydro facilities are well below $50/MW-hr.

A wide array of US energy laws and regulations now promote the build-out of wind and solar facilities and effectively mandate the closure of existing hydrocarbon facilities, in order to "tackle" global warming. Twenty-nine states adopted Renewable Portfolio Standards (RPS) laws, requiring utilities to purchase an increasing amount of electricity from renewable sources or else be fined.[36] The EPA's Clean Power Plan (CPP), a regulation finalized in 2015 but under court challenge, establishes goals for each of the 50 states to force large reductions in greenhouse gas emissions from utilities. US federal and state governments also provide generous subsidies to renewables, including the Wind Production Tax Credit. These subsidies, the RPS laws, the CPP, and other regulations force the premature closure of coal (and sometimes nuclear) power plants with decades of useful life remaining. The forced substitution of new high-cost renewables for perfectly good existing low-cost facilities will certainly raise US electricity rates. But as we discussed in Chapter 5, this switch to renewables won't change global temperatures.

## RENEWABLE MANTRA AND REALITY

Despite the wind and solar deficiencies of low-energy density, intermittent operation, and high cost, advocates of sustainable development demand the substitution of wind and solar energy for traditional hydrocarbon facilities. Many believe such a shift is possible. The November 2009 cover of *Scientific American*, which might better be called "Scientific American Fiction," announced, "A Plan for a Sustainable Future: How to get all energy from wind, water and solar power by 2030." The article, written by Mark Jacobson and Mark Delucci of Stanford University, called for the construction of millions of wind turbines, millions of tidal turbines and wave convertors, and literally billions of rooftop solar systems, as well as an "electric vehicle economy." It also proposed that these wind, water, and solar technologies could provide 100 percent of world energy by 2030.[37]

Sadly, the governments of developed nations have adopted this renewable mantra. In June 2015, German Chancellor Angela Merkel announced that the G7 nations had committed to "decarbonize the global economy in the course of this century."[39] Leading businesses have also adopted renewables, despite the deficiencies. The World Wildlife Fund reports: "Sixty percent of the largest US businesses have set public climate and energy goals to increase their use of renewable energy." Amazon, DuPont, IKEA, Kaiser

**Believe This? Then I've Got A Bridge to Sell You**

"Wind, water and solar technologies can provide 100 percent of the world's energy, eliminating all fossil fuels."
—Mark Jacobson and Mark Delucci, Stanford University, 2009[38]

Permanente, Sprint, Volvo, and 3M are just a few of these firms.[40]

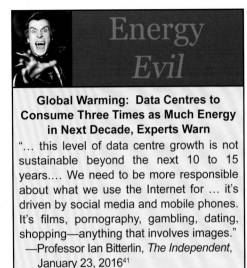

**Global Warming: Data Centres to Consume Three Times as Much Energy in Next Decade, Experts Warn**

"... this level of data centre growth is not sustainable beyond the next 10 to 15 years.... We need to be more responsible about what we use the Internet for ... it's driven by social media and mobile phones. It's films, pornography, gambling, dating, shopping—anything that involves images."
—Professor Ian Bitterlin, *The Independent*, January 23, 2016[41]

But contrary to all of the sustainable rhetoric, the developing nations, and even some of the developed nations, are building vast numbers of new coal-fired power plants. A December 2015 study published by *EndCoal. org* noted that more than 2,400 new coal-fired power plants were planned or in construction around the world. China led with 1,179 new coal plants announced or pre-planned, a 50 percent addition to their fleet of existing coal-fired stations. India followed with 446 new planned coal plants, a 75 percent addition to existing coal facilities. Additional countries with coal plants in the works include Indonesia (119), Pakistan (51), the Philippines (60), South Africa (31), South Korea (26), Turkey (92), and Vietnam (80). Even wealthy nations are adding to the build-out, including Japan (45) and Germany (5).[42] Coal will likely remain the leading fuel for electricity production for decades to come.

But mounting evidence also shows that forced addition of wind and solar can seriously degrade national electrical grids. A renewable energy debacle is unfolding in Europe.

## EUROPE'S RUSH FOR RENEWABLES

In June 2000, the EU launched the European Climate Change Programme (ECCP). The program was adopted to:

> … identify the most environmentally effective and most cost-effective policies and measures that can be taken at European level to cut greenhouse gas emissions.[43]

The short-term goal of the ECCP was to allow European countries to meet emissions reduction targets set by the 1997 Kyoto Protocol agreement. The ECCP was followed by the Second European Climate Change Programme in 2005, which established the European Emissions Trading System, a market for trading carbon dioxide emissions credits from 11,500 electrical power and manufacturing companies.[44] In 2009, the EU issued a directive calling for 20 percent of Europe's energy to come from renewable sources by 2020.[45]

Renewables included biofuels for transportation, but with a special emphasis on wind and solar for electricity generation. These initiatives forced wide-ranging changes in European agriculture, industry, and transportation, but especially in the electrical power sector.

Dr. Benny Peiser, director of the Global Warming Policy Foundation, pointed out in US congressional testimony that the ECCP was based on two false assumptions. First, European leaders were convinced that global warming was an urgent problem to be halted at all costs. Second, leaders assumed that the world was running out of oil and natural gas and that the price of hydrocarbons would continue to rise, making renewable energy competitive. If true, early investment in wind and solar might provide European firms with a first-mover advantage in world markets.[46]

Nations of Europe established two fundamental policies to promote the build-out of wind and solar capacity. First, feed-in tariffs (FITs) established high prices for electricity fed into the grid from wind farms and solar systems. The FITs paid a price far above the market electricity rate with guaranteed payments for decades. In Spain, wind generators were paid 90 percent over the market rate and solar generators were paid 575 percent over the market rate for a period of 25 years. With the generous FIT price, Spanish solar investors could earn a 17 percent compounded annual return for decades.[47] Germany established its Electricity Feed-In Law in 1991, which became a model for other European nations and the ECCP, and followed with the Renewable Energy Act of 2000 (Erneuerbare Energien Gesetz, or EEG). German on-shore wind turbines were paid twice the market rate, and solar producers received a tariff about eight times the market rate, both guaranteed for 20 years.[48] By 2010, 21 European nations used FITs as the primary policy to promote renewable energy.[49] Quota systems for renewables were also used. Quotas required production or consumption a specified amount of renewable energy set by the government, a system similar to US RPS laws. By 2013, quota systems were used in Belgium, Italy, Poland, Romania, Sweden, and the UK, which also used FITs.[50]

Second, electricity from renewables received priority among generating sources. The 2009 Renewable Energy Directive from the European Parliament stated:

> Member states shall also provide for either priority access or guaranteed access to the grid-system of electricity produced from renewable energy sources.[51]

In Germany, and most other nations with feed-in tariffs, utilities are legally required to accept green energy fed into the grid. This means that other power plants must be scaled back or shut down when solar and wind fields generate electricity.

The ECCP forced a massive build-out of wind and solar in Europe. From 1990 through 2014, Europe built 130 gigawatts of wind and 89 gigawatts of nameplate solar capacity. Over the period, wind and solar installations provided the majority of a 70-percent increase in electricity capacity on the continent, while electricity demand increased by only 26 percent.[52] This massive investment ignored the fact that wind and solar fields operate relatively poorly on the continent of Europe. During 2014, the combined capacity factor for Europe's solar systems was a meagre 12 percent, with the output from wind systems less than 22 percent of rated output.[53] This huge renewable build-out produced a number of uneconomic and even bizarre results.

Denmark constructed over 5,200 wind turbines, one for every thousand Danish residents, the highest density in the world. Today a backpacker can hike from one end of Denmark to the other with a 200- to 500-foot wind tower always in view. With a footprint of about 0.2 square kilometers for each turbine, the 5,200 turbines blanket an area of about 1,000 square kilometers. But together these turbines produce an average output of only about 1.5 gigawatts.[54] They could all be replaced by a single large conventional power plant on a site covering only 4 square kilometers. Wind turbines helped Denmark achieve the highest household electricity prices in the developed world, over 30 euro cents per kW-hr.[55]

Germany, the largest energy market in Europe, led the push for renewable electricity, establishing the Energiewende (energy transition) initiative in the 1990s. Energiewende gained broad political consensus after the 2011 nuclear accident in Fukashima, Japan. The Energiewende seeks a transformation of German energy systems to provide a nuclear-free and low-carbon economy. Energiewende calls for 80 percent of Germany's electricity from renewables by 2050 and the closure of all nuclear, most coal, and many natural gas power plants.[56] By 2015, eleven of the nation's nuclear plants were shut down, with the remaining eight reactors to be closed by 2022.

Germany's generous FIT rates stimulated over one million rooftop solar installations, more than any other nation. But Germany is not exactly located in the sun belt. The city

Destroying
The Environment
To Save It?

**Millions of Trees Felled in Pursuit of Energy Targets**

"Millions of trees have been felled to clear the way for wind farms ... 2,510 hectares of woodland—the equivalent of five million trees—have been destroyed since 2007 as the Scottish Government pursues tough renewable energy targets."
—*The Times*, January 2, 2014[57]

of Erfurt in central Germany sits at 50°59′ north latitude, as far north as Calgary, Canada. Due to cloudy weather and the northern latitude, Germany's solar systems produced only 10.4 percent of rated output in 2014, comprising 6 percent of Germany's electricity.[58]

Germany now finds the cost of this green miracle unsustainable. The EEG levy, the renewable subsidy paid for by German electricity consumers, rose to €24 billion ($31 billion) per year by 2014. Through 2014, subsidies to the German renewables industry paid, or obligated in the future, totalled over 300 billion euros (over $400 billion).[59] Environment Minister Peter Altmaier estimated that the German energy revolution could cost Germany up to €680 billion by 2022 and up to an astonishing trillion euros by 2040.[60] These numbers include subsidies for FITs only and do not account for network expansion or other costs.

On the cold day of October 28, 2008, in the middle of the earliest London snowfall since 1922, the United Kingdom House of Commons passed the UK Climate Change Act to stop global warming, calling for an 80 percent emissions cut by 2050.[61] The Brits then pursued hideously expensive offshore wind, installing 4,500 megawatts by the end of 2014, almost one-half the world's total.[62] Cloudy and farther north than Germany, the nation also provided large incentives for the installation of solar systems. In 2014, UK solar installations provided only 8.6 percent of their rated output.[63] But, of course, a nation *must* deploy solar to be sustainable. And in a shining act of sustainable folly, Britain is converting the coal-burning Drax power station, the largest power plant in Europe, to wood fuel, ferried 3,000 miles from the southern US.

The feed-in tariffs and mandates produced an impressive boom in renewable electricity across the continent. In 2014, the percentages of electricity generated by renewable energy were: Denmark (48.5 percent), France (18.3 percent), Germany (28.2 percent), Italy (33.4 percent), and the UK (17.8 percent), with 27.5 percent of electricity from renewables for total Europe, including biomass, geothermal, hydropower, solar, and wind generation.[64]

But Europe's total bill for renewable energy is staggering. Including research, biofuels, and renewable capacity build-out, Europe spent over $850 billion dollars from 2000 to 2014.[65] This massive spending boosted renewables from 1.4 percent to 27.5 percent of Europe's electricity and from under 8 percent to 16 percent of the continent's energy.[66] While environmental groups celebrate this renewable "success," consumers and business suffer.

Drax power station, North Yorkshire, England[67]

## Drax Power Station Folly

The Drax power station in North Yorkshire, England, is the largest power station in Europe, delivering up to 3,960 megawatts of electrical power. Drax was formerly a coal-fired station, consuming 36,000 tons of coal per day, delivered by 140 coal trains each week. But because the UK government and the EU do not count carbon dioxide emissions from the burning of wood, Drax is being converted to burn wood chips instead of coal. Because Europe does not have enough wood to supply the plant, forests are cut down in the US and shipped more than 3,000 miles to North Yorkshire. Forests covering 4,600 square miles are needed to feed the plant's voracious appetite.[68]

The first-phase conversion of one-half of the Drax facility to wood cost £700 million ($1.1 billion). British consumers now pay roughly twice as much for electricity from the new wood-fired plant as from the previous coal station. Drax Group plc receives an annual subsidy of over £1 billion ($1.6 billion) for this forest-consuming monster.[69]

## EUROPE'S RENEWABLE ENERGY LESSON

The European drive for renewable energy, and particularly wind and solar, created an energy system where everyone loses. Consumers, industry, traditional electrical utilities, and even renewable energy companies lose in the new energy regime.

Europe is learning that the intermittent capacity of wind and solar is disruptive. Wholesale electricity prices, once driven by market demand, are now driven by the weather. When the wind blows and the sun shines, large amounts of electricity from wind and solar fields are dumped onto the grid, forcing wholesale prices to go negative. Conversely, prices rise during cloudy days with low wind, even during periods of low demand. Wind and solar generators receive guaranteed subsidy payments from FITs, regardless of market demand. The renewable build-out forced European wholesale markets into disequilibrium, no longer responsive to the need for electricity by consumers and businesses, and caused a steady decline in wholesale prices. Also, as fluctuating wind and solar output rises, grid operators must increasingly intervene to maintain electricity voltage and frequency within normal operating ranges. German grid operator Tennet reports that the number of stabilization interventions soared from 2 in 2003, to 387 in 2007, to 1,213 in 2013.[70]

Consumers lose big in the new age of renewables. Europe's FITs are typically paid by boosting electricity rates for households. Green energy subsidies more than offset the wholesale electricity price decline, spurring a dramatic rise in residential electricity prices. From 2004 to 2014, European consumers saw prices rise more than 50 percent, from 14 to 22 euro cents per kW-hr. The UK suffered a 141 percent rise over the ten-year period, with hefty increases in Germany (74 percent), Ireland (93 percent), Portugal (69 percent), and Spain (114 percent).[71] A plot of installed wind and solar capacity and household electricity prices shows a strong association for European nations. The more wind and solar capacity, the more consumers pay for electricity. Spanish households now pay three times the US price. Households in Denmark and Germany pay almost four times the US price.[72]

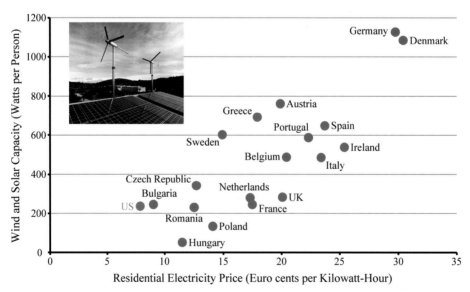

**Wind and Solar Capacity and Electricity Prices in Europe, 2014.** Installed wind and solar capacity per person and residential electricity price for nations of Europe, compared to the US. Higher prices are strongly associated with higher amounts of wind and solar capacity. (Eurostat, 2015; EurObserv'ER, 2015; World Bank, 2015, US EIA, 2015)[73]

European industrial companies also lose in the era of sustainable energy. From 2007 to 2014, the continent's average industrial electricity prices climbed by 30 percent, compared to a 12 percent rise in the US. Over the same period, major rises occurred in France (59 percent), Germany (47 percent), and the UK (27 percent).[74] But these industrial rates should be even higher. To prevent the migration of major companies, governments shield energy-intensive businesses from higher electricity rates. For example, Germany's EEG levy, the renewable fee added to electricity bills, increased from 0.19 euro cents/kW-hr in 2000 to 6.24 euro cents/kW-hr in 2014. Large German industrial companies are exempt from the EEG levy, amounting to a huge €5 billion per year, leaving consumers to pay most of the bill for green energy.[75]

European industry also faces comparatively high costs for natural gas. Unlike petroleum markets, which trade on a world price, natural gas prices continue to be set in regional markets. Nevertheless, back in 2007, natural gas spot prices in Europe and the US were comparable at about $6–8 per million British Thermal Units (BTU). But Europe's gas prices rose to about $9 per million BTU in 2014, while the US gas price fell to just above $4, driven by the US hydrofracturing revolution.[76] Fracking for natural gas has not yet been deployed in Europe. Bulgaria, France, Germany, and the Netherlands adopted fracking bans. Shale projects in Poland and Romania have been slow to achieve success. Fracking efforts slowly move forward in the UK against strong community opposition.

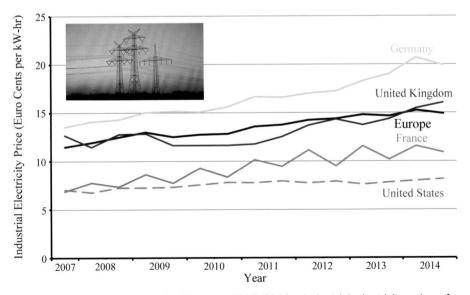

**Industrial Electricity Prices in Europe, 2007–2014.** Industrial electricity prices for Europe (EU28) and selected nations compared to the US in euro cents per kilowatt-hour. US prices are the EIA commercial end-use sector. (Eurostat 2016; EIA, 2016)[77]

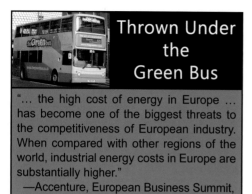

**Thrown Under the Green Bus**

"… the high cost of energy in Europe … has become one of the biggest threats to the competitiveness of European industry. When compared with other regions of the world, industrial energy costs in Europe are substantially higher."
—Accenture, European Business Summit, May 16, 2013[78]

As a result, Europe's high cost of industrial natural gas is likely to continue, a competitive disadvantage for European firms in world markets. For example, the UK chemical industry delivers 16 percent of the nation's industrial output and energy accounts for about 30 percent of chemical production costs, much of it from natural gas. Since 2009, 22 UK chemical plants have closed, with no new builds.[79]

European industries lead the world in the export of energy-intensive goods, providing more than one-third of world exports in 2013, according to the International Energy Agency.[80] But European industries now stagger under the burdens of high electricity prices, high natural gas prices, and a mounting bill to purchase carbon credits. Electricity accounts for a large portion of production costs in industries such as aluminum (40 percent), cement (21 percent), paper (7 percent) and steel (8 percent).[81]

Lakshmi Mittal, CEO of ArcelorMittal, the world's largest steel company, stated:

> … EU energy and climate policy is punishing the steel sector and other energy-intensive industries, which is having a profound impact on our competitiveness.… there is no realistic prospect of renewables powering the European steel industry soon. Despite many improvements, the available technologies are currently limited, placing the EU's unrealistic emissions reduction requirements out of reach for even the most advanced plants.[82]

Within the last five years, ArchlorMittal halted iron and steel production at plants in Liege, Belgium, in Florange, France, and in Schifflange, Luxembourg, and stopped operations at a plate mill in Galati, Romania.

Despite efforts to shield companies from higher electricity rates, Europe's climate policies are driving a migration of industry from the continent. As energy-intensive plants age and need to be replaced, operations managers often choose non-European locations. In 2013, automobile giant BWM chose Moses Lake, Washington, in the US for their new energy-intensive plant to manufacture carbon fiber auto parts. A large factor in site selection was the low three cents per kilowatt-hour electricity from nearby dams on the Columbia River.[83]

The European drive for renewable energy is devastating traditional electrical utilities. RWE, a major German power generator, suffered a net loss of €2.8 billion in 2013, the company's first net loss since 1949.[84] E.ON, German's largest electricity producer, reported a record €3.2 billion loss for year 2014, followed by a €7 billion loss for a single quarter of operation in November 2015.[85] From 2008 to 2013, long-term corporate bond ratings for Europe's five largest utilities, EDF, GDF Suez, Enel, E.ON, and RWE were all downgraded by Moody's credit rating agency.[86] Over the same five-year period, the total market value of European utilities declined by half a trillion euros.[87] Share prices have recovered somewhat but continue to under-perform other European stocks.

Conventional coal- and gas-fired power plants are no longer profitable in much of Europe, hammered by the double whammy of declining wholesale electricity prices and forced output reduction. The massive construction of generating capacity, driven by the only-too-successful renewable expansion policies, produced a steady decline in wholesale electricity prices. In 2008–2009, wholesale prices varied around 50–70 euro cents per kW-hr, declining to 35–45 euro cents per kW-hr by 2015.[88] This price decline affected utilities in most nations, since Germany and Denmark export large amounts of power when wind and solar generators are producing.

Mandates prioritizing renewable-generated electricity force conventional power plants to reduce output. Conventional plants increasingly provide only a back-up role to renewables. In 2010, E.ON launched units four and five of the company's Irsching gas-fired power plant, both operating at 60 percent efficiency, the highest in the world. But by 2012, output from these new units dropped severely, replaced by renewable generation. E.ON then signed an agreement with grid operator Tennet to keep the Irsching plants open to provide back-up power, in exchange for annual subsidy payments of over €10 million.[89]

Coal and gas plants can hardly break even due to low wholesale prices. No one will invest in new conventional plants that run less than half of the time and are forced to accept low wholesale prices. But these plants are needed to keep the lights on when the wind and sunshine disappear. So, like the Irsching plant, utilities now demand "capacity payment" subsidies, and governments are granting such payments.

Capacity remuneration mechanisms (CRMs) now operate in France, Germany,

**Sustainable Subsidies?**

"You have a wholesale price that is not actually the driver of investments any longer. If you look at renewables, the money doesn't come from the actual energy price, it comes from subsidies. In a market with low demand, that puts pressure on the whole system with the merit order pricing system that we have. It makes it difficult to see how you could invest in conventional generation under these circumstances."
—Magnus Hall, CEO of electrical utility Vattenfall AB, December 10, 2014[90]

Italy, Spain, the UK, and at least five other nations.[91] CRMs subsidize utilities to operate coal and natural gas plants that would otherwise be shut down. So Europeans now
subsidize both renewable facilities and also the conventional power plants that must back
up the renewables. The costs of CRM payments to back-up plants and the costs of grid
interventions are hidden costs attributable to the installation of wind and solar energy.

E.ON and Vattenfall AB, a Swedish utility, now pursue a new corporate solution to
counter the green assault. They've reorganized their energy businesses into the "good
energy" (renewables) and the "bad energy" (coal and gas). The bad-energy subsidiaries are
being spun off into separate companies and put up for sale.[92] But who will buy conventional power plants that can't turn a profit? To keep the lights on, governments must either
pay large capacity subsidies or will be forced to nationalize these conventional utility assets.

Even renewable companies now struggle in Europe's green energy "miracle." Supported
by two decades of government subsidies and mandates, European company sales of capital
equipment for renewable energy, including biofuels, biogas, solid biomass, geothermal,
heat pumps, small hydropower, solar and wind, grew to a total of €143 billion in 2012.
But renewable energy equipment sales fell in 2013 to €138 billion and are expected to
decline again in 2014 and 2015.[93] Renewable energy employment, both direct and indirect
jobs, soared from 50,000 in 2000 to 1.2 million in 2012, but began a decline in 2013 to

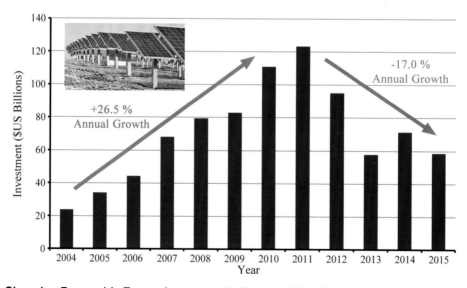

**Changing Renewable Energy Investment in Europe 2004–2015.** Annual investment in
renewable energy, including generating systems, and corporate and government research
and development. (Bloomberg New Energy Finance, 2014, 2016)[94]

1.1 million.[95] Investment in renewables grew from 2004 to 2011 at a 26.5 percent annual rate, but has declined since 2011 at an annual rate of 17 percent, with 2015 investment less than half of the peak 2011 year.[96] An important factor in the declining numbers for equipment sales and investment is the falling cost of solar photovoltaic cells and other renewable system prices, but a larger factor is the cut back in government subsidies.

The renewable-driven impact of rising electricity prices and bloated national budgets forced governments of Europe to slash renewable subsidies and roll back mandates. Spain's generous subsidies stimulated an explosion in wind and solar installations, but also an explosion in an unsustainable government-financed subsidy obligation that totaled €28.7 billion ($37 billion) annually by 2008.[97] In September 2008, the government of Spain retroactively reduced subsidy payments and established a quota system for renewables. Solar installations dropped 90 percent by 2013, and 55,000 solar and 20,000 wind jobs disappeared.[98] Italy's electricity rate-payers accumulated renewable debt obligations of €200 billion ($260 billion) for solar installations that provided less than 10 percent of Italy's electricity. In 2012, Italy introduced a tax on renewable-produced electricity and eliminated its FIT in 2013, causing solar investment to plummet and bankruptcies to surge.[99] Subsidy cuts and tax hikes in Belgium, Bulgaria, France, Germany, Greece, the UK, and other nations force renewable companies to look for "greener" pastures.

Europe also faces a growing prospect of a shortfall in electric power availability. With reactor shut downs in Germany and Spain, Europe's nuclear generating capacity has fallen since 2011. Coal and gas generating capacity has fallen since 2012.[100] Every year, additional conventional generating capacity is closed. On days with little sun and wind, fewer

---

### Mr. Brown and Mr. Green

Suppose you are an employer, considering to hire two different employees. Mr. Brown requires wages of $10 per hour and Mr. Green requires wages of $8 per hour. Mr. Brown will work full time, five days per week, but Mr. Green will work only part time, one or two days per week, and you'll never know which days Mr. Green will show up for work. Would you hire Mr. Green? In the analogy, Mr. Brown represents conventional hydrocarbon or nuclear power, while Mr. Green represents intermittent wind and solar energy.

Further, suppose government policies imposed mandates on employers requiring that all intermittent employees like Mr. Green *must be hired*. In addition, the labor of intermittent employees must be accepted on any day they show up, requiring Mr. Brown and other regular employees to be sent home randomly on a daily basis. Mr. Brown would soon look for another job. European grid priority laws and some US net metering laws impose similar mandates. Wind and solar capacity is disruptive capacity.

**Era of Constant Electricity at Home is Ending, Says Power Chief**

"The grid is going to be a very different system in 2020, 2030. We keep thinking that we want it to be there and provide power when we need it…. As a society, we all need to be clear about what we can and cannot afford."

—Steve Holliday, UK National Grid CEO, *The Daily Telegraph*, March 2, 2011[101]

reliable power stations remain to keep the lights on. Britain recently introduced emergency measures to prevent winter blackouts. UK businesses now receive payments to shut down operations between 4 PM and 8 PM on cold winter days.[102] Shortfall in electricity supply, once the mark of an underdeveloped nation, may soon be rampant in Europe, courtesy of sustainable development.

Europe's dismal green energy experience provides a lesson for everyone. For expenditures nearing a trillion dollars, and with obligations of additional trillions, Europe created an energy system where everyone loses. Consumers pay among the highest household electricity rates in the industrialized world. Businesses face uncompetitive costs for electricity and natural gas, electing to move energy-intensive facilities to the US or other locations. Conventional coal and gas-fired utilities, beset by falling wholesale prices and plant utilization rates, face operating losses and plummeting stock values, with dim prospects for needed investment in new facilities. And renewable companies that no longer receive fat subsidies for wind and solar projects, now pursue business in other nations that have not yet learned Europe's renewable lesson.

## SHALE SHOCK—THE WORLD HAS CHANGED

The world is only slowly beginning to realize how profoundly the energy industry has changed. The revolution in production of oil and gas from shale altered the course of global energy, affecting most of the world's people. Individuals, business, and countries will be impacted for decades to come.

Over the last 20 years, US exploration companies perfected the technologies of hydraulic fracturing and horizontal drilling, enabling the cost-effective production of oil and gas from shale rock fields. Oil in shale is called "tight oil." Rather than pooling in porous rocks between shale rock layers, shale oil is tightly held within the shale itself. Fracking employs water and sand, injected under pressure, to fracture the rock and release the oil. Horizontal wells, drilled radially outward from a single vertical shaft, maximize the capture of oil and gas from horizontal shale layers.

Fracking is not new technology. A veteran oil and gas industry executive told me about ad-hoc fracking techniques used in the Appalachian Mountains during the 1960s. At that time, some companies dropped armor-piercing bullets followed by nitroglycerine into mine shafts to squeeze more oil from existing wells. Today's frackers use water and sand.

By boosting US production back above 9 million barrels per day, the shale shock triggered a plunge in global crude oil prices, from over $100 per barrel in summer 2014 to under $30 per barrel by early 2016.[103] For the first time in four decades, the world oil price was determined by competition. OPEC could no longer control the price of petroleum by restricting production. Low prices clobbered oil-baron nations, such as Nigeria, Russia, and Venezuela, slashing export revenues, forcing national budget cuts and fostering civil unrest. Results from the global glut of oil in 2016 continue to unfold, but major traditional oil companies are hard hit, with many oil investments, such as the deep-water oil fields in the North Sea, no longer profitable. More than 100,000 jobs disappeared in the US oil industry, many shed from the fracking companies that created the shale revolution.[104]

In a 2013 study, the US Energy Information Administration stated, "the world shale oil and shale gas resource is vast."[105] Argentina, Brazil, Canada, China, India, Mexico, Pakistan, Poland, Russia, the UK, and other countries contain shale basins with technically recoverable oil and natural gas deposits. With the fracking genie out of the bottle, non-US fracking fields will soon be under development, adding to the available supply.

World oil prices rise and fall in cycles. The low crude prices in 2016 will soon rise in response to growing global demand and recent price-driven reductions in production. But technology used by the oil and gas industry has improved by orders of magnitude in terms of cost and cycle time. As energy expert Daniel Yergin points out, "It takes $10 billion and five to ten years to launch a deep-water project. It takes $10 million and just 20 days to drill for shale."[106] It's likely that production from shale fields, which can be quickly ramped in response to rising prices, will put a lid on world oil prices for the next decades.

But fracking is now the devil to be slain for the sustainability movement. The shale shock means low-cost hydrocarbon energy for the world. Unless foolish government programs artificially raise the price of hydrocarbons, people will enjoy access to low-cost fuel for transportation, low-cost gas for home heating, and low-cost energy for industry. Hydrocarbon energy will fuel economic growth for decades, a prospect scorned by the anti-growth sustainability crowd. Low-cost natural gas diminishes the competitiveness of wind and solar. Low-cost petroleum means inexpensive gasoline and diesel fuel for vehicles, diminishing the competitiveness of biofuels. For these reasons, environmental groups will fight hydraulic fracturing to the death.

## THE WAR ON HYDROCARBONS

We live in the age of NOPE. Past protests against energy production and transmission facilities were local in nature and labeled NIMBY, or "not in my backyard." Today, protests are based on the philosophy of NOPE, "not on planet Earth." Any project to build a mine, a power plant, a pipeline, a refinery, an electrical transmission line, an airport runway, or anything else that involves hydrocarbons, will be opposed by the sustainability movement.

An example is the rejection of the Keystone XL pipeline. The pipeline project proposed to transport more than 800,000 barrels of crude oil per day from Canadian oil sands, Montana, and North Dakota to US Gulf Coast refineries. Environmental groups viciously attacked the project, claiming that construction of the pipeline would pollute water aquifers, increase global warming, and even cause cancer. Seven years of review by the US State Department concluded that Keystone XL would neither harm aquifers nor significantly increase greenhouse gas emissions. The 875-mile Keystone XL, a follow-on to the Keystone and other pipelines already transporting oil from Canadian oil sands, proposed only a small addition to the 50,000 miles of US oil pipelines already in operation. But in November 2015, President Obama rejected the project, stating:

> America is now a global leader when it comes to taking serious action to fight climate change. And frankly, approving this project would have undercut that global leadership.[107]

Instead, rail cars transport oil from Canadian oil sands, a method more expensive, less safe, and emitting more greenhouse gases than transportation by pipeline.

Businesses often serve as willing accomplices in the war on hydrocarbons. In 2007, the Sierra Club announced their "Beyond Coal" campaign, with the objective:

Union: Obama Threw Workers 'Under the Bus' in Keystone Decision
—*The Hill*, November 9, 2015[108]

> … to replace dirty coal with clean energy by mobilizing grass roots activists in local communities to advocate for the retirement of old and outdated coal plants and to prevent new coal plants from being built.[109]

The club claims that the campaign succeeded in closing more than 200 US coal-fired power plants. One of the funding organizations for the Beyond Coal campaign was natural gas producer Chesapeake Energy, contributing a total of $26 million over four years. Apparently Chesapeake hoped to gain share in the power plant fuel market as utilities switched from coal to natural gas. But then in May 2012, the Sierra Club announced their "Beyond Gas" campaign. As Winston Churchill said, "An appeaser is one who feeds the crocodile, hoping

**Feed the Green Crocodile!**

**Gas Firm Funded Sierra Club Campaign**
"From 2007 to 2010, Chesapeake Energy poured $26 million into the anti-coal campaign by the Sierra Club, a tax-exempt environmental group."
—*Charleston Gazette-Mail*, February 15, 2012[110]

it will eat him last." Natural gas, nuclear, and other industries with a vested competitive interest provide ammunition to environmental groups for the war on hydrocarbons.

## THE FOOLISH AND THE DESTRUCTIVE

Sustainability promotes energy policies that are uneconomical beyond the point of being foolish. Some are even harmful to Earth's environment. Governments and businesses eagerly pursue these policies in the quest to be green. The most notable involve biofuels, electric cars, utility-scale battery storage, and carbon capture and storage.

Fuel for transportation remains a big hole in the drive for a zero-carbon society. Transportation accounts for 30–40 percent of energy consumption in developed nations, and more than 90 percent of vehicle fuel comes from oil. To try to close this hole, advocates promote biofuels and electric vehicles as the sustainable answer for transportation energy.

Biofuels primarily consist of ethanol, which is blended with gasoline, and biodiesel, which is blended with diesel fuel, as substitutes for vehicle fuel from crude oil. After the OPEC oil embargo of the 1970s, Europe and the US pursued biofuels to reduce dependence on foreign oil. The sustainable movement subsequently adopted biofuels as a method to combat global warming and to reduce hydrocarbon energy use.

Headlines We Expect to See?

*Post-Herald*

Sierra Club Announces 'Beyond Prosperity' Campaign[111]

But a problem remained. Scientific studies show that combustion of biomass emits more carbon dioxide than burning coal.[112] In 1996, the Intergovernmental Panel on Climate Change (IPCC) developed a solution. They published guidelines for greenhouse gas emissions accounting, stating "biomass consumption is assumed to equal its regrowth."[113] The IPCC assumed that, as biofuel plants grow, they absorb $CO_2$ equal to the amount released when burned, making biofuels "carbon neutral." If correct, the substitution of biofuels for hydrocarbon fuels would reduce net emissions.

Governments soon embraced and promoted "carbon neutral" biofuels as the answer for low-carbon transportation energy. President George W. Bush, Prime Minister Tony Blair, and Chancellor Angela Merkel became public cheerleaders for green, leafy petrol. The European Community's Biofuels Directive of 2003 called for 2 percent of vehicle fuel from biofuels by 2005, later raised to 10 percent by 2020.[114] The ethanol share of the US corn crop ballooned from 6 percent in 2001 to 38 percent in 2014, but still provided only about 10 percent of US vehicle fuel.[115]

The biofuel push rapidly became the most destructive of sustainable energy policies. About 2.7 gallons of ethanol is produced from each bushel of corn. A single 25-gallon tank of E85 fuel (up to 83 percent ethanol) for a Sport Utility Vehicle consumes as much as 8 bushels of corn, which can feed a person in the developing world for most of a year.[116] From 2001 to 2012, world corn and soybean prices doubled, driven by the mad rush to produce biofuels.[117] According to the UN Food and Agriculture Organization, biofuel production is a major factor boosting grain prices.

Biofuel mania also harms the environment. Field runoff of nitrogen fertilizer used to grow corn for ethanol flows down the Mississippi River and adds to eutrophication (oxygen depletion) in the Gulf of Mexico. Rain forests in Indonesia are cut down and replaced with palm oil plantations, so that feedstock for biodiesel can be shipped 10,000 miles to Germany to meet biofuel targets.[119] Higher food prices, ocean eutrophication, and deforestation are apparently a small price to pay so US and European motorists can burn food derivatives in cars, rather than hydrocarbons.

People of poor nations don't need biofuels, but they do need affordable food prices.[118]

To top it all off, scientists now realize that biofuels *do not* reduce $CO_2$ emissions when substituted for gasoline or diesel fuel. A 2011 paper by the European Environment Agency pointed out that, when land-use changes are considered, biofuel production is not carbon neutral:

> It is widely assumed that biomass combustion would be inherently "carbon neutral" because it only releases carbon taken from the atmosphere during plant growth. However, this assumption is not correct and results in a form of double-counting, as it ignores the fact that using land to produce plants for energy typically means that this land *is not producing plants for other purposes*, including carbon otherwise sequestered.[120]

Biofuel production may also add to air pollution. A 2011 study from the National Academy of Sciences concluded:

> The production and use of ethanol from biomass is projected to result in the higher release of air pollutants such as particulate matter, ozone, and sulfur oxide than petroleum-based fuels.[121]

Electric cars, a second questionable policy, receive purchase subsidies in most developed nations in the name of sustainability. In 2008, President Barack Obama pledged to put one million electric cars on the road by 2015. The US provides a $7,500 tax credit to purchasers of electric cars.[122] The US Department of Transportation and the EPA adopted a 54.5-mile-per-gallon Corporate Average Fuel Economy standard, to be phased in by year 2025, intended to force adoption of plug-in electric vehicles (PHEVs).[123]

But electric cars face a big hurdle—the physics of batteries. The energy density of today's lithium-ion batteries is about 120 watt-hours per kilogram, or only one percent of the energy density of gasoline or diesel fuel.[124] Electric motors are about four times as efficient, but petroleum-fueled internal combustion cars still have at least a 20-to-1 power advantage over PHEVs. The poor energy density of batteries causes the sub-100-mile driving range of most of today's electric cars.

Another big issue is the poor life span of today's automobile batteries. The average age of a US car reached 11.5 years in 2015, but electric car batteries struggle to last half that long.[125] Automobile engines age, but the energy in a gallon of gasoline remains the same throughout the life of a vehicle. In contrast, electric car batteries begin to degrade the day an electric car leaves the showroom. Chemical reactions within a battery continuously work to remove its charge. Complete charging, rapid charging, frequent charging, and hot temperatures degrade batteries faster. At the end of five years, an electric car may get only 80 percent of its original driving range.

Most electric car warranties don't cover loss of battery power. The Tesla Model S 85-hour battery "unlimited mile" warranty states, "Loss of battery energy or power over time or due to or resulting from battery usage, is NOT covered under this Battery Limited Warranty."[126] Like most other electric car manufacturers, Tesla only warrants that the battery will move the car. The price of replacement batteries is huge, from $5,500 for a Nissan Leaf to a whopping $44,000 for the Tesla S 85-hour battery.[127]

Nor are electric cars doing well in the new age of lower gasoline prices from fracking. As the price of gasoline dropped to $2 per gallon, US PHEV sales declined 6 percent from 2014 to 2015, and sales gains in 2016 are likely to be small.[128] Despite generous government subsidies and mandates, the shortcomings of short driving range, lack of charging stations, poor battery life spans, and high prices will relegate electric vehicle demand to green advocates or the bountifully rich for coming decades.

Utility-scale batteries are another proposed foolish energy policy. Sustainable advocates recommend huge batteries to store intermittent wind- and solar-generated electricity for electrical power systems. Utility-scale storage of electricity, they claim, will allow wind and solar to completely replace hydrocarbon-fueled power plants. The problem again is cost. Battery-backed solar systems increase the cost of electricity by a factor of four or five, compared to current electrical power.[129] As in the case of electric cars, the five- to ten-year life spans of utility-scale battery banks compare poorly to life spans of today's power plants, which operate for more than 30 years.

**To Die a Green Death**

Internal Combustion Engine

Germany Wants All Europe to Ban Non-Electric New Cars by 2030
—*ItechPost*, October 31, 2016[130]

Since the invention of just-in-time manufacturing by Toyota in the 1960s, manufacturing industries pursued inventory reduction on a global scale. Firms adopted waste elimination, kanban, zero inventory, lot sizes of one, and many other programs to reduce in-process and finished-goods inventory. In the same spirit, electricity is the ultimate just-in-time good. Large-scale electrical power is produced only when demanded. It's true that a limited amount of low-cost storage can benefit electrical system operation, but adding large amounts of storage will be costly and counterproductive. In fact, hydrocarbon and nuclear plants already use storage. Energy is stored in the chemical bonds of coal, natural gas, and nuclear fuels both on site and in delivery systems. Storage of electricity is only required to compensate for the shortfalls of wind and solar.

The green energy revolution produced many bizarre technologies, but carbon capture and storage (CCS) wins the top prize. CCS requires capturing emitted carbon dioxide from industrial plants, transporting it by pipeline, and storing it underground to prevent release into the atmosphere. EPA Administrator Gina McCarthy says CCS "is a technology that is feasible and it's available today."[131]

"The near-universal failure to make the connection between energy-intensive lifestyles and ecological disaster is a disturbing illustration of collective amnesia. As a consequence, an increasing majority of the population is inadvertently complicit in a process that is already reducing the quality of life of literally billions of people, and which will almost certainly cause the deaths of millions in the near and longer-term future."
—Mayer Hillman, Senior Fellow Emeritus, Policy Studies Institute, 2005[132]

CCS may be feasible on a small scale, but it's very expensive and not feasible on a large scale. Power plant capacity must be increased by about 30 percent just to provide energy to capture $CO_2$ from the combustion process. The US Department of Energy estimates that CCS increases coal-fired electricity cost by about 70 percent.[133] But the volume of the carbon dioxide to be captured crushes any ideas about feasibility. As we discussed in Chapter 5, the amount of $CO_2$ produced by industry is small in global terms, only about five percent of what nature releases to and absorbs from the atmosphere every day. But the amount of industrial $CO_2$ produced is huge in human terms. Think of the mile-long train of hopper cars filled with coal that is consumed by a large power plant every day. Picture more than double this volume to estimate the amount of $CO_2$ to be captured and stored, since combustion adds two oxygen atoms for each carbon atom. The volumes and costs are staggering.

In November 2015, Shell Oil began operating the state-of-the-art Quest CCS project in Alberta, Canada. The system captures 1.2 million tons of $CO_2$ per year from chemical processing, transports the $CO_2$ 64 kilometers, and injects it into deep saline aquifers. The carbon capture facility costs US$1.35 billion, with $771 million provided by Canadian government subsidies. Operating the facility costs about $41 million per year to capture and put $CO_2$ in the ground.[134] But 1.2 million tons of $CO_2$ per year is tiny compared to sustainable plans for CCS. Models of the International Energy Agency estimate that 6,000 million tons of $CO_2$ must be captured and sequestered *each year* by 2050 to meet the IPCC goal of a maximum global temperature rise of 2°C.[135] This would require about 5,000

Quest projects and a global capital investment of an astonishing $6.75 trillion dollars and annual operating costs of $205 billion dollars, just to capture the $CO_2$.

Like other green remedies, CCS is headed for failure. Carbon dioxide can enhance oil recovery and has other industrial uses, but otherwise captured $CO_2$ has zero commercial value. CCS is hugely expensive, and large-scale implementation is probably not feasible. When the world finally realizes that human emissions play only an insignificant role in global temperatures, CCS facilities will be discarded on the junk heap of human history.

## A LESSON FOR ENERGY EXECUTIVES

As we discussed in earlier chapters, there is neither evidence that rising energy use increases pollution, nor that hydrocarbon energy is in short supply. Empirical evidence does not show that human greenhouse gas emissions produce a measurable change in global temperatures. Nevertheless, local, state, provincial, and national governments continue to force adoption of renewable energy by consumers and businesses.

Renewables, and particularly wind and solar energy, can't provide the energy needed by modern society. Wind and solar are dilute, intermittent, and costly. Forced adoption of wind and solar results in higher electricity costs and reduced grid reliability. For more than 20 years, the nations of Europe promoted and mandated wind and solar energy. Europe's result is the disruption of wholesale electricity markets, rising consumer and industrial electricity prices, the migration of energy-intensive industries, the financial demise of traditional electrical utilities, bloated national budgets from renewable subsidies, and the eventual decline of renewable investment. Other countries should learn from Europe's lesson and adopt policies to allow energy sources to compete on a level playing field on capability, reliability, price, and environmental quality.

Electrical utilities should deliver the lowest-cost electricity with excellent reliability, along with adoption of sensible environmental protection measures. Policies to force renewable adoption should be opposed. Wind and solar should be paid wholesale market prices for delivered energy, not inflated feed-in tariff or net metering prices. Companies should pursue environmental policies that reduce real air and water pollutants. Energy should be used as a factor in production along with labor and capital to produce products and services with the highest benefit and lowest cost for customers. Policies that reduce energy use for energy's sake, count carbon footprints, and tout renewables produce negligible actual benefit for the environment. Adopting biofuels, switching to electric vehicles, and capturing carbon dioxide emissions is foolish and in some cases even environmentally damaging.

CHAPTER 8

# AGRICULTURE UNDER ATTACK

*"Cultivators of the earth are the most valuable citizens. They are the most vigorous,
the most independent, the most virtuous, and they are tied to their country and
wedded to its liberty and interests by the most lasting bands."*

—THOMAS JEFFERSON (1785)[1]

Agriculture is under attack. The green movement warns that, like energy usage, modern agriculture pollutes the planet and destroys the climate. They complain that farmers use too much land and water. Ecological schizophrenics label biofuel production sustainable, but meat production unsustainable. Organic pesticides are good, but synthetic pesticides cause cancer. Genetically modified farming technology threatens humanity. Deforestation and overfishing put us on the road to calamity. Alarmists demand that farmers be "climate-smart." Consumers must plant trees, buy locally, eat less meat, and never, ever eat genetically modified foods. But instead, trends show that today's farmers are using less land, water, fertilizer, and pesticides to feed the world's billions.

## AGRICULTURE SUCCESS AND SCORN

Modern agriculture has been remarkably successful. From 1961 to 2013, world population more than doubled from 3.1 billion to 7.2 billion.[2] But over the same period, world agricultural production more than tripled, according to data from the United Nations Food and Agriculture Organization (FAO).[3]

The success of modern agriculture means that humanity is slowly winning the battle against world hunger. About 30 percent of the world's population was chronically undernourished in 1950. That number has fallen to about 11 percent today. During the last 20 years, the number of undernourished people declined by more than 200 million, but 800 million people still do not get enough to eat.[4]

Not only the quantity, but the quality and variety of food is much better than in past ages. Ferdinand Magellan's round-the-globe voyage in 1519 searched for a westerly route to the spice islands. Today's common food spices, such as black pepper, cinnamon, cloves, and nutmeg, were uncommon, expensive, and only available by long journey from the Far East. Modern foods come from all over the world. Coffee was first brewed in Arabia in the 1400s.[5] Columbus encountered the pineapple during his second voyage to the Caribbean in 1493.[6] Oranges first arrived in Europe from Asia in the 1400s.[7] Today we enjoy Valencia, Cara Cara, Navel, Tangerine, Clementine, Seville, Bergamot, Naruto, Sanbo, Kitchli, and other varieties of orange. Corn (maize) was domesticated by Native Americans 2,500 years ago and carried to Europe during the 1500s. Now farmers grow dozens of varieties of corn, including dent corn, flint corn, flour corn, pod corn, popcorn, and sweet corn. A 2015 Stockholm University study compared modern food to food of the Middle Ages, including recipes from the chef of King Richard II of England. The study concluded that people of today's developed nations eat better than kings of old.[8]

But some say that modern agriculture is unsustainable. Sustainable advocates scorn the farmer's use of water, land, pesticides, and energy. From a 2010 United Nations Environment Programme document:

> Agricultural production accounts for a staggering 70% of the global freshwater consumption, 38% of the total land use, and 14% of the world's greenhouse gas emissions… The use of agrochemicals is related to ecotoxicity, eutrophication and depletion of phosphorus stocks. Intensive agriculture is related to substantial energy use. The loss of soil and biomass carbon can contribute to climate change.[9]

Climatists further warn that global warming will degrade agricultural yields. The 2014 Fifth Assessment Report of the IPCC projected an average "impact" of a two percent yield

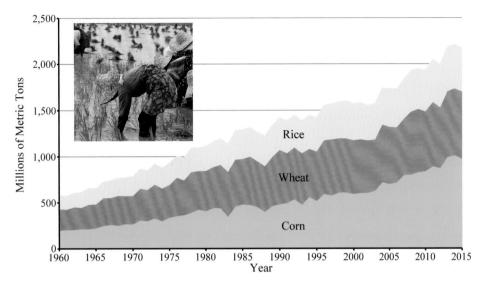

**World Corn, Rice, and Wheat Production, 1960–2015.** Rising world corn, rice, and wheat production in millions of metric tons per year. Yearly data is across a two-year agricultural season (i.e. 1960 for 1960/1961). Image of rice farming in Iran. (USDA, 2016)[10]

loss per decade throughout this century, with larger yield losses near the year 2100. The report stated that negative aspects of climate change are already "evident in several regions of the world."[11] But global production figures do not show these impacts. World output of corn, rice, and wheat continues to rise.

Some sustainable ideologues think it's terrible that we import agricultural products from foreign lands. They dislike the fact that petroleum powers the international shipment of food. Last year I attended a lecture by a professor from Scotland, who visited Chicago courtesy of a hydrocarbon-consuming carbon dioxide-emitting jet. He proposed that everyone should buy locally and eat locally-grown foods to solve the "climate crisis." Should Illinois farmers try to grow pineapples so that Chicagoans can "eat locally"? Should Scots grow their own coffee?

Production and consumption of meat now tops the list of farming evils. Environmentalist Jeremy Rifkin lectures us:

In the past half a century, we have erected an artificial, worldwide protein ladder, with grain-fed beef and other meats on the top rung. Affluent populations, especially in Europe, North America and Japan, devour the bounty of the planet. The transition of world agriculture from food grain to feed grain represents a new form of human evil, with consequences possibly far greater and longer lasting than any past wrongdoing inflicted by men against their fellow human beings.[12]

But contrary to all the sustainable alarm, today's farmers are boosting the quantity and quality of agricultural output, while simultaneously *reducing* the impact on the environment. New agricultural techniques and technologies produce greater output on less land, with less water usage, and with greater variety and quality.

## PEAK AGRICULTURAL LAND

According to UN data, land used for agriculture is now declining. Total agricultural area, the sum of crop land and pasture land, peaked in 2000 at 4.955 billion hectares and declined about one-half percent through 2013. Over the same period, world agricultural production increased 37 percent.[13] While land used for agriculture continues to increase in most developing nations, farm land has been shrinking in developed countries since the mid-1980s.[14] The recent decline in total agricultural land use occurred despite 41.3 million hectares added for "sustainable" biofuel production, an area larger than Germany.[15]

The astounding improvement in agricultural yields provides growing output without use of additional land for farming. Gains in US corn yield are a remarkable example. Open-pollenated varieties of corn planted in the US in the late 1800s produced an average yield of less than 2,000 kilograms per hectare. Four-parent hybrids planted as early as 1925 boosted yields to 3,000 kg/ha by 1960. Two-parent corn hybrids introduced in the 1950s increased average yields to 7,000 kg/ha by 1980. Modern genetically modified hybrids raised yields to 9,000 kg/ha by 2005. US land used to harvest corn peaked in 1917. Today, farmers produce five times more corn on 11 percent less area than 100 years ago.[17]

In 1968, Paul Ehrlich remarked about India, "I don't see how they could possibly feed two hundred million more people by 1980."[18] But Ehrlich was wrong. India became an example of vast agricultural improvement. In 1961, the population of India was 459 million. The average Indian consumed 2,010 kilocalories of food per day, just above the average minimum UN requirement of 1,800 kcals per day. By 2013,

**James Cameron and Wife to Launch Campaign Advocating Sustainable Plant-Only Based Diet**
—*The Guardian*, July 4, 2014[16]

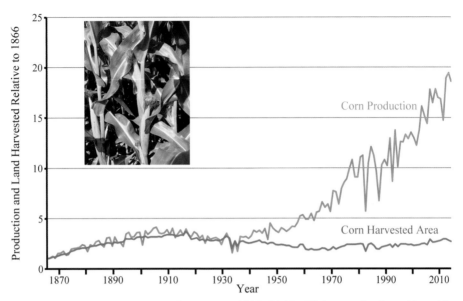

**US Corn Production and Land Harvested, 1866–2015.** Rising production with stable harvested area, relative to year 1866 (1866=1). The recent rise in harvested area coincides with corn production for ethanol vehicle fuel. (US Department of Agriculture, 2016)[19]

India's population more than tripled, to almost 1.3 billion. But farm output more than quadrupled and GDP increased by ten times. Daily food consumption increased 20 percent to 2,459 kcals per person. From 1961–1970, India imported a net average of 6.3 million tons of cereals per year, but *exported* 11.3 million tons per year from 2001–2013. These tremendous gains were achieved using only three percent more land in 2013 compared to 1961, with farm land peaking in 1991. Today India's people are better fed and have higher incomes, and the country exports cereals, using only three percent more land than 52 years ago.[20]

Indeed, the world appears to have passed the point of peak agricultural land use. Advanced farming techniques, including fertilizers, pesticides, irrigation, and new seed hybrids continue to boost farm productivity gains. As we discussed in Chapter 4, higher levels of atmospheric $CO_2$ are also increasing crop yields. As developing nations join the ranks of the developed nations, their farm land use will peak and also begin to decline. The world can look forward to the return of large amounts of land to nature.

## FRESH WATER CRISIS?

Ocean salt water comprises 97.5 percent of Earth's water. Polar ice caps, glaciers, and deep underground reservoirs hold most of the fresh water, totaling another 2.2 percent of

Earth's water. Only about 0.3 percent of our planet's water is readily available to humanity, the fresh water held in lakes, rivers, and accessible underground reservoirs.[21]

The water used by society isn't used up. Consumed water flows to the oceans as waste water, evaporates, and returns to the land by rainfall, as part of the hydrological cycle. But the sustainability movement warns that the world will soon run out of fresh water.

In recent decades, environmentalists led by the United Nations raised fears that the world faced a water crisis. A 1997 paper by the World Meteorological Organization, a UN division, asked, "The World's Water: Is There Enough?" The paper called water a "diminishing resource" and pointed out that 70 percent of all fresh water is used by agriculture.[22] A 1999 UN press release listed fresh water as one of the world's "full-scale emergencies" and warned, "The world water cycle seems unlikely to be able to cope with demands in the coming decades."[23] The 2006 UN Human Development Report concluded:

> The unsustainable exploitation of water resources represents a growing threat to human development, generating an unsustainable ecological debt that will be transferred to future generations.[24]

Sustainable advocates point out that, while the daily drinking water requirement per person is about 2–4 liters, production of one kilogram of grain requires 1,000–2,000 kilograms of water, and one kilogram of meat from livestock requires an average of 16,000 kg of water.[25] They warn that, as consumption and industrial needs grow in developing nations, demands for water will overwhelm the available fresh water sources of Earth.

We are certainly consuming more water. Human water consumption more than doubled from 1950 to 2000.[26] World irrigated land area increased 80 percent from 1961 to 2011, according to the FAO.[27] Global water consumption is increasing about one percent per year and is projected to grow at 10–12 percent per decade over the next 30 years.[28]

**Signs of the End Times?**

**Earth to RUN OUT of Water by 2050: Leaked Report Shows "Catastrophic" Fate Facing World**
—*Daily Express*, April 30, 2016[29]

Earth's water is unevenly distributed. A measure of water scarcity for a nation is per capita renewable water per year. A country is said to be water stressed when renewable water falls below 1,700 cubic meters per person per year, and in a state of chronic water scarcity when supplies drop below 1,000 m³ per person.[30] New Zealand enjoys abundant water resources with 72,000 m³ of water per person, while Israel ranks near the bottom with only 93 m³ per person.³¹ Over a third of the world's nations are classified as water stressed, with most located in Africa and the Middle East. The UN estimates that global water demand will increase 55 percent by the year 2050.³²

But fears that we'll run out of fresh water are misguided. Water consumption has stabilized or slightly declined in many of the world's developed nations, including Australia, Canada, Japan, Russia, the US, and most nations of Europe, even while farm output grows.³³ Improved water pricing policies in advanced nations reduce water over-use. Treatment of waste water and other pollution control measures improve water availability. Aqueducts move water from locations of abundance to locations of scarcity.

The developing nations also have growing access to water. In 2015, an estimated 663 million people lacked clean sources of drinking water, and as many as 2.4 billion did not use proper sanitation facilities.³⁴ But this situation is much improved since 1990. Over the last 25 years, more than 2 billion people gained access to clean drinking water, and almost 2 billion more people now use improved sanitation facilities.³⁵

Modern agriculture is adopting methods to produce greater output with less water. Drip irrigation systems reduce water use and improve yields by reducing the growth of weeds and incidence of disease. Advanced hybrid seeds produce larger harvests in dry regions. Water use efficiency continues to improve through innovations in agriculture technology.

Like other resources, fresh water can be created by people. The 99.7 percent of Earth's water currently unavailable provides a huge opportunity to expand society's water supply. Desalination of sea water is now a practical process used across the world. Despite higher costs than traditional methods of water withdrawal, more than 18,000 desalination plants, operating in more than 25 countries, supply about one percent of the world's consumed fresh water.³⁶ Desalination produces over 50 percent of fresh water consumed in Israel.³⁷ Treatment of waste water provides an additional potential source of recycled fresh water.

Humanity will always have sufficient water, if we are willing to pay for it. Growing incomes, low-cost energy for desalination, and advanced agricultural technology hold the keys to sufficient fresh water for generations to come. Artificial water restrictions on agriculture and society in the name of sustainability are only counterproductive.

## FERTILIZER TO FEED THE WORLD

Fertilizer to boost soil fertility has been central to agriculture throughout history. The Babylonians, Egyptians, Romans, and early Germans spread animal manure or minerals to increase crop yields. Manure served as the primary source of fertilizer for thousands of years. Ground-up bison bones were used as fertilizer in early US history.[38] Guano from seabirds of Peru was the world's most important source of commercial fertilizer for decades during the mid-1800s.[39]

Justus von Liebig, a German chemist of the nineteenth century, ushered in the era of modern agricultural chemistry. He determined that nitrogen, phosphorus, and potassium are essential for plant growth. All modern fertilizers provide compounds containing some or all of these elements to enrich the soil. In the early twentieth century, German scientists Carl Bosch and Fritz Haber developed the Haber-Bosch process for synthesizing nitrogen-containing ammonia from methane gas and gaseous nitrogen. Later, chemists used a process developed by Wilhelm Ostwald to produce nitric acid from ammonia on a commercial scale. Ammonia and nitric acid form basic components of many chemical fertilizers.[40]

During World War II, large factories were erected to produce nitrogen, a principal ingredient in explosives. After the war, these facilities were converted to produce low-cost ammonia and nitric acid for agricultural fertilizer. From 1961 to 2013, annual world consumption of chemical fertilizers increased by five times, from 31 million metric tons to 183 million tons.[41] Studies show that 40 to 60 percent of global agriculture yield today is attributable to the use of chemical fertilizer, with nitrogen the most important element.[42]

Advocates of sustainable development attack the farmer's use of chemical nutrients. An example is a 2013 article titled, "A Brief History of Our Deadly Addiction to Nitrogen Fertilizer." The article condemns US-farmer use of cheap nitrogen fertilizer produced from fracking of natural gas and warns of algae blooms and global warming from nitrous oxide gas.[43] Agricultural firms, such as Monsanto, are favorite targets for attacks by environmental groups. Greenpeace warns that "corporate fertilizer companies are the only winners" in our modern age of intensive farming.[44]

It's true that overuse of nitrate and phosphate fertilizer can harm the environment.

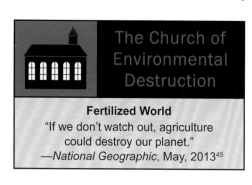

**The Church of Environmental Destruction**

**Fertilized World**
"If we don't watch out, agriculture could destroy our planet."
—*National Geographic*, May, 2013[45]

Nitrogen and phosphorus are nutrients. Fertilizer runoff into lakes and rivers can produce eutrophication, a condition of excess nutrients, which can also lead to hypoxia, a depletion of dissolved oxygen. Excess levels of nutrients stimulate the growth of algae. When bacteria eat the algae, much of the water's oxygen is used up, creating a "dead

## Artificially Synthesized Nitrogen: Essential for Modern Society

Although used only in small quantities by living organisms, nitrogen is an essential part of plant growth and human nutrition. Nitrogen is part of every living cell, present in the nucleic acids of genetic chromosomes, in chlorophyll that absorbs energy from light for photosynthesis, in the amino acids of proteins, and in enzymes that drive biochemical reactions in cell tissue. Humans must ingest ten amino acids from plant and meat diet that our bodies cannot synthesize, all of which contain nitrogen.[46]

Most of Earth's natural nitrogen is not usable by plants and animals. The nitrogen that comprises 78 percent of Earth's atmosphere is locked in stable nonreactive $N_2$ molecules. Few natural methods exist to transform $N_2$ to usable reactive compounds. Most of agricultural history was a struggle to increase use of the relatively small available supplies of reactive nitrogen found in human and livestock manure, animal bones, bird guano, and natural deposits of sodium nitrate, along with the planting of leguminous crops. When the Haber-Bosch process for synthesizing ammonia from atmospheric nitrogen was invented in the early 1900s, it was clear that natural supplies of reactive nitrogen were severely inadequate to support human population growth.[47]

Synthesized nitrogen transformed world food production. Today, commercially-produced nitrogen delivers about half of global agricultural output. Three billion of the world's people could not survive without modern chemical fertilizer, and this population will grow in the twenty-first century.[48]

zone." In hypoxic dead zones, fish, shrimp, and other species become less abundant or die out.

During the second half of the twentieth century, fertilizer runoff, sewage, and industrial waste produced aquatic dead zones in rivers, lakes, and dozens of ocean locations. Sizeable dead zones developed in coastal areas of the Chesapeake Bay, the Adriatic, Baltic, Black, and East China Seas, and the Gulf of Mexico, particularly at the mouth of major rivers, such as the Danube River and the Mississippi River. It is estimated that 50 percent of nitrogen fertilizer eventually runs off into bodies of water.[49]

But growth in global consumption of fertilizer is slowing. World fertilizer consumption increased at an annual average of 5.9 percent per year from 1961 to 1988. But since 1993, consumption grew by only 2 percent per year.[50] Fertilizer use in many developed nations is no longer rising. US annual consumption peaked

**ECO-INSIGHT?**

**Is Your Lawn Accelerating Climate Change?**
"A study published in the *Journal of Environmental Management* ... found, 'the total $CO_2$ emissions from lawns in the US is about 25 million tons annually.' These emissions are primarily released from the 2.2 billion gallons of fossil fuels used for gas-powered mowing and the manufacturing/application of synthetic fertilizers in the US each year."
—*Clean Air Lawn Care*, 2016[51]

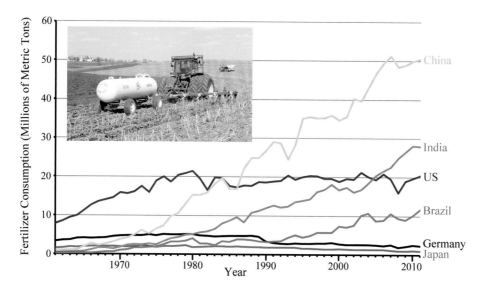

**Fertilizer Consumption for Selected Nations, 1961–2011.** Fertilizer consumption is flat or declining in advanced nations, such as Germany, Japan and the US, but still rising in developing nations, such as Brazil, China, and India. Image of fertilizer application in Iowa. (Earth Policy Institute, International Fertilizer Industry Association, 2013)[52]

in 1981 at 21 million metric tons and has been flat for the last 30 years. Fertilizer use peaked in Western Europe in 1986 at an estimated 29 million tons and declined 50 percent over the last three decades. Fertilizer consumption peaked in Japan in 1979, in Germany in 1980, and in South Africa in 1981.[53]

Society is beginning to reduce the occurrence of eutrophication. As we discussed in Chapter 4, water quality is improving in the Great Lakes, the Rhine and Danube Rivers, and below the Danube Delta in the Black Sea. Treatment of waste water in Europe, the US, and other developed countries is reducing the nutrient load on water systems. Today, about 80 percent of the world's waste water continues to be discharged untreated into water bodies, primarily in developing nations.[54] But this will change in future years with the installation of modern water treatment systems worldwide.

No farmer wants to waste fertilizer. Fertilizer costs money. Today, farmers increasingly use advanced techniques to provide targeted applications of fertilizer to minimize cost and reduce environmental impact. Conservation tillage reduces soil erosion and runoff. Cover crops are planted off-season to recycle nitrogen and reduce soil erosion. Improved farming techniques apply the right amount of fertilizer at the right time in the growing season. Farmers in advanced nations are boosting yields while using the same or reduced amounts of fertilizer, and farmers in developing nations will learn improved techniques as well.

## PESTICIDE FEARS

Farmers have long sought to reduce damage from agricultural pests. Pesticides in the form of sulphur compounds were used by the Sumerians as early as 4,500 years ago. Ancient Persia used a powder of pyrethrum, derived from dried chrysanthemum flowers, as an insecticide.[55] Pyrethrum remains a frequently used non-synthetic insecticide. However, modern chemical pesticides are labeled unsustainable and are widely feared by the public.

In her 1962 best-selling book *Silent Spring*, Rachel Carson leveled an attack on agricultural pesticides that has continued until today, stating:

> Since the mid-1940's over 200 basic chemicals have been created for use in killing insects, weeds, rodents, and other organisms described in the modern vernacular as "pests" … These sprays, dusts, and aerosols are now applied almost universally to farms, gardens, forests, and homes…. Can anyone believe it is possible to lay down such a barrage of poisons on the surface of the earth without making it unfit for all life?[56]

Carson's book targeted the widespread spraying of dichlorodiphenyltrichloroethane (DDT), a remarkably effective pesticide against malarial mosquitoes, typhus-carrying lice, farm pests, and other insects. Carson falsely claimed that DDT was killing birds and causing cancer in humans. Due to a rising tide of public concern, the EPA banned DDT use in 1972, followed by bans in most developed countries.[57]

DDT became one of the most heavily analyzed substances in history. But DDT use was not found to be harmful to people, and with the possible exception of the thinning of raptor egg shells, no environmental impacts of DDT have been identified. In 2006, the World Health Organization lifted its ban on DDT and authorized indoor spraying of DDT to control malaria.[58] Nevertheless, because of Carson's book and fears promoted by environmental groups, synthetic pesticides are wrongly blamed for a wide range of human health problems.

Pesticides are poison. At high levels of exposure, pesticides can be harmful to people. Cancers of the blood, brain, breast, lung, kidney, pancreas, prostrate, ovaries, and stomach are associated with high levels of pesticide exposure.[59] Pesticides are also associated with skin damage, nervous system damage, and genetic and reproductive issues.[60]

Like any poison, pesticide health dangers are strongly correlated with the size of the dose from exposure. Pesticide risks today are almost entirely associated with people that handle pesticide chemicals as part of their occupation, including farmers, pesticide applicators, workers in pesticide factories, and landscapers. These workers need to take special precautions when handling pesticide chemicals. *But actual pesticide risks to the general public are very low to negligible*, because few people are exposed to high doses.

The US Department of Agriculture (USDA) annually analyzes samples from thousands of foods to detect pesticide residues. Laboratory methods detect the lowest possible levels of residues, down to low parts-per-billion levels. In 2014, the USDA collected and analyzed 10,619 samples from fruits, vegetables, infant formula, fish, and other foods. Over 41 percent of the samples found no detectable pesticide residue, and over 99.6 percent of the samples tested had residues below the limits set by the EPA.[61] US and European safety limits are set at extremely low levels of exposure, typically 100 times below the no observed adverse effect level found in laboratory experiments with animals. US and European limits for pesticides in water are yet hundreds of times lower than food-limit levels. Food and water in developed nations today is remarkably free of pesticide residues.

Despite the extremely low level of synthetic pesticides in food and water, today's consumers fear that industrially-produced pesticides cause health problems. What they don't realize is that the vast majority of pesticides that people consume are natural, produced by plants. Pesticides produced by plants include aflatoxin, nicotine, pyrethrum, and strychnine. Dr. Bruce Ames of the University of California, Berkeley, estimates that 99.99 percent of pesticides in our diet are naturally present in plants. Only 0.01 percent of dietary pesticides are the synthetic pesticides produced by industry that Rachel Carson so feared. A single cup of coffee contains natural carcinogens equal in weight to a year's consumption of synthetic pesticide residues.[62] This does not mean that coffee is hazardous, only that dietary dangers from synthetic pesticides are vastly overstated.

One of the early concerns about DDT and some other organochloride pesticides was their tendency to persist in the environment. DDT is fat soluble and accumulates in the tissues of birds and animals. But newer pesticides are designed to break down quickly in farm fields to minimize any long-term environmental impact. As an example, glyphosate, the active ingredient in the herbicide RoundUp, breaks down within a few weeks of application.

Synthetic pesticide use has begun to decline in some advanced nations like the US, particularly where genetically modified (GM) crops are used. GM crops can be engineered to allow reduced use of pesticides and fertilizer. According to the FAO, US use of pesticides

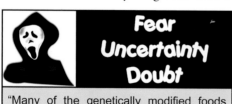

Fear
Uncertainty
Doubt

"Many of the genetically modified foods will be safe, I'm sure. Will most of them be safe? Nobody knows."
—Jeremy Rifkin, *PBS* interview, August, 2010[63]

and fertilizer per hectare is now lower than nations that restrict GM crops, including in France, Germany, Japan, Netherlands, and the United Kingdom.[64]

## GENETICALLY MODIFIED FEARS

One of the most destructive tenants of sustainable development is the rejection of genetically modified (GM) crop technology. Environmental groups brand GM (or GMO) agriculture as risky and harmful to people and the environment. Greenpeace warns:

> While scientific progress on molecular biology has a great potential to increase our understanding of nature and provide new medical tools, it should not be used as justification to turn the environment into a giant genetic experiment by commercial interests. The biodiversity and environmental integrity of the world's food supply is too important to our survival to be put at risk.[65]

But agriculture is a human invention. The vast majority of crops planted and foods consumed today were never a part of wild nature. Thousands of years of plant cross-pollinating and hybridization produced improved drought- and pest-resistant crops with higher yields. Selective breeding and domestication delivered new animals for human consumption. Genetically modified agriculture is only the next step in the process.

In 1971, Stanford University biochemist Paul Berg started the field of GM agriculture with the first splicing of DNA, enabling the moving of genes from one organism to another. Genetic modification allows introduction of traits into crop plants that significantly improve pest resistance, nutrition, and yields. Since the introduction of the first GM crop in 1996, biotech crops have become the fastest-adopted agricultural technology in history. Acreage annually planted with biotech crops now covers about 180 million hectares, about 13 percent of global arable land.[66]

Farmers that adopt biotech crops gain tremendous agricultural benefits. A 2014 analysis by Wilhelm Klumper and Matin Qaim of the University of Göttingen, aggregated results from 147 studies of GM crops from around the world. The analysis found that GM technology increased crop yields by 22 percent, reduced pesticide use by 37 percent, and increased farmer profits by 69 percent.[67]

Herbicide resistance, the most commonly planted GM trait, is available for all major crops. Soybeans, maize, cotton, and other crops are genetically engineered for resistance to the pesticides glyphosate (Roundup) or glufosinate-ammonium (Liberty), allowing farmers to kill unwanted weeds and boost yields, while reducing pesticide application. Corn

**Chemicals, Toxics, And Scares! Oh My!**

**Groups Press Costco to Reject "Frankenfish"**

"Food safety and environmental organizations are pushing retail giant Costco to refuse to stock a brand of genetically engineered salmon awaiting approval by the Food and Drug Administration. Target, Kroger, Safeway, Trader Joe's and other companies have already committed to refrain from selling the salmon, dubbed "Frankenfish" by opponents of food made with genetically modified organisms."
—*The Hill*, March 18, 2014[68]

and cotton bioengineered with toxins from the bacteria Bacillus thuringiensis (Bt) provide increased insect resistance, the second leading transgenic trait.[69] GM crops include disease-resistant potatoes, bruise-resistant fruit, and vitamin-enhanced grains. In 2015, the US Food and Drug Administration approved the first GM animal for human consumption, a faster-growing salmon. The fish is to be raised in specific land-based hatcheries. Pigs are being developed to resist deadly viral diseases. Other biotech animals are now under development.[70]

Environmental groups oppose GM crops based on fears of potential environmental consequences. Suppose a bioengineered salmon escapes into the wild and multiplies? Suppose exotic new plants spread and upset ecosystems? These concerns are valid, but society is already dealing with issues from the spread of non-native natural species such as the European starling, the Asian carp, and the kudzu vine.

For the last three decades, environmentalists have pursued a media fear campaign against biotech foods. The American Academy of Environmental Medicine warns:

> … several animal studies indicate serious health risks associated with GM food consumption including infertility, immune dysregulation, accelerated aging, dysregulation of genes associated with cholesterol synthesis, insulin regulation, cell signaling, and protein formation, and changes in the liver, kidney, spleen and gastrointestinal system.[71]

Sustainable advocates brand GM foods as unhealthy, unnatural, dangerous, and harmful, even using the colorful term "frankenfoods."

However, *there is no evidence that any person has ever been harmed by the genetic modification of foods.* The National Academy of Sciences, the British Royal Society, and the American Association for the Advancement of Science all conclude that GM foods are safe. A 2010 analysis by the European Commission stated:

> The main conclusion to be drawn from the efforts of more than 130 research projects, covering a period of more than 25 years of research, and involving more than 500 independent research groups, is that biotechnology, and in particular GMOs, are not per se more risky than e.g. conventional plant breeding technologies.[72]

## The Tragedy of Opposition to Golden Rice

According to the World Health Organization, an estimated 250 million preschool children suffer from vitamin A deficiency worldwide. Each year 250,000 to 500,000 of these children become blind, with half of them dying within one year of losing their sight.[73]

In 1999, two European researchers, Peter Beyer and Ingo Potrykus, developed golden rice, a genetically-modified common rice with two inserted genes that caused rice to accumulate beta-carotene, an effective source of vitamin A for humans.[74] In 2005, a team of researchers at agricultural firm Syngenta produced a commercially-ready version of golden rice that accumulates higher levels of beta-carotene.[75] Adoption of golden rice promised vitamin A to poor world populations suffering from vitamin A deficiency. To reduce opposition, Syngenta granted royalty-free access to its technology.

But Greenpeace, the Sierra Club, and other environmental groups conducted a tragically successful 10-year opposition campaign against use of the crop. As part of the effort, protesters in the Philippines destroyed an experimental golden rice field in 2013.[76] As of June, 2016, golden rice had not been commercially planted in any country.

Over the last 20 years, hundreds of billions of servings of GM foods have been safely consumed by billions of people across dozens of nations. Today biotech crops dominate US agriculture, with GM adoption rates for corn (92 percent), soybeans (94 percent), and cotton (94 percent). India is the world's leading producer of cotton, and 95 percent of the crop is GM cotton. By 2015, GM foods were approved for consumption in 40 nations, and 28 countries grew GM crops, with 87 percent of biotech acreage in North and South America, 11 percent in Asia, 2 percent in Africa, and less than one percent in Europe.[77]

Europeans have been captured by sustainable environment ideology, largely rejecting genetically modified crops and foods. Planting of biotech crops is banned in 19 of 28 European nations, including Denmark, France, Germany, Italy, and the Netherlands. Marketing of GM foods requires specific European Union approval, but since 2001 the EU has withheld approvals, effectively banning GM foods.[78]

Proper testing and regulatory oversight should be required for introduction of GM crops and foods. But history now shows 20 years of GM planting without environmental impacts and billions of meals without harmful health effects. The evidence supports use of GM agriculture to expand and improve world food supplies.

## ORGANIC FOOD MYTHOLOGY

Demand for organic food is an outgrowth of opposition to modern agriculture technology. Today, there is widespread public belief that organic foods are safer, better tasting, and more nutritious than food produced using modern agricultural methods. As a result,

**Did You Know Organic Underwear Could Look This Good?**

"Fabrics like organic cotton, bamboo and hemp are so soft and comfortable they are perfect for underwear and what better way to add organic fabrics to your wardrobe …"
—*Natural Living for Women*, 2016[79]

organic foods are a fast-growing segment of food supply. Thousands of organic products fill store shelves in wealthy nations, with novelties such as organic vodka and even organic underwear, made from organically-grown cotton.

Organic foods require certification by the governments of the European Union, Canada, Japan, the US, and other nations in order to be marketed as organic. For certification, the USDA requires that organic operations:

> …maintain or enhance soil and water quality, while also conserving wetlands, woodlands, and wildlife. Synthetic fertilizers, sewage sludge, irradiation, and genetic engineering may not be used.[80]

My local supermarket features a variety of organic foods, including organic bananas for $1.27 per pound. But my wife and I generally choose to buy the conventional bananas priced at $0.27 per pound, grown using modern farming methods. If the usual bananas are short and we buy the organics instead, the size, appearance, and taste of the organic bananas is about the same, but at more than four times the price.

Despite claims to the contrary, there is no scientific evidence that organic foods are safer, more nutritious, or taste better than foods grown using synthetic fertilizer, synthetic pesticides, and genetically modified seeds. A 2010 study by the London School of Hygiene and Tropical Medicine reviewed 162 peer-reviewed papers and concluded:

> An independent systematic review of the available published literature has shown that there are no important differences in the nutrition content of, or any additional health benefits deriving from, organic food when compared with conventionally produced food.[81]

It's publicly believed that organic farming is pesticide-free, but this is not true. The USDA's National Organic Program recommends that "preventive, cultural, and physical methods must be the first choice for insect and disease control."[82] But USDA also issues its National List of many natural and synthetic substances that can be used for pest control in organic farming.[83] Organic farms frequently use pesticides, usually of natural composition, and sometimes in greater quantities than conventional farms. Bt is the organic insecticide most widely sprayed on US organic crops.[84] Conventional farming uses biotech crops engineered with Bt genetic traits, instead of spraying Bt on fields. Rotenone is a natural organic pesticide commonly used in Europe that is harmful to humans in high doses. Spinosad and copper sulfate are widely used organic pesticides that are very toxic to bees.

Natural fertilizers, such as animal manure and compost, contain less nitrogen than synthetic fertilizers, producing lower organic crop yields than modern agriculture. Widespread adoption of organic methods would lower crop yields and require use of more land to feed world populations. Use of natural fertilizer (manure) in organic farming may also result in higher risk of fecal contamination of food crops from transmitted E. coli and other bacteria.[85] In summary, organic foods are comparable to foods produced with conventional farming methods, but with lower crop yields, and without pesticide-free health benefits that are widely claimed.

## COMING GLOBAL FOREST REGROWTH

Deforestation has long been an important environmental issue. US President Theodore Roosevelt voiced concern in 1907:

> We are consuming our forests three times faster than they are being reproduced. Some of the richest timber lands of this continent have already been destroyed, and not replaced, and other vast areas are on the verge of destruction.[86]

The United Nations informs us:

> Deforestation and forest degradation, through agricultural expansion, conversion to pastureland, infrastructure development, destructive logging, fires etc., account for nearly 20% of global greenhouse gas emissions, more than the entire global transportation sector and second only to the energy sector.[87]

Throughout history, people have felled forests to clear land for farms and to gather wood for fuel. An estimated 60 percent of Europe's forests were cut down during the last 2,000 years. About one-third of US forests disappeared, with most vanishing during the 1800s. Earth has lost about 30 percent of original forests since agriculture began.[88]

Today, world forested areas are still shrinking, but at a decreasing rate. The UN reports that from 1990 to 2015, global forested area declined by about 3 percent, but that the net rate of forest loss decreased by about 50 percent from previous decades.[89] Developing nations in South America, Africa, and Southeast Asia continue to fell forests, but forests are stable or growing in North America, Europe, and much of Asia. Today, forested area is declining in about one-third of the world's countries, stable in one-third, and growing in one third. Forests are stable or regrowing in more than 100

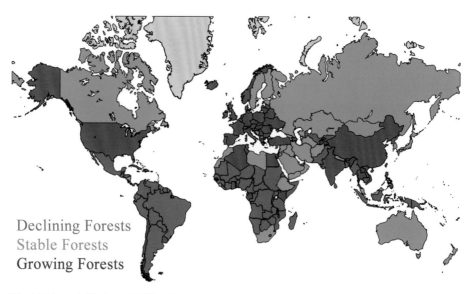

**World Forest Status, 2013.** Forests are declining in roughly one-third of the world's nations (red), stable in one-third of the nations (light green), and growing in one-third of the nations (dark green). (United Nations FAO, 2016)[90]

countries, including Australia, Canada, China, India, Japan, New Zealand, Russia, the US, and in most of Europe.

As we discussed in Chapter 4, deforestation appears to follow the inverted U-shape of an Environmental Kuznets Curve. As the income of nations rises, modern high-yield agriculture techniques reduce the need for additional farmland. Modern fuels, such as propane, butane, and natural gas, replace wood fuel for heating and cooking. Deforestation eventually slows and then changes to forest regrowth. In 2013, according to UN FAO and World Bank data, 61 of the 67 nations with annual per-person incomes of over $10,000 enjoyed stable or growing forests.[91] The great promise of global forest regrowth can best be achieved by boosting the income of developing nations and the adoption of high-yield farming techniques, not by coercive sustainable policies to restrict agriculture.

By the way, company promotional campaigns urging customers to "go electronic and save a tree" have little factual basis, at least in the US. More than 90 percent of US paper comes from high-yield forests planted specifically to be harvested.

## OVERFISHING AND THE RISE OF AQUACULTURE

Fish are the last wild animal that humans capture in large numbers. From 1950 to 2014, global seafood consumption increased by a factor of seven, to 167 million metric tons.

Consumption of seafood exceeded 20 kilograms (44 pounds) per-person in 2014. Each person annually eats about three times more fish today than in 1950.[92] Seafood increasingly provides the high-protein portion of the diet of people in developing nations.

Some complain that modern commercial fishing methods are unsustainable. An example article warns, "How the World's Oceans Could be Running Out of Fish."[93] Indeed, fish populations declined in many locations during the last century. In 2014, the FAO classified 31 percent of the world's fish stocks as overfished. As a severe example, fish catches in the Mediterranean and Black Seas dropped by one-third since 2007. Global production from wild fish catches has been flat since 1995.[94]

But people are learning how to farm the lakes and oceans. Aquaculture is booming, providing more than 50 percent of the world's seafood supply for the first time in 2014, up from only 7 percent in 1974.[95] Companies breed new fish varieties for faster growth, better conversion of feed into weight, and resistance to disease. Aquaculture is among the world's fastest growing categories of food production.

Sustainable development advocates attack aquiculture in even stronger measure than capture fishing. They argue that farmed fish are fatty, stuffed with antibiotics, and polluting. They're alarmed that farmed carnivorous fish, such as salmon and tuna, require capture of large numbers of smaller fish to serve as feed, further taxing marine life.

---

### Haida Salmon Open-Ocean Farming Experiment

In 2012, the Native American Haida tribe established the Haida Salmon Restoration Corporation (HSRC), a controversial effort to restore salmon populations along the west coast of British Columbia, Canada. The Haida financed an effort by entrepreneur Russ George, whose team deposited 120 tons of iron sulfate over 5,000 square kilometers of ocean, 300 km offshore, across sockeye salmon migration paths.[96]

Within a few months, satellite imagery showed a massive bloom of phytoplankton across the ocean where the iron was deposited. The phytoplankton bloom provided food for baby pink salmon, which grew and returned to Alaskan and Canadian rivers in record numbers the following year. In 2013, the Southeast Alaska pink salmon catch totalled a record 226 million, more than four times the expected total.[97]

Both scientists and environmental groups denounced the Haida experiment as unsanctioned and dangerous geoengineering. Environment Canada declared the project to be a violation of the Canadian Environmental Protection Act. Offices of the HSRC were raided and documents seized by the Canadian government.[98]

Nevertheless, it appears that the Haida experiment produced an unexpected bloom in east Pacific salmon populations. The seeding of the open oceans appears to be the major factor causing the enormous salmon run of 2013. Open-ocean farming holds great potential for future harvests from the sea.

Today, the fish farming industry is an infant compared to the sophistication of modern land agriculture. Just as land agriculture boosts yields and reduces the environmental impact of today's farms, aqua-farmers are beginning to develop advanced high-yield, lower-impact technologies. New feed formulations are more digestible and leach less waste into the environment. Antibiotic and chemical use is being reduced in many aqua farms. Soy and other land-produced feed ingredients are growing, reducing the need for large quantities of smaller fish for food.[99]

The twenty-first century will be the aquaculture century, as humanity learns to farm the oceans as we have learned to farm the land. Society will harness the almost unlimited potential of the oceans to feed the world.

## MODERN AGRICULTURE: IMPROVING THE ENVIRONMENT

Modern agriculture is a remarkable success. World agricultural output continues to rise faster than population growth, shrinking the number of people suffering from malnutrition. Today, people in developed nations eat food of the highest quality, lowest cost, and best variety in history.

But proponents of the ideology of sustainable development decry the farmer's use of land, water, fertilizer, pesticides, energy, and genetically modified seeds. Environmentalists call for horse-and-buggy solutions to halt a feared environmental crisis from agriculture. They demand locally grown organic foods, vegetarian diets, and the elimination of synthetic fertilizer, pesticides, and GM foods. Without such nineteenth-century procedures, they tell us, degradation or destruction of Earth's environment is assured.

Yet the trends show something else. Human ingenuity is boosting agricultural yields while using less land, and soon to be using less water, fertilizer, and pesticide. Genetically modified foods serve billions of people each year, without evidence of human harm or environmental damage. Contrary to widespread belief, dietary dangers from synthetic pesticides are negligible. The world is moving toward the promise of global forest regrowth, reversing a centuries-long trend of declining forests. Modern agriculture promises to continue to feed the world's billions, while humanity continues to improve the environment.

CHAPTER 9

# BUSINESS ENVIRONMENTAL POLICY—
# SENSIBLY GREEN

*"There is nothing so useless as doing efficiently that
which should not be done at all."* —PETER DRUCKER[1]

Today, every major business must be green. Many industries face intense public pressure to be sustainable. But, if you've been following our discussion, it's clear that the concept of sustainable development is based on false foundations. Population growth is slowing, pollution trends are positive, humanity is not running short of material or energy resources, and global temperatures are dominated by natural factors—not emissions from industry. How then, should a business structure its corporate environmental policy? Let's discuss elements of a sensible, fact-based environmental policy for business and then look at a few applications in major business and industrial segments.

## SENSIBLY GREEN ENVIRONMENTAL POLICY

Every major business needs an effective environmental policy. Corporate social responsibility is expected and demanded by shareholders, customers, suppliers, employees, and other stakeholders. But corporate environmental policy should be "sensibly green," based on sound science and sound economics, not irrational fears promoted by sustainable ideology.

Key elements of a sensible environmental policy include:

1. **Use the lowest-cost mix of process elements** to produce the lowest-cost, highest-value products and services. Sensibly reduce the use of energy, materials, water, labor, and capital. Energy should be conserved like any other process input. Water should be used rationally, based on local availability and cost.

2. **Reduce waste** from processes to minimize cost and environmental impact. Use recycled materials where advantageous to reduce production cost.

3. **Minimize the discharge of hazardous air and water pollutants** to reduce environmental impact. Limit the release of lead, mercury, sulfur oxides, nitrous oxides, and particulate emissions into the air and the discharge of natural and synthetic chemicals into the water. This does not include carbon dioxide, which at today's low atmospheric levels is not harmful to humans or the environment.

4. **Design and test products** to minimize danger to humans or nature.

5. **Prepare** for severe weather or natural disaster events. Contrary to the claims of some, neither society or industry can control the frequency or severity of weather, so companies must adapt and prepare for changing conditions.

6. **Restore nature** after completion of mining or construction activities.

7. **Comply** with environmental laws and regulations.

The elements listed above are already part of many corporate environmental plans. But most plans are foolish in the execution of policy. Companies invest huge sums in environmental projects that actually do nothing for the environment.

Your company's environmental policy should *not* include:

- **Counting carbon dioxide emissions.** Unless required by law or for possible public relations benefit, totaling your firm's carbon footprint is a waste of resources.

- **Purchasing carbon offsets.** There is no evidence that purchasing carbon offsets to invest in "carbon-soaking" projects has the slightest effect on global temperatures.

- **Special efforts to reduce energy consumption.** Like any resource, energy should not be wasted, but neither should extraordinary or expensive efforts be taken to conserve energy. Nations that use the most energy per person discharge the lowest levels of harmful pollutants. Low-cost energy is the foundation of economic growth, generating capital to fund air and water pollution control measures. There is no evidence that energy production hurts the environment or that energy resources face exhaustion.

**A GREEN MARKET IN HERE SOMEWHERE?**

**Green Ideas:**
**Making Concrete from Rice**
"Concrete accounts for about 5% of all human-related $CO_2$ emissions.... But what if there was a way to make concrete that was more environmentally friendly? A team of researchers in Texas thinks there might be—by adding rice to concrete."
—*Phys.org*, July 21, 2009[2]

- **Payment of a premium to use renewable energy.** Electricity from a 120-volt or 240-volt outlet is identical whether renewable or from hydrocarbon fuels. Energy does not have color. No company should pay a premium for "green" energy unless the public relations benefits outweigh the increased electricity cost.

- **Payment of a premium to use biofuels or electric vehicles.** Electric vehicles and biofuels should be adopted only when they offer superior cost/benefit for your firm. Many studies show that biofuels consume more land and water and emit more pollutants than use of gasoline or diesel fuel for vehicles.

- **Special efforts to use natural or renewable materials**. Today's engineers are amazing. They can make plates from pig urine, furniture from hay, and concrete from rice. But why do so if the foundations of sustainable development are wrong? Products that intentionally use natural materials or shun petroleum-based materials offer negligible actual environmental benefit.

Policies that count carbon dioxide emissions, purchase carbon offsets, promote use of renewable energy, needlessly reduce energy consumption, and promote adoption of natural materials do little for the environment. If your company pursues any of these policies, they belong in only one place in your budget—that's your public relations department—*because they don't do anything else*. Let's look at some industry cases.

## STEEL INDUSTRY BOWS TO SUSTAINABLE ATTACKS

Steel, the world's most important building material, requires substantial amounts of coal, coke, natural gas, and energy to produce. The majority of world production of steel from iron ore requires coke, which is produced from coal or petroleum refining. Coke heats

## Drinking The Green Cool-Ade

**Belgian "CO$_2$ Champion" Plant Bought Off Forged Chinese Carbon Credits**
"The Arcelor Mittal steel plant in Ghent is Belgium's leading 'polluting permits' buyer. But those CO$_2$ credits are largely bought from a Chinese chemicals plant that forged its emissions scheme."
—*MobileReporter*, September 23, 2015[3]

blast furnaces to 2,200°C. Coke also acts as a reducing agent to remove oxygen from iron ore, an essential step in steel production. Energy can amount to 20 to 40 percent of the cost of steel production. Because of this intensive use of hydrocarbon materials and energy, the industry serves as cannon fodder for attacks from the forces of green ideology.

The steel industry surrendered to pressure, now dwelling in the green box of sustainable development. Press releases admit that the industry "accounts for approximately 6.7% of world CO$_2$ emissions," but claim a 60 percent reduction in energy use per ton of steel since 1960. The industry developed a method to estimate the CO$_2$ footprint of steel plants and a database for reporting emissions to help move to a "low-carbon future."[4] The World Steel Association states, "Climate change is the biggest issue for the steel industry in the 21st century."[5] But an outside observer might conclude that chronic steel industry overcapacity ranks as the biggest issue. The industry produced over 1.6 billion metric tons of crude steel in 2014, but contained capacity to produce over 2.3 billion tons.[6] The excess capacity in China alone in 2014 exceeded Europe's total production.[7] Substitution of aluminum, carbon composites, and plastics for steel in products and structures may be the largest competitive issue. Another key issue should be the rising cost of energy due to misguided energy and climate policies.

The steel industry is shooting itself in the foot. The G7 nations, in a fit of sustainable madness, agreed to eliminate *all* CO$_2$ emissions by the year 2100.[8] Steel can't be made with energy from wood, solar, and wind. Wind turbines require steel, but wind turbines can't power the steel industry. Hydrocarbons and low-cost energy are essential. The steel industry should argue that energy use does not pollute the planet and that natural factors dominate climate change, not human industrial emissions.

## PLASTICS AND CHEMICALS UNDER ATTACK

Plastics and chemicals are essential to modern life. We fabricate food containers, boat paddles, shoes, heart valves, pipes, toys, and smart phones from plastic. Our chemical industry provides cosmetics, medicines, lubricants, clothes dye, house paint, and fuels. Most plastic and chemical products are produced from oil or natural gas refining, therefore a target in the war on hydrocarbons.

## The Seeds of Our Destruction

From an objective point of view, plastics are a miracle material. Plastics are composed of long synthetic molecules of carbon and hydrogen, derived from petrochemicals, with amazing chemical properties. Plastics are moldable, impervious to water, inert in normal room temperature conditions, light weight and strong, able to deform without breaking, and relatively inexpensive.

"I sometimes think there is a malign force loose in the universe that is the social equivalent of cancer, and it's plastic. It infiltrates everything. It's metastasis. It gets into every single pore of productive life. I mean there won't be anything that isn't made of plastic before long. They'll be paving the roads with plastic before they're done. Our bodies, our skeletons, will be replaced with plastic."
—Author Norman Mailer, 1983[9]

World plastics production increased from tiny volumes in 1950 to 311 million tons in 2014, and plastics production may equal the tonnage of global steel production by the end of this century.[10] Plastics comprise over 15 percent of the weight of today's automobile. Low-cost, convenient, and sanitary plastic packaging displaced animal skin, glass, metal, paper, and wood packaging historically used throughout the world. Every day, society consumes approximately 450 million plastic bottles and 2.7 billion plastic bags.[11]

But the valuable characteristics of plastic, a low-cost, non-reactive material with wide applicability, produce both misguided and justified fears about impacts to the environment. The 2016 World Economic Forum raised concerns about plastic volumes going to landfills, about fossil fuel feedstock for plastic, and about "leakage" of plastic into the environment.[12] The landfill and fossil fuel concerns are overstated, but the concern about plastic accumulation in the environment is valid.

As we discussed in Chapter 4, recycling rates for plastics and other materials are rising, reducing pressure on landfill sites. Landfill space is not in short supply for large-area nations. In smaller nations, combustion can be used to dispose of plastics not recycled. Regarding petroleum use for plastic feedstock, the Earth Policy Institute states:

> Manufacturing of the nearly 28 billion plastic bottles used each year to package water in the United States alone requires the equivalent of 17 million barrels of oil.[13]

This sounds alarming, but it's mistaken. Plastic is a by-product, made from the waste stream of petroleum and natural gas refining. Only about four percent of the world's oil is used to produce plastic, with only about one percent used for plastic bottles.[14] If plastic bottle production were halted, the volume of petroleum used in refining would hardly change, continuing to produce fuel and other products.

A valid concern, however, is the accumulation of plastic in the environment, particularly the oceans. Dr. Jenna Jambeck and others at the University of Georgia estimated that 4.8 to 12.7 million tons of plastic waste entered the world's oceans in 2010, or about 1.7 to 4.6 percent of total plastic production.[15] These waste numbers are rising with increasing global consumption of plastic. Only about two percent of the plastic that ends up in the ocean originates in Europe and the US, where waste disposal is well-controlled. But an estimated 82 percent originates in Asia and another 16 percent from the rest of the world.[16]

Over time, plastic breaks down into smaller particles, but because of the chemical inertness of the material, it can remain in the environment for decades. Some scientists warn of a growing Pacific Ocean garbage patch, a huge area of ocean current whirlpool north of Hawaii, where plastic is said to be accumulating.[17] Contrary to some reports, an observer gazing at this ocean area *does not see* accumulating plastic waste. But scientists do measure a growing concentration of tiny plastic particles. Sea birds, which mistake plastic for food, are often found with plastic fragments in their stomachs. European nations, California, states of Australia, and dozens of cities across the world have enacted bans or taxes on single-use plastic bags. Environmental groups push for plastic bottle restrictions to try to solve the problem.

Unfortunately, companies now promote technologies to solve the non-problem of global warming, rather than the real problem of accumulating plastic in the oceans. For example, Coca-Cola uses its PlantBottle technology to produce soda bottles composed of up to 30 percent plant material from Brazilian sugar cane. Since 2009, the company shipped over 35 billion PlantBottle packages, claiming to have saved 315,000 tons of carbon dioxide.[19] But the new bottles are no more biodegradable than traditional plastic, and the emissions savings provide only public relations value. Instead of petroleum-free plastics, biodegradable plastics are needed to solve the growing problem of plastic in the oceans.

Industrial chemicals, and chemical additives in plastics, are wrongly blamed for health problems. Donella Meadows, author of *Limits*

**Wonderfully Sustainable!**

**France Bans All Plastic Dishware Starting in 2020**

"… France has enacted a ban on all plastic dishes, cups, and utensils. The ban goes into effect in 2020, after which all disposable utensils and dishes must be made of biological, rather than petroleum-based, material."

—*Fortune*, September 17, 2016[18]

*to Growth* and professor at Dartmouth College, warned in 1996:

> If we emit massive quantities of untested chemicals into the environment, some of them are bound to end up in places that surprise us, doing things that endanger us.[20]

Today's society suffers from "chemophobia," the fear of human-made chemicals. News reports warn of dangerous levels of lead in lipstick, carcinogens in sunscreen, pesticides on vegetables, and chemical poison in plastic baby bottles. Environmental groups promote chemical fears to grow funding and influence. Political leaders strive to remove any trace of chemical risk from daily life.

Chemophobia is closely tied to the sustainability movement. Along with concern for the environment, advocates of sustainable development tend to hold anti-technology and anti-industry views. Chemicals naturally produced by plants are regarded as good, but industrially made chemicals are labeled as toxic and harmful. Synthetic pesticides and fertilizers, plastics, food additives, and materials produced by industry are under attack. Big corporations must be bad and out to poison you.

Scientists can now detect trace amounts of chemicals down to small parts per billion (ppb) levels, soon detectable to parts per trillion levels. When a scientist detects a few ppb trace of a toxin in water, newspapers ring with alarm. But one ppb is exceedingly small. It's equivalent to one drop in 16,000 gallons of water (larger than a tanker truck) or equal to one kernel of corn in a 45-foot-high, 16-foot-diameter silo.[22]

The size of the dose makes the poison. Paracelsus, a Swiss physician of the 1500s regarded as the father of toxicology, stated:

> All substances are poison. There is none which is not a poison. The right dose makes the difference between a poison and a remedy.

**Chemicals, Toxics, And Scares! Oh My!**

**Toxic Dangers in Plastic Baby Bottles**
"In the latest assault on plastics widely used in consumer products, a coalition of advocacy groups says that heating plastic baby bottles releases harmful quantities of Bisphenol A (BPA) into milk."
—*MinnPost*, February 7, 2008[21]

**Fear Uncertainty Doubt**

**Our Polluted Bodies**
"Clearly, the system is broken when our health is threatened by everyday activities and products. Current federal and state laws do not adequately prevent harmful toxic chemicals from entering products, food and the environment. Of the 82,000 chemicals in use today, a mere fraction has been tested for toxicity."
—Senator Lisa Brown and Senator Bill Finkbeiner, *Seattle Times*, July 18, 2006[23]

Dennis Avery of the Hudson Institute points out that even sunlight and water are poisons in high doses.[24] Most synthetic chemicals regarded as toxins are encountered at doses far below levels that can cause harm.

Professor Bruce Ames, of the University of California at Berkeley (C.U.), observes:

> … over the years I have repeatedly found that environmental economics students at C.U. enter my class with strongly-held beliefs that 1) cancer is a growing threat to mankind and 2) pollution, pesticides, food additives and other "synthetic chemicals" are the principle cause of the cancer epidemic. I am not sure why these beliefs are so strongly held (brainwashing?) but it turns out that both beliefs are demonstrably wrong.[25]

Cancer can be a terrible illness. Cancer ranks as the number two cause for US mortality behind heart disease. But the idea that chemicals or plastics produced by our industry are the cause of a cancer epidemic is irrational.

The leading causes of cancer are: 1) smoking, which causes about 90 percent of lung cancer and more than one quarter of all cancers in the US, 2) dietary imbalances, including a lack of fruits and vegetables, and 3) chronic infections, which are mostly a cause in developing countries.[26] But the exact causes of cancer are still not well understood. A 2012 study found that breast cancer in women was caused by 40 different mutated genes, probably due to ten different diseases.[27]

Nor are cancer tests in rodents a valid measure of a chemical's ability to cause cancer in humans. More than half of all chemicals, whether synthetic or natural, that are tested in high doses with laboratory rodents, produce cancer. Natural chemicals that are rodent carcinogens occur in apples, bananas, cabbage, carrots, chocolate, coffee, grapes, honey, lettuce, mushrooms, mustard, onions, potatoes, soybeans, tomatoes, and many other common foods. Evidence is mounting that the use of *extremely high chemical doses* may be the primary cause of cancer in laboratory rodent tests, rather than the chemical itself.[28]

As Dr. Ames pointed out, about 99.9 percent of chemicals that humans ingest are natural. About 99.99 percent of ingested pesticides are naturally produced by plants.[29] The idea that natural chemicals are good and that synthetic chemicals are bad is kindergarten logic. It makes no difference where a substance comes from, just the chemical properties of the substance itself. The good news is that our bodies have many excellent natural defenses that protect us from toxins. Except in the case of high-dose exposure in occupational situations, neither natural nor synthetic chemicals in the daily lives of people cause cancer.

Cancer is usually a disease of old age. According to the National Cancer Institute, the incidence of cancer in those over age 65 is 10 times greater than those younger than 65.[30]

## Don't Sweat the Chemicals!

Over the last five decades, the world media frequently exploded with horror stories about synthetically produced chemicals, human health, and the environment. A small number of these episodes, such as the Bhopal, India, chemical leak in 1984 and birth defects caused by the over-the-counter drug Thalidomide in 1961, became tragic health concerns. But the vast majority of alarmingly predicted chemical disasters never occurred.

Phthalates are plastics ingredients used for more than 50 years in hundreds of products to make vinyl flexible. Phthalates have been attacked repeatedly by environmental groups and the scientific community over fears they cause childhood cancer, infertility, and human obesity. But phthalates are one of the most thoroughly studied compound families in the world. Studies by the EPA, the US Product Safety Commission, and the European Union found no risk from phthalates. The Centers for Disease Control found average phthalate exposures 100 to 1,000 times below health-concern levels.[31]

Bisphenol A (BPA) is a compound used to harden polycarbonate plastic in water bottles and food containers that has been in use since 1957, and one of the highest volume chemicals produced worldwide. Sensational headlines claimed that BPA was released into milk for infants by heating plastic baby bottles. Numerous scientific studies show that BPA injected into or ingested by laboratory rats and mice in high doses causes changes to rodent genitals, breasts, prostrate glands, and various types of cancers. Canada and the European Union banned the use of BPA in plastic baby bottles. In the face of huge public pressure, plastics manufacturers removed BPA from baby-bottle plastic. But numerous world agencies have since concluded that BPA does not pose a health problem to adults, children, or infants at normal dose levels, including the European Food Safety Agency, the US Food and Drug Administration, and the US EPA.[32]

Formaldehyde ($CH_2O$) is a commonly used chemical in flooring, insulation materials, and adhesives. Formaldahyde is also the leading volatile organic compound released into indoor air from home construction materials. In 2011, the US National Toxicology Program concluded that formaldehyde was a known human carcinogen, based on occupational studies of pathologists, embalmers, and industrial workers who received high doses at companies that used or produced formaldehyde. But formaldehyde is also a natural substance exhausted by plants and found in the air above all forests. This substance is created in the human body and naturally present in all human cells in tiny amounts. Inhaled formaldehyde typically breaks down in about one minute. Formaldehyde is a poison in high concentrations but not harmful to humans in usual daily doses.[33]

Alar, a chemical sprayed on apples during the 1980s to prevent pre-harvest fruit drop was banned in 1989 by the EPA. High dose tests produced cancer in laboratory rodents. Millions of US citizens stopped buying apples and apple products. But the lab tests that prompted the scare required consumption of over 5,000 gallons of apple juice each day to produce a cancer risk in people.[34]

Lead in lipstick, additives to sun screen, mercury in fish, pesticides on vegetables, artificial sweetener in soft drinks, and hundreds of other chemical scares, feared by the same sustainable crowd that promoted peak oil and global warming mania, have not produced adverse human health effects. People should avoid smoking and pursue balanced diets, moderation in eating habits, and exercise, but don't sweat the chemicals!

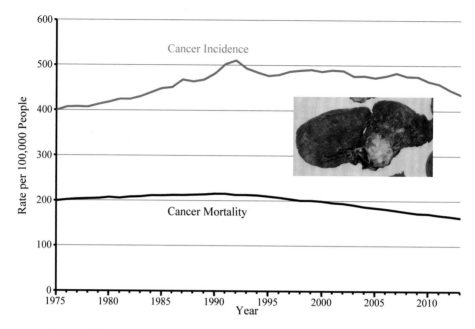

**Age-Adjusted US Cancer Incidence and Mortality 1975–2013.** The rates of cancer incidence and mortality per 100,000 United States population are shown, age-adjusted for year 2000 US population. Incidence and mortality rates peaked about 1990. Image of a cancerous human lung. (National Cancer Institute, 2015)[35]

If you live long enough, you'll likely get cancer. But *age-adjusted* cancer incidence and mortality rates are falling in developed nations. Age-adjusted cancer incidence and mortality rates in the United States have fallen since 1990, even though use of synthetic chemicals and plastics continues to rise.[36]

Plastics and chemical companies should focus on reducing dangers to human health, reducing pollutants released into the environment, and providing maximum cost/benefit to customers in delivered products and services. Plastic fabricated from plant material provides no inherent environmental advantage compared to plastic produced from hydrocarbons. Synthetic chemicals are no more hazardous to health than natural chemicals produced by plants. We await the day when chemophobia recedes and society returns to common-sense ideas about sustainability and health issues.

## INSURANCE AND FINANCIAL SUSTAINABLE MANIA

Mark Carney, governor of the Bank of England, delivered a speech to the Lloyd's of London insurance market on September 29, 2015, claiming:

Since the 1980s the number of weather-related loss events has tripled … and on an inflation-adjusted basis, insurance losses from these events have increased from around ten billion per year during the 1980s to around fifty billion annually over the last decade.[37]

Governor Carney went on to attribute rising insurance losses to human-caused climate change. Insurance giant Munich Re sponsors an "extreme weather congress," where insurance executives and environmental groups meet to discuss how power plants and SUVs cause stronger storms and hurricanes.[38] Munich Re, Swiss Re, Zurich Insurance Group, and other leading firms point to higher insurance losses as evidence of dangerous climate change. There is no doubt that weather-related loss events and damages increased faster than inflation over recent decades, but there is enormous doubt that $CO_2$ is the cause.

Such conclusions are about as valid as concluding that our health care is poor because many more people die each day today than died each day in the year 1900. As we discussed in Chapter 5, historical evidence shows that today's storms, droughts, floods, and blizzards are neither more frequent nor more extreme than in past decades. Higher claims and losses result from larger population, higher property values, higher incomes, the trend of people moving to coastal areas, and the increasing concentration of population in coastal cities. As Professor Roger Pielke, Jr., pointed out in congressional testimony, US flood damage losses as a percentage of GDP have declined over the last 70 years.[39]

The insurance industry now offers green policies and discounts for insulated houses, electric and hybrid cars, and solar rooftops. The Farmers Insurance Group even filed suit on the city of Chicago for failing to prepare for heavy rains and associated flooding.[40] But it's amusing that real estate markets don't share the insurance industry's concern for stronger storms and rising seas. The prices of oceanfront property continue to rise rapidly in coastal cities such as Miami and Boston that would flood if climate warnings come to pass.

In 2007, former Vice President Al Gore joined the board of venture capitalist Kleiner Perkins to promote investment in green energy companies. From 2006 to 2010, Kleiner Perkins invested in more than 60 "cleantech" firms, along with many other leading venture companies (VCs). But US venture investors subsequently received a dose of reality, losing over half of the $25 billion invested over a five-year period. Few cleantech companies achieved success, compared to many disasters, such as A123 Systems, Abound Solar, Fisker

**The Seas Are Rising…**

Price of Oceanfront Property Up More than 20 Percent This Year
—*VeroNews*, Vero Beach, FL, October 16, 2014[41]

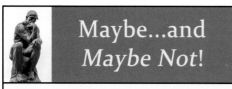

"Green technologies—going green—is bigger than the Internet. It could be the biggest economic opportunity of the 21st century."
—John Doerr, Kleiner Perkins, 2007[42]

Automotive, Range Fuels, and Solyndra. US VC cleantech investments dropped from a peak of $5 billion per year in 2008 to only $2 billion per year by 2013. Poor economics of green products determined the fate of many cleantech firms. VCs subsequently moved investment money out of green-energy companies and back into the software and medical industries.[43]

Over the last two decades, world financial industries embraced sustainable development hook, line, and ledger. ABN Amro, Barclays, Citibank, and other leading banks succumbed to pressure from environmental groups and adopted the Equator Principles, surrendering to "responsible" lending practices in the name of green ideology. The Principles resulted in reduced lending for coal, gas, oil, hydroelectric, and nuclear power plants, projects that provide low-cost electricity to poor peoples of the world.[44] Banks have been misguided supporters of carbon markets, renewable energy, and other green policies, which are based on shaky science and poor economics. Decisions involving trillions of lending dollars are now skewed by faulty advice from the doctrine of sustainable development.

## SENSIBLY GREEN, NOT SUSTAINABLY GREEN

Businesses should rethink their acceptance of environmental policies recommended by the teachings of sustainable development. Counting carbon dioxide emissions, purchasing carbon credits, paying premiums for renewable energy, needlessly reducing energy use, and redesigning products to replace hydrocarbon materials with plant-based materials are policies that have negligible positive effect on the environment. Instead, firms should continue to reduce emission of real air and water pollutants.

Steel and other energy-intensive industries need to advocate for low-cost energy, not low-carbon energy. Citizens should realize that, except in rare cases, ingested synthetic chemicals are not a hazard in our modern society, even if produced from hydrocarbons. Plastic-borne chemicals do not pose a health hazard at normal daily exposure levels. Engineers need to develop cost-effective biodegradable plastics to reduce accumulation of plastic in the environment, rather than petroleum-free plastics. Financial industries should deliver products and services that solve real-world problems, not those that pursue solutions to global warming and other imaginary sustainable fears.

CHAPTER 10

# UPHEAVAL—COMING CHANGES IN ENERGY AND CLIMATE REGULATION

*"Everybody loves a tree and hates a businessman."*
—ECONOMIST PAUL SAMUELSON (1976)[1]

The ideology of sustainable development reigns supreme. Despite shaky foundations, government and university leaders tout environmental sustainability as the only way forward for humanity. Nations pursue a mad rush for renewables. Businesses are trapped in the green box of sustainability, forced to pursue policies that raise the cost of products and services with little positive effect on the environment. But the winds of change are blowing. Powerful trends against the ideology of sustainable development grow in strength. It appears that the pendulum is beginning to swing back toward environmental common sense. An upheaval in energy and climate regulation is coming.

## NOT CALAMITY, BUT STEADY IMPROVEMENT

Much of government policy, academic thought, and public opinion stands on fears created and promulgated by environmental sustainable development. The philosophy that humans are too many, too polluting, climate destroying, and profligate wasters of natural resources holds today's society in a powerful psychological grip. Thousands of energy and environmental laws are justified on these misconceptions. Let's briefly review why these ideas are incorrect.

As we discussed in Chapter 2, trends show steady improvement in almost all aspects of the quality of human life. Over the last 200 years, human life spans more than doubled, from 30 years to more than 70 years. Infant mortality rates dropped to one-fifth of the rates in the 1800s. Per-person world incomes rose 10 times from the year 1800, driven by world energy production up 26 times and world trade volumes up 1,800 times. Food output continues to grow faster than population growth, with 11 percent of the world's people undernourished today, the smallest percentage in history. Eighty percent of the world's population can now read and write, double the percentage in 1900. The number of democratic nations increased from zero in 1750 to about 90 today, with the elimination of indentured servitude and chattel slavery, and the establishment of rule of law, freedom of speech and religion, women's suffrage, and gender equality in many countries. We enjoy an improving golden age, rather than a journey on a road to calamity.

Strong, Ehrlich, and others warned that overpopulation would lead to disaster and that humans were a "species out of control." But as we discussed in Chapter 3, global fertility rates declined from 5 children per woman in 1950 to fewer than 2.5 children per woman today. It's now clear that all societies undergo a natural demographic transition from high birth and death rates to low birth and death rates with eventual population stabilization. Rather than be out of control, world population will likely stabilize by the second half of the twenty-first century.

"Humanity's collective demands have exceeded the Earth's regenerative capacity by 26 percent. It is fearful that there are still large numbers of people dreaming the 'American Dream,' hoping to consume like the Americans."
—Lester Brown, *People's Daily Online* interview, September, 2005[2]

Over the last 200 years, humanity struggled with increasing levels of air and water pollution. Today, the UN and environmental groups demand an end to "overproduction" and "overconsumption," an end to the economic growth of developed nations, and constraints on energy use to halt "environmental destruction." Carbon dioxide is branded a pollutant, and the air over developed nations is labeled "too dangerous to breathe."

## Maybe...and *Maybe Not!*

"The story is one of growth in populations and consumption (in most countries) compounded by inertia stemming from inadequate governance and policy responses. The result is degradation of the environment and social stress."
—World Business Council for Sustainable Development, 2010[3]

But as we discussed in Chapter 4, actual trends tell a different story. Over the last century, most people gained access to clean drinking water, eliminating viruses, bacteria, and parasites. Air pollution above wealthy nations has been declining for three decades. Water quality in the Rhine and Danube Rivers, the Great Lakes, and other water systems improves with each passing year. Communities dispose of solid waste using environmentally friendly processes, including recycling, incineration, composting, and lined-landfill sites. Water purification systems, lead-free gasoline, catalytic converters, exhaust scrubbers, double-hulled tankers, and mining land reclamation are now employed by advanced countries. Air and water pollution remains problematic in poor nations, but they are also moving to cleaner environments. Evidence shows that countries eventually reduce pollution as part of economic development.

Energy consumption is not a villain. Nations that consume the most energy per person discharge the lowest level of air and water pollutants per person. Low-cost energy provides economic growth and generates capital for pollution control. Carbon dioxide is not a pollutant. Hundreds of peer-reviewed studies show that increased levels of $CO_2$ result in faster and larger plant growth. The recent rise in atmospheric $CO_2$ is actually greening the Earth.

Over the last 30 years, climate change ideology became the core of sustainable development and the green movement. Most scientific organizations, most leading universities, most of the Fortune 500 companies, faith-based organizations, and the majority of the news media have publicly endorsed this theory. Climatists call carbon dioxide a "dirty pollutant," call coal trains "death trains," and brand those who don't accept the ideology "climate deniers." Thousands of energy and climate laws across hundreds of nations aim to reduce $CO_2$ emissions from transportation, industry, agriculture, and even light bulbs.

But from Chapter 5, scientific data shows that natural forces, not human emissions, dominate Earth's climate. Water vapor, not carbon dioxide or methane, is Earth's dominant greenhouse gas. Human industry contributes less than two percent to the greenhouse effect. Earth's temperatures 1,000 years ago were naturally warmer than today and have

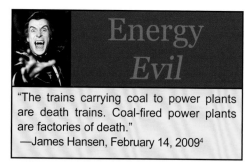

"The trains carrying coal to power plants are death trains. Coal-fired power plants are factories of death."
—James Hansen, February 14, 2009[4]

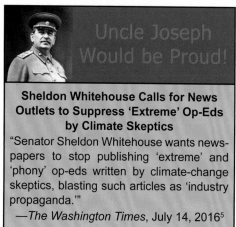

**Sheldon Whitehouse Calls for News Outlets to Suppress 'Extreme' Op-Eds by Climate Skeptics**
"Senator Sheldon Whitehouse wants newspapers to stop publishing 'extreme' and 'phony' op-eds written by climate-change skeptics, blasting such articles as 'industry propaganda.'"
—*The Washington Times*, July 14, 2016[5]

been gently cooling over the last 8,000 years. Contrary to warnings, history shows that today's storms, floods, and droughts are neither more frequent nor more intense than in past centuries. According to satellite data, surface temperatures show no significant warming over the last eighteen years, evidence that the world's climate models are in error.

From Chapter 6, sustainable disciples have long warned that Earth is finite and that natural resources will soon be depleted. Growing population, affluence, production, and consumption must cause peak oil, deforestation, food and water shortages, rising resource prices, and shrinking resource reserves. Humanity faces inevitable economic decline unless we limit growth and adopt sustainable practices.

But resource trends show no such coming exhaustion. World metal production rose five times over the last 50 years, accompanied by flat prices and expanding reserves. The hydrofracturing revolution slew the gremlin of peak oil, with oil and natural gas reserves rising faster than consumption over the last three decades. Despite warnings from many, agricultural output continues to outpace population. Global agricultural land peaked in 2000 and, on net, farm land is now being returned to nature. Over the next 50 years, deforestation will end and the world will enter a period of modest forest regrowth.

Raw materials are natural, but resources are created by people. The level of available resources is not based on the amount of wild fruit on trees or the number of rocks on the ground, but instead on the level of human skill and technology. Access to resources will continue to grow, with resource exhaustion only an unsustainable myth.

## INDICATIONS OF A COMING UPHEAVAL

An upheaval approaches. After 35 years of growing support for restrictive and sometimes bizarre energy laws and regulations, policy changes are on the horizon. Four major trends—the failure of renewables, the abundance of low-cost hydrocarbons, flat to cooling global temperatures, and changing world leadership—challenge the core beliefs of sustainable development. World opinion appears to be to moving back toward sensible energy and environmental policy.

Renewable energy companies continue to be darlings of the media, but their investment quality is shaky. If stock prices are a leading indicator of future trends, then the trend for renewables is not good. The RENIXX index aggregates the stock prices of the world's 30 largest renewable energy companies based on market capitalization. In 2007–2008, when Al Gore and the IPCC received the Nobel Peace Prize for work on climate change, the index exceeded 1,800. Since then, the index has fallen more than 75 percent to just above 400 in 2016. When created in 2002, the RENIXX index was over 1,000, but after fourteen years it stands at less than half of the original value.[6]

Climate policy advocates regard carbon emissions trading as a vital tool to reduce $CO_2$ emissions as part of cap-and-trade systems. Carbon credits, or rights to emit $CO_2$, must be submitted to government agencies each year based on actual industrial emissions. Emissions credits are issued by the government and traded between companies. By controlling and reducing the number of credits traded, governments seek to force firms to reduce actual $CO_2$ emissions. Carbon permit prices indicate the success of climate control policies.

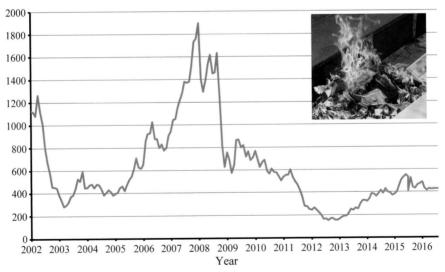

**RENIXX (Renewable Energy Industrial Index) 2002–2016.** RENIXX index of the world's 30 largest renewable energy companies from 2002 to 2016. Index value remains far below the original value in 2002. (*Financial Times*, 2016)[7]

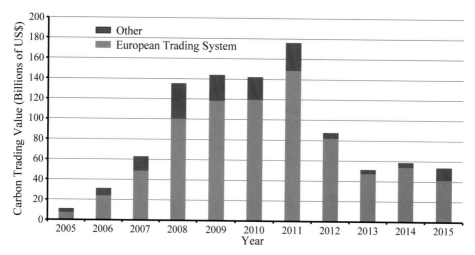

**World Carbon Markets 2005–2015.** The rise and fall in the value of carbon emissions permit trading for the world (full bar height) and the European Trading System. (World Bank, 2012; *Reuters*, 2016)[8]

The European Trading System (ETS), the world's largest cap-and-trade system, began operation in 2005 covering more than 10,000 European companies. Driven by growth in ETS trading, the value of world carbon trading soared to over $170 billion dollars. For several years up to 2012, the World Bank annually published glowing reports on carbon trading progress. But then in 2013, the World Bank did not issue a carbon trading report for year 2012. The reason was that the value of European carbon trading crashed, dropping the value of world carbon trading more than 60 percent in a single year. The value of carbon trading, the vaunted tool to stop global warming, totaled only $54 billion in 2015, less than one-third of the value in 2011.[9]

Renewable energy, particularly wind and solar, is failing in the attempt to replace traditional energy sources. As we discussed in Chapter 7, renewable growth can't even provide for the annual growth in world energy consumption, let alone replace traditional hydrocarbon and nuclear energy sources. Wind and solar energy, with all costs included, and excluding subsidies, costs double to triple the price of hydrocarbon fuels. High levels of wind and solar penetration reduce electrical grid reliability. Wind energy shut down played a key role in the September 2016 state-wide blackout in South Australia, causing Prime Minister Malcolm Turnbull to criticize the renewables "obsession" of state administrations.[10] Governments are now rethinking the renewable energy revolution.

Europe led the world in renewables installation and learned a costly lesson. Hundreds of billions of euros in renewable investment disrupted wholesale electricity markets, ballooned consumer electricity prices, destroyed the balance sheets of utilities, hiked industrial electricity prices, forced the migration of energy-intensive industries, and broke government budgets. A 2016 report placed the cost of the German energy transition at 25,000 euros for each family of four.[11] Unable to cope with the cost, beginning about 2010, more than a dozen countries in Europe slashed renewable subsidies. This caused a 50-percent

**Faulty Forecast**

"Investment in sustainable energy ... is expected to reach $450 billion per year by 2012, rising to more than $600 a year from 2020."
—United Nations Environment Programme, 2008[12]

drop in European renewable investment from 2011 to 2015. With Europe's pullback, world investment in renewable energy has been flat since 2011, after rising almost 30 percent per year for a decade.[13]

As discussed in Chapter 5, Earth's climate does not appear to be cooperating with the theory of human-caused climate change. Two natural temperature cycles, the Pacific Decadal Oscillation (PDO) and the Atlantic Multi-decadal Oscillation (AMO) indicate flat to cooling temperatures ahead. The PDO entered a cool phase early this century after being in a warm phase since 1975.[14] As of 2016, the AMO remains in its warm phase but should begin to cool over the next decade.[15] These ocean cycles play a powerful role in

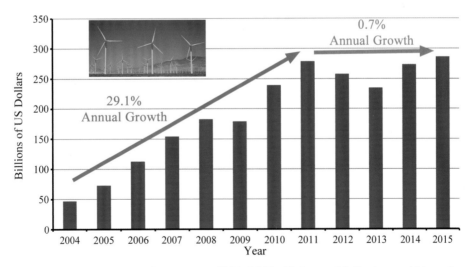

**World Renewable Energy Investment 2004–2015.** Rising and flattening world investment in renewable energy over the last 12 years. Image of wind farm in Palm Springs, California. (UN Environmental Programme and Bloomberg New Energy Finance, 2016)[16]

global temperatures. Another important factor, sunspot activity, languishes at the lowest level in 200 years.[17] Some scientists theorize that sunspot activity influences temperatures by affecting the level of Earth's cloud formation, with high sunspot activity producing warmer global temperatures.[18] The combination of cooling ocean cycles and low sunspot activity indicates flat to cooling temperatures in coming decades. If true, climate model predictions will drift further and further from reality, causing the eventual collapse of the theory of human-caused global warming.

The US hydrofracturing revolution opened a new age in access to hydrocarbon energy. By using fracking and horizontal drilling, oil and gas can now be economically recovered from shale, a common rock formation found all over the world. Recent low petroleum prices appear to be the new normal trend, rather than the exception. Oil and gas extraction cost and cycle time has improved by more than an order of magnitude over conventional techniques. Along with globally abundant coal deposits, the hydrofracturing revolution means low-cost abundant energy for humanity for at least another century.

The global implications are huge. The world's one billion cars today will likely double to two billion by 2050, boosted by low-cost vehicle fuel. Low-cost coal and natural gas will enable access to electricity for the 1.2 billion people who lack electricity today. Wind, solar, and biofuels must push against the powerful headwinds of low-cost hydrocarbon energy. Low-cost hydrocarbon energy means renewables are likely to provide only a small part of world energy consumption for many decades.

A growing number of world leaders now challenge accepted energy and climate assumptions. In 2009, soon-to-be Australian Prime Minister Tony Abbott stated that the argument behind the theory of human-caused warming was "absolute crap."[20] On his first day in office in 2013, Abbott introduced legislation to repeal Australia's carbon tax. He cut government-funded climate research in 2014[21] and cancelled wind farm subsidies in 2015.[22] After the Brexit vote to leave the European Community in 2016, Teresa May became the UK's new prime minister. On her first day in office, she closed down the Department of Energy and Climate Change, the architect

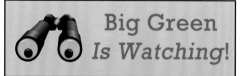

**Big Green Is Watching!**

**EPA Wants to Monitor Your Hotel Showers**

"The Environmental Protection Agency (EPA) is looking to develop a wireless shower monitoring system that would measure the length of guests' showers and water use ... 'This device will be designed to fit most new and existing hotel shower fixtures and will wirelessly transmit hotel guest water usage data to a central hotel accounting system.'"

—*The Daily Caller*, April 9, 2015[19]

of UK energy and climate regulations since 2008.[23] Nicolas Sarkozy, 2016 candidate for President of France, stated:

> Climate has been changing for four billion years.… You need to be as arrogant as men are to believe we changed the climate.[24]

The biggest change may be in the US. By fall of 2016, about half of US Congress, mostly Republicans, disputed the theory of dangerous human-caused warming. The election of climate-skeptic Donald Trump as President in November 2016 portends major US policy reversals. Trump is likely to withdraw from the 2015 Paris Climate Agreement and roll back numerous energy and climate regulations, such as the pending Clean Power Plan.

The powerful trends of failing renewable energy policies, low-cost hydrocarbon energy, flat-to-cooling global temperatures, and changing leadership have already begun an upheaval in energy and climate regulation. The roll-back of subsidies in Europe and Australia will be followed by cuts in the US and other nations. The mad rush for renewables is over and the ideology of sustainable development will return to Earth.

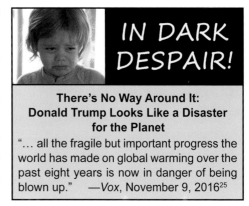

**IN DARK DESPAIR!**

**There's No Way Around It: Donald Trump Looks Like a Disaster for the Planet**

"… all the fragile but important progress the world has made on global warming over the past eight years is now in danger of being blown up."   —*Vox*, November 9, 2016[25]

## LET'S GET REAL

When society pursues the wrong path, as in the case of many of the aspects of sustainable development, business can play a role in restoring sensible policy.  Here are a few more simple recommendations for business.

**Push for low-cost energy, rather than low-carbon energy.** Low-cost energy is the basis for cost-effective products and services in many metal, material, heavy equipment, and transportation market segments, while low-carbon energy is of negligible real value.

**Stop selling guns to the renegades.** Payments to environmental groups may keep them off your back in the short term, but such payments only perpetuate destructive environmental policies in the long term. Promotions touting the green credentials of your firm versus another company may help short-term sales, but also provide tacit support for green ideology that may injure your industry in the long run. Support for a carbon tax, or lobbying to force another industry to adopt renewable energy, only aids the zealots.

**Get the language right.** It may be correct to state that your firm "reduced carbon dioxide emissions to comply with regulations," but it's clearly wrong to say that your company's efforts "help prevent global warming." Don't say "carbon" when you mean "carbon dioxide."

**Put effort into learning the facts.** It's amazing that leading technology firms such as HP, IBM, and Intel continue to support the foolish idea that humans are causing dangerous climate change. A little scientific investigation shows the error of this position.

**Stop shooting your own company in the foot.** The acceptance of human-caused climate change by the American Petroleum Institute and the World Steel Association is bizarre. This can hardly be good for the long-term health of these industries. As philosopher Rollo May said, "… the opposite of courage in society is not cowardice, but conformity."[26]

## TIME FOR BUSINESS TO PUSH BACK?

I speak frequently to US business groups about energy, sustainability, and public policy. I "outrageously" provide evidence against commonly held energy and climate misconceptions and challenge the false foundations of sustainable development. Afterwards, I'm often told that I was "preaching to the choir."

In my experience, most business and industry executives consider energy laws and regulations that restrict energy use and force adoption of renewables to be misguided. They do not accept the theory of dangerous man-made climate change. But it also appears that these executives *don't realize that their views are actually part of a silent common-sense majority.* University professors, government officials, and self-professed green firms such as Apple and Google grab the headlines and promote sustainable ideology, while most of the business community remains silent.

Is it time for world business to come out of the green box of sustainability? New products and services that provide customers with high benefit at low cost offer superior value to green offerings. Corporate philanthropic efforts to reduce poverty, fight disease, and provide clean water, health care, nutritious food, and low-cost energy to people in need merit high value, while purchasing renewable energy and carbon credits brings little value. Reducing discharge of real air and water pollutants protects the environment, but reducing carbon dioxide emissions does nothing.

Join the coming upheaval, and let's return to sensible environmental policy.

# RECOMMENDED READING

Ron Bailey, *The End of Doom: Environmental Renewal in the 21st Century* (Thomas Dunne Books, 2015)

Joseph L. Bast, *Eco-sanity: Common-Sense Guide to Environmentalism* (Madison Books, 1994)

Larry Bell, *Climate of Corruption: Politics and Power Behind the Global Warming Hoax* (Greenleaf Book Group, 2011)

Christopher Booker and Richard North, *Scared to Death: From BSE to Global Warming: Why Scares are Costing Us the Earth* (Bloomsbury Academic, 2008)

Robert L. Bradley, Jr., *Capitalism at Work: Business, Government, and Energy* (M&M Scrivener Press, 2008)

Peter Brimblecombe, *The Big Smoke* (Methuen, 1987)

Robert Bryce, *Power Hungry: The Myths of "Green Energy" and the Real Fuels of the Future* (Public Affairs, 2011)

Robert Bryce, *Smaller, Lighter, Faster, Denser, Cheaper: How Innovation Keeps Proving the Catastrophists Wrong* (Public Affairs, 2016)

James Delingpole, *Watermelons: The Green Movement's True Colors* (Publis Books, 2011)

Paul Driessen, *Eco-Imperialism: Green Power, Black Death* (Merril Press, 2010)

Alex Epstein, *The Moral Case for Fossil Fuels* (Portfolio, 2014)

Giovanni Federico, *Feeding the World: An Economic History of Agriculture, 1800-2000* (Princeton University Press, 2008)

Steve Goreham, *Climatism! Science, Common Sense, and the 21st Century's Hottest Topic* (New Lenox Books, 2010)

Steve Goreham, *The Mad, Mad, Mad World of Climatism: Mankind and Climate Change Mania* (New Lenox Books, 2012)

Howard C. Hayden, *Solar Fraud: Why Solar Energy Won't Run the World* (Vales Lake, 2005)

Peter Huber and Mark P. Mills, *The Bottomless Well: The Twilight of Fuel, the Virtue of Waste, and Why We Will Never Run Out of Energy* (Basic Books, 2006)

Craig Idso, Robert Carter, and S. Fred Singer, *Why Scientists Disagree About Global Warming: The NIPCC Report on Scientific Consensus* (Heartland Institute, 2015)

James Inhofe, *The Greatest Hoax: How Global Warming Conspiracy Threatens Your Future* (WND Books, 2012)

Bjorn Lomborg, *The Skeptical Environmentalist: Measuring the Real State of the World* (Cambridge University, 2001)

Stephen Moore and Kathleen Hartnett White, *Fueling Freedom: Exposing the Mad War on Energy* (Regnery, 2016)

Stephen Moore and Julian Simon, *It's Getting Better All the Time: 110 Greatest Trends of the Last 100 Years* (Cato Institute, 2001)

Alan Moran, editor, *Climate Change: The Facts* (Stockdale Books, 2015)

Matt Ridley, *The Rational Optimist: How Prosperity Evolves* (Harper Perennial, 2011)

Julian L. Simon, *The Ultimate Resource 2* (Princeton University Press, 1998)

S. Fred Singer and Dennis Avery, *Unstoppable Global Warming: Every 1500 Years* (Rowman & Littlefield, 2007)

Vaclav Smil, *Energy Transitions: History, Requirements, Prospects* (Praeger, 2010)

Vaclav Smil, *Enriching the Earth: Fritz Haber, Carl Bosch, and the Transformation of World Food Production* by (NIT Press, 2001)

Roy Spencer, *Climate Confusion: How Global Warming Hysteria Leads to Bad Science, Pandering Politicians, and Misguided Policies that Hurt the Poor* (Encounter Books, 2010)

Robert Zubrin, *Merchants of Despair: Radical Environmentalists, Criminal Pseudo-Scientists, and the Fatal Cult of Anti-Humanism* (New Atlantis Books, 2012)

# NOTES

## Introduction

1. Secretary of State Hillary Rodham Clinton presentation to the United Nations Conference on Sustainable Development, June 22, 2012
2. "Golf Ball With Carbon Dioxide Absorbents," US 20120046126 A1, http://patft.uspto.gov/netacgi/nph-Parser?Sect1=PTO2&Sect2=HITO FF&p=1&u=%2Fnetahtml%2FPTO%2Fsearch-bool.html&r=1&f=G&l=50&co1=AND&d=PTXT&s1=8475297.PN.&OS=PN/8475297&RS= PN/8475297; tree image by Cruiser under GNU Free Documentation License
3. "A Great Freeze Over the Great Lakes: Image of the Day," NASA, February 19, 2014, http://earthobservatory.nasa.gov/IOTD/view. php?id=83169
4. "Hearings Before the Subcommittee on Energy and Power," US House of Representatives, Feb., 1975, https://babel.hathitrust.org/cgi/pt?id=m dp.39015081210620;view=1up;seq=1; 8-ball image by nicubunu
5. Stephen Dinan, "Obama administration issues permits for wind farms to kill more eagles," *The Washington Times*, Dec. 6, 2013; Eagle killed by wind turbine image by Stefan Hedgren

## Chapter 1: The Capture of Global Business

1. *Extraordinary Delusions and the Madness of Crowds* by Charles MacKay, (Wordsworth Editions, 1995), p. xvi
2. Intel Corporation, 2012 Corporate Responsibility Report, http://www.intel.com/content/www/us/en/corporate-responsibility/corporate-responsibility-2012-report.html?wapkw=2012+sustainability+report; demonstrator image from Pedro Ribeiro Simoes under Creative Commons License
3. Daisuke Wakabayashi, "Cook Raises, Dashes Hopes for Excitement at Apple Annual Meeting," *The Wall Street Journal*, Feb. 28, 2014, http://blogs. wsj.com/digits/2014/02/28/cook-raises-dashes-hopes-for-excitement-at-apple-annual-meeting/
4. "Tim Cook to Apple Investors: Drop Dead," The National Center for Public Policy Research, Feb., 28, 2014, http://www.nationalcenter.org/PR-Apple_ Tim_Cook_Climate_022814.html
5. "Environmental Responsibility Report, 2015 Progress Report, Covering FY2014," Apple Inc., 2015, https://www.apple.com/environment/pdf/ Apple_Environmental_Responsibility_Report_2015.pdf
6. Bill DiBenedetto, "Apple Invests $3 Billion in Solar Energy," *triplepundit.com*, Feb. 13, 2015, http://www.triplepundit.com/2015/02/apple-goes-invest-3-billion-solar-energy/
7. Environmental Responsibility Report, (See no.5)
8. Chris Martin, "Google Is Making Its Biggest Ever Bet on Renewable Energy, *Bloomberg*, Feb. 26, 2015, http://www.bloomberg.com/news/ articles/2015-02-26/google-makes-biggest-bet-on-renewables-to-fund-solarcity
9. "Google cans concentrated solar power project," evwind.es, Nov. 24, 2011, http://www.evwind.es/2011/11/24/google-cans-concentrated-solar-power-project/14860
10. Devin Henry, "Solar energy project killed 3,500 birds," *The Hill*, Apr. 15, 2015, http://thehill.com/policy/energy-environment/240015-solar-energy-project-killed-3500-birds
11. Pete Danko, "More Problems for CSP: Ivanpah Solar Plant Falling Short of Expected Electricity Production," *GreenTechMedia.com*, Oct. 30, 2014, http://www.greentechmedia.com/articles/read/ivanpah-solar-plant-falling-short-of-expected-electricity-production
12. "Guide for Responsible Corporate Engagement in Climate Policy," by the United Nations Global Compact, the United Nations Framework Convention on Climate Change, and the United Nations Environment Programme, 2013,https://www.unglobalcompact.org/docs/issues_doc/ Environment/climate/Guide_Responsible_Corporate_Engagement_Climate_Policy.pdf
13. "Deserts 'greening' from rising CO2," Commonwealth Scientific and Industrial Research Organization, Jul. 3, 2013, http://www.csiro.au/Portals/ Media/Deserts-greening-from-rising-CO2.aspx; plant image by Tanheiheimandy under Creative Commons License
14. Chipotle 2013 Annual Report, p. 16, http://ir.chipotle.com/phoenix.zhtml?c=194775&p=irol-reportsAnnual; annual report image by Wikimedia Deutschland under Creative Commons License; Kate Taylor, "Chipotle Says Global Warming May Mean the End of Guacamole," *Entrepreneur*, Mar. 5, 2014, http://www.entrepreneur.com/article/231976
15. Bill Gates, "Innovating to zero!," TED lecture, Feb. 20, 2010, http://www.ted.com/talks/bill_gates/transcript?language=en, Bill Gates image from Flickr and World Economic Forum under Creative Commons License
16. Mark Tercek, "Q&A With Sir Richard Branson: Dialogues on the Environment," *Huffington Post*, May 28, 2013, http://www.huffingtonpost.com/ mark-tercek/qa-with-sir-richard-branson_b_3347067.html; Richard Branson image by D@LY3D under Creative Commons License
17. Jeff Immelt, presentation at the University of Cambridge, Oct. 28, 2010, http://www.cisl.cam.ac.uk/Resources/Videos/Jeff-Immelt.aspx; Jeffery Immelt image by Katarzyna Czerwinska under Creative Commons License
18. Rupert Murdock speech to News Corporation employees, 2007, The Aspen Institute, http://www.caseplace.org/d.asp?d=2328; Rupert Murdoch image by Flicker, World Economic Forum under Creative Commons License

19. Bryan Walsh, "Five Questions with DuPont CEO Ellen Kullman," *Time.com*, Feb. 13, 2014, http://time.com/9072/dupont-ceo-ellen-kullman-q-and-a/;Ellen Kullman image by Flickr, World Economic Forum under Creative Commons License

20. "Letter from global investor networks to the governments of the world's largest economies," Nov. 20, 2012, http://www.iigcc.org/files/publication-files/2012_Open_letter_from_global_investor_networks.pdf

21. Larry Bell, "EPA's Wood-Burning Stove Ban Has Chilling Consequences For Many Rural People," *Forbes*, Jan. 29, 2014, http://www.forbes.com/sites/larrybell/2014/01/29/epas-wood-burning-stove-ban-has-chilling-consequences-for-many-rural-people/; graveyard silhouette image by naoshika; stove image by hatalar205

22. Merck 2012 Corporate Responsibility Report, http://www.csrwire.com/reports/1321-Merck-2012-Corporate-Responsibility-Report

23. BP 2013 Sustainability Review, http://www.bp.com/en/global/corporate/sustainability/about-our-reporting/report-library.html

24. Nestle 2013 Creating Shared Value Report, http://www.nestle.com/asset-library/documents/library/documents/corporate_social_responsibility/nestle-csv-summary-report-2013-en.pdf

25. Barbara Boland, "Sen. Boxer Links Keystone Pipeline to Cancer," *CNSNews*, Feb. 27, 2014, http://cnsnews.com/mrctv-blog/barbara-boland/sen-boxer-links-keystone-pipeline-cancer

26. American Petroleum Institute website, 2014, http://www.api.org/environment-health-and-safety/climate-change

27. Tesco PLC Corporate Responsibility Review 2012, http://www.tescoplc.com/files/pdf/reports/tesco_cr_review_2012.pdf

28. Panasonic 2014 Sustainbility Report, http://www.panasonic.com/global/corporate/sustainability/downloads.html

29. *The New Hacker's Dictionary, Third Edition* edited by Eric Raymond, (MIT Press, 1996), p. 208

30. BBC Radio 4 interview with Sir John Beddington, Apr. 1, 2014, https://sites.google.com/site/mytranscriptbox/home/20140104_r4; Ghost image by netalloy

31. "Rio Declaration on Environment and Development," Jun., 16,1992, http://www.unep.org/Documents.Multilingual/Default.asp?DocumentID=78&ArticleID=1163

32. Chicken image by paweo111

33. Michal Nachmany, et al., "The 2015 GLOBE Climate Legislation Study," Grantham Research Institute on Climate Change and the Environment, May 31, 2015, http://www.lse.ac.uk/GranthamInstitute/publication/2015-global-climate-legislation-study/

34. Ibid

35. "Environmental Reporting Guidelines: including mandatory greenhouse gas emissions reporting guidance," Oct. 3, 2013, https://www.gov.uk/government/publications/environmental-reporting-guidelines-including-mandatory-greenhouse-gas-emissions-reporting-guidance

36. "Greenhouse gas reporting program," US Environmental Protection Agency, 2013, http://www.epa.gov/ghgreporting/ghgdata/reported/index.html

37. P Byrne, "Fact Sheet No. 9.371," Colorado State University, Sep. 2010, http://www.ext.colostate.edu/pubs/foodnut/09371.html

38. California Proposition 65 warning label for firewood, https://www.flickr.com/photos/raludwick/9177955397; firewood image by Motai-juku, Saku, under Creative Commons License

39. "Global Trends in Renewable Energy Investment 2016, " UN Environment Programme, Boomberg New Energy Finance, Mar. 2016, http://fs-unep-centre.org/publications/global-trends-renewable-energy-investment-2016

40. Christian Hiller, "Deutsche Bank, Al Gore and the $10 Billion Climate Fund," *Frankfurter Allgemaine Zeitung*, Nov. 15, 2010, http://www.thegwpf.com/deutsche-bank-al-gore-and-the-10-billion-climate-fund/; money image from *deviantart.com* under Creative Commons License

41. *Renewables 2013: Global Status Report*, REN21, www.ren21.net

42. Siemens Environmental Portfolio Report, 2014, http://www.siemens.com/about/sustainability/pool/de/umweltportfolio/ep_report.pdf

43. Bank of America Corporate Social Report 2012, http://about.bankofamerica.com/en-us/global-impact/corporate-social-responsibility.html#fbid=hpKwi48WV8b

44. Citibank 2012 Global Citizenship Report, http://www.citigroup.com/citi/about/data/corp_citizenship/global_2012_english.pdf

45. Morgan Stanley 2012 Sustainability Report, http://www.morganstanley.com/globalcitizen/pdf/sReport_2012.pdf?v=07222013

46. "Carbon Market Monitor," Thomson Reuters, Jan. 11, 2016, https://climateobserver.org/wp-content/uploads/2016/01/Carbon-Market-Review-2016.pdf

47. LOHAS Background, http://www.lohas.com/about

48. A. K. Streeter, "No-petroleum sunglasses crafted form castor bean oil," *Treehugger.com*, May 16, 2013, http://www.treehugger.com/sustainable-product-design/plant-based-sunglasses-eliminate-crude-oil-plastic.html

49. "Sustainability & Resource Productivity Practice," McKinsey & Company, 2014, http://www.mckinsey.com/client_service/sustainability

50. "Energy and Environmental Consulting," Booz Allen Hamilton, 2014, http://www.boozallen.com/consultants/civilian-government/energy-environmental

51. Jeff Immelt, presentation at the University of Cambridge, (See no. 17)

52. "Eroding Alaska town sues oil, power companies," *Associated Press*, Feb. 27, 2008, http://www.nbcnews.com/id/23367934/ns/us_news-environment/t/eroding-alaska-town-sues-oil-power-companies/#.VEk9S5V0xOg; steel plant image from US Environmental Protection Agency

53. Richard Heede, "Tracing anthropogenic carbon dioxide and methane emissions to fossil fuel and cement producers, 1954-2010, *Climatic Change*, Nov. 22, 2013, http://www.climateaccountability.org/pdf/Heede%20TracingAnthropogenic%20ClimCh%20Nov13.pdf

54. Keith Stewart, "Corporate executives could be personally liable for undermining action on climate change," Greenpeace, May 28, 2014, http://www.greenpeace.org/canada/en/Blog/corporate-executives-could-be-personally-liab/blog/49417/

55. Jonathan Amos, "Arctic summers ice-free 'by 2013'", *BBC News*, Dec. 12, 2007, http://news.bbc.co.uk/2/hi/7139797.stm, Eight ball image by nicubunu

56. "Responsible Industry," Forest Ethics, 2014, http://www.forestethics.org/responsible-industry

57. Brian Clark Howard, "Washing Hands in Hot Water Wastes Energy, Study Says," National Geographic, Dec. 12, 2013, http://news.nationalgeographic.com/news/energy/2013/12/131213-washing-hands-hot-water-wastes-energy-health/; question mark image from semjaza

58. Andy Serwer, "(Say wha???) The CEO who writes her employees' parents," *Fortune*, Jan. 28, 2014, http://fortune.com/2014/01/28/say-wha-the-ceo-who-writes-her-employees-parents/; green bus image by Alan Sansbury under Creative Commons License

59. Marianne Veach, "Pressure on the Paper Production Industry," University of California, San Diego, Fall 2007, http://irps.ucsd.edu/assets/021/8434.pdf

60. Evan Perez, "Royal Caribbean Alters Waste-Treatment Tack," *Wall Street Journal*, May 6, 2004, http://online.wsj.com/articles/SB108379551432603177

61. "Shifting the Paradigm," Rainforest Action Network, 2014, http://www.ran.org/shifting-paradigm

62. Rhett Butler, "An Interview with Michael Brune," *Mongabay.com*, Jan. 29,2007, http://news.mongabay.com/2007/0130-ran.html

63. Neil Harb, "A Sign of Things to Come?," Frontiers of Freedom Institute, Summer 2004, http://www.cei.org/pdf/4079.pdf

64. Amanda Carey, "Green Bullies: How Environmental Groups Use the Tactics of Intimidation," Capital Research, May 8, 2011, http://capitalresearch.org/2011/05/green-bullies-how-environmental-groups-use-the-tactics-of-intimidation/

65. Margie Kelly and Molly Haigh, "Revlon Under Fire for Cancer-Causing Chemicals in Makeup," Safe Cosmetics, Oct. 25, 2013, http://safecosmetics.org/article.php?id=1162

66. Jane Levere, "In an Overhaul, Clorox Aims to Get Green Works Out of Its Niche," *New York Times*, Apr. 21, 2013, http://www.nytimes.com/2013/04/22/business/media/cloroxs-green-works-aims-to-get-out-of-the-niche.html?_r=0
67. "NAD Examines Clorox 'Green Works' Claims, Following Challenge by Method Products," ASRC, Oct. 27, 2009, http://www.asrcreviews.org/2009/10/nad-examines-clorox-green-works-claims-following-challenge-by-method-products/
68. "Cleaning Products - Natural Household Cleaners," Clorox, 2014, http://linkis.com/com/IPcS
69. "Is Revlon Filled With Cancer-Causing Crap? (Hint: No)," brightestbulbinthebox.com, Nov. 30, 2013, http://www.brightestbulbinthebox.com/2013/11/is-revlon-filled-with-cancer-causing.html
70. Richard Brownlee and Allison Elias, "Coca-Cola, World Wildlife Fund team up for water conservation," *Washington Post*, Oct. 17, 2014, http://www.washingtonpost.com/business/coca-cola-world-wildlife-fund-team-up-for-water-conservation/2014/10/16/144c7046-5305-11e4-892e-602188e70e9c_story.html
71. Lowe's 2012 Social Responsibility Report, http://responsibility.lowes.com/2014/wp-content/uploads/2014/04/2012-Annual-Report-PDF-English1.pdf
72. "Where We Give," Wells Fargo, 2014, https://www.wellsfargo.com/about/csr/charitable/where
73. Joe Stephens, "Nature Conservancy faces potential backlash from ties with BP," Washington Post, May 24, 2010, http://www.washingtonpost.com/wp-dyn/content/article/2010/05/23/AR2010052302164.html
74. Anne Landman, "BP's 'Beyond Petroleum' Campaign Losing its Sheen," PR Watch, May 3, 2010, http://www.prwatch.org/news/2010/05/9038/bps-beyond-petroleum-campaign-losing-its-sheen
75. "A mandate for change is a mandate for smart," IBM, 2014, http://www.ibm.com/smarterplanet/global/files/us__en_us__general__smarterplanet_overview.pdf
76. "The compliance market," RWE, 2014, http://www.rwe.com/web/cms/en/595982/rwe-supply-trading/industrial-customers/commodity-solutions/commodities/the-compliance-market/
77. Presentation by Sam Warburton of RWE Power AG, 2013, http://www.fao.org/fileadmin/user_upload/rome2007/docs/Promoting%20Renewable%20Energy%20and%20the%20use%20of%20Biomass%20in%20Power%20Generation.pdf
78. "Overview of the UN Global Compact," UN Global Compact, 2014, https://www.unglobalcompact.org/aboutthegc/
79. "Ceres In Brief," Ceres, 2014, http://www.ceres.org/files/in-briefs-and-one-pagers/ceres-in-brief
80. "CEO Statement," Allianz, 2014, https://www.allianz.com/en/sustainability/approach/ceo_statement.html; Lemonade image by Michael Fludkov under Creative Commons License
81. CDP: Driving Sustainable Economies, 2014, https://www.cdp.net/en-US/Pages/HomePage.aspx
82. The Climate Group, 2014, http://www.theclimategroup.org/who-we-are/about-us/
83. "Carbon Footprint Calculator for Printing," HP, 2014, http://www.hp.com/large/ipg/ecological-printing-solutions/carbon-footprint-calc.html
84. Timothy, Cama, "Tech leaders urge State to reject Keystone XL," *The Hill*, Apr. 1, 2014, http://thehill.com/policy/energy-environment/202276-tech-leaders-urge-state-to-reject-keystone-xl
85. "Microsoft, Sprint Call for Extension to Wind Power Tax Credit," *Environmental Leader*, June 15, 2012, http://www.environmentalleader.com/2012/06/15/microsoft-sprint-call-for-extension-to-wind-power-tax-credit/
86. UNEP, (See no. 40)
87. "Key World Energy Statistics, 2012," International Energy Agency, 2014, http://www.iea.org/publications/freepublications/publication/KeyWorld2014.pdf
88. Robert Roy Britt, "Extreme Green: Reusable Toilet Wipes," *Livescience*, Feb. 27, 2009, http://www.livescience.com/7688-extreme-green-reusable-toilet-wipes.html; flower image by Hakani
89. Sam Batkins, "Piling On: The Year in Regulation," American Action Forum, Jan. 2013, http://americanactionnetwork.org/sites/default/files/2012%20in%20Regs.pdf
90. "Car refrigerant rejected by Daimler is safe, EU scientists say," Automotive News Europe, Mar. 10, 2014, http://europe.autonews.com/article/20140310/ANE/140319998/car-refrigerant-rejected-by-daimler-is-safe-eu-scientists-say
91. "Corn supply, disappearance, and share of total corn supply used for ethanol," US Department of Agriculture, www.ers.usda.gov/datafiles/US_Bioenergy/Feedstocks/table05.xls
92. "World Agriculture Outlook Database," Food and Agriculture Policy Institute, 2012, http://www.fapri.iastate.edu/tools/outlook.aspx
93. Karen Lo, "Swiss Chocolatier Barry Callebaut Creates Heat-Resistant Chocolate to Survive Global Warming," Daily Meal, Dec. 28, 2016, http://www.thedailymeal.com/cook/swiss-chocolatier-barry-callebaut-creates-heat-resistant-chocolate-survive-global-warming/122815

## Chapter 2: Environmental Apocalypse or Golden Age?

1. U Thant, statement at the Commemorative Session of the UN General Assembly, Oct. 24, 1970, http://www.uthantinstitute.org/index.php?option=com_content&view=article&id=130:human-environment&catid=67:human-environment&Itemid=126
2. "Message for the New Millenium," The Dalai Lama, 2014, http://www.dalailama.com/messages/world-peace/millennium-message
3. *Silent Spring* by Rachel Carson, (Penguin Books,1968), p.6
4. *Earth in Balance: Ecology and the Human Spirit* by Al Gore, (Houghton Mifflin, 1992), p. 269
5. "Outdoor Air Pollution," World Health Organization, July 2008, www.ipa-world.org/uploadedbyfck/OUTDOOR_AIR.ppt
6. Peter Brimblecombe, "A History of Urban Air Pollution," *Korean Journal of Atmospheric Sciences*, 6, p. 40-46, 2003, http://ocean.kisti.re.kr/downfile/volume/komes/KSHHDL/2003/v13n2/KSHHDL_2003_v13n2_40.pdf
7. *World Atlas of Atmospheric Pollution* edited by Ranjeet Sokhi, (Anthem Press, 2011), p. 9
8. Brimblecombe, (See no. 8)
9. Photograph of Widnes, England in the late 19th Century from *A History of the Chemical Industry in Widnes* by D.W.F. Hardie, (Imperial Chemical Industries, 1950)
10. *Principles of Environmental Science: Inquiry & Applications 4th Edition* by William and Mary Ann Cunningham, (McGraw-Hill, 2007), p. 210
11. "Ecology Becomes Everybody's Issue," *Life Magazine*, Jan. 30, 1970, p. 22-30
12. *The Limits to Growth: A Report to The Club of Rome's Project on the Predicament of Mankind* by Donella Meadows et. al, (Potomac Associates, 1972), p. 23
13. Uri Friedman, "The Norwegian Military Is Fighting Climate Change with 'Meatless Mondays,'" *Atlantic*, Nov. 21, 2013, http://www.theatlantic.com/international/archive/2013/11/the-norwegian-military-is-fighting-climate-change-with-meatless-mondays/281729/; flower image by Hakani
14. United Nations Environment Programme, 2016, http://web.unep.org/about/who-we-are/overview
15. "Report of the World Commission on Environment and Development," United Nations General Assembly, Dec. 11, 1987, http://www.un.org/documents/ga/res/42/ares42-187.htm
16. "Report of the World Commission on Environment and Development: Our Common Future," The Brundtland Commission, 1987, http://www.un-documents.net/our-common-future.pdf
17. "Policymakers Summary of the Scientific Assessment of Climate Change: Report to IPCC from Working Group I," June 1990, p. xi, https://www.ipcc.ch/ipccreports/far/wg_I/ipcc_far_wg_I_spm.pdf

18. "Agenda 21," United Nations Conference on Environment & Development, Rio de Janeiro, Brazil, 1992, http://sustainabledevelopment.un.org/content/documents/Agenda21.pdf

19. "Sustainable Lifestyles and Education for Sustainable Consumption," United Nations, http://www.docstoc.com/docs/160402702/Issues_Sus_Lifestyles

20. Maurice Strong opening statement at the 1992 Rio de Janeiro Earth Summit, June 3, 1992, http://www.mauricestrong.net/index.php/opening-statement6; explosion image is US Navy photo

21. Xan Brooks, "I'm the last crazy artist," *Guardian*, Apr. 4, 2007, http://www.theguardian.com/film/2007/apr/05/1

22. Ann Landers, *Washington Post*, Apr. 16, 1989, p. F7

23. President Jimmy Carter's Farewell Address, Jan. 14, 1981, http://www.jimmycarterlibrary.gov/documents/speeches/farewell.phtml

24. "GY121 Sustainable Development" course description, London School of Economics, 2013/2014, http://www.lse.ac.uk/resources/calendar/courseGuides/GY/2014_GY121.htm

25. "ENVR E-117 Hybrid: Catalyzing Change--Sustainability Leadership for the Twenty-First Century," Harvard University, 2014, http://www.extension.harvard.edu/courses/hybrid-catalyzing-change-sustainability-leadership-twenty-first-century

26. Next Generation Science Standards, 2014  http://www.nextgenscience.org/sites/ngss/files/NGSS%20Combined%20Topics%2011.8.13.pdf

27. Ibid

28. Samuel Preston, "American Longevity: Past, Present, and Future," Center for Policy Research, 1996, http://surface.syr.edu/cgi/viewcontent.cgi?article=1035&context=cpr

29. 1960-2010 data from World Bank World Development Indicators, http://data.worldbank.org/data-catalog/world-development-indicators; France, India, and US data prior to 1960 from Human Life Table Database and official national statistics, http://www.lifetable.de/; UK data is England data from *Aging in the Past: Demography, Society, and Old Age* by David Kertzer and Peter Laslett (Berkeley Press, 1995); old man image from Ahmet Demirel

30. Ibid

31. "Abraham Lincoln's Family," http://www.abrahamlincolns.com/abraham-lincolns-family.php

32. 1960-2010 data from World Bank World Development Indicators, http://data.worldbank.org/data-catalog/world-development-indicators; Chile, Mexico, and US data prior to 1960 from Rodwan Abouharb and Anessa Kimball, "A New Dataset on Infant Mortality Rates, 1816-2002," *Journal of Peace Research*, Nov. 2007, http://jpr.sagepub.com/content/44/6/743.abstract

33. Bradford De Long, "Estimates of World GDP, One Million B.C.--Present," 1998, http://delong.typepad.com/sdj/2014/05/estimates-of-world-gdp-one-million-bc-present-1998-my-view-as-of-1998-the-honest-broker-for-the-week-of-may-24-2014.html

34. *It's Getting Better All the Time: 110 Greatest Trends of the Last 100 Years* by Stephen Moore and Julian Simon, (Cato Institute, 2001), p. 58

35. Angus Maddison, "Historical Statistics of the World Economy," 2010, http://www.ggdc.net/maddison/maddison-project/home.htm

36. Ibid

37. Infant mortality, (See no. 32); infant image from Azoreg under Creative Commons License

38. Maddison, (See no. 35); moneybags image by Southern Railway System

39. "Vision 2050: The new agenda for business," World Business Council for Sustainable Development, Feb. 2010, http://www.wbcsd.org/pages/edocument/edocumentdetails.aspx?id=219; fist image by Worker

40. "Standard Bank report confirms strong growth in Africa's rising middle class—and even faster future growth," Standard Bank press release, Aug. 19, 2014, http://appablog.wordpress.com/2014/08/19/standard-bank-report-confirms-strong-growth-in-africas-rising-middle-class-and-even-faster-future-growth/

41. United Nations International Trade Statistics, 1900-1960, https://unstats.un.org/unsd/trade/imts/Historical%20data%201900-1960.pdf; World Trade Organization Statistics Database, 1950-2010,http://www.wto.org/english/res_e/statis_e/trade_data_e.htm

42. *101 Ways to Save the Planet* by Deborah Underwood, (Heinemann-Raintree Books, 2012), p. 8; question mark image from semjaza

43. UN Food and Agriculture Organization, http://www.fao.org/docrep/018/i3107e/i3107e00.htm, FAOSTAT, UN FAO, 2014, http://faostat3.fao.org/home/E

44. "Human Development Report 2014," United Nations, http://hdr.undp.org/en

45. Trade Statistics, (See no. 41); container ship photo from Huhu Uet under Creative Commons License

46. Food production data computed from Indur Goklany, "Meeting Global Food Needs: The Environmental Trade-Offs Between Increasing Land Conversion and Land Productivity," *Technology*, Vol. 6, 1999, p. 107-130, http://goklany.org/library/Global%20Food%20Needs%20Technology%201999.pdf and "World Indices of Agricultural and Food Production," US Department of Agriculture, Economic Research Service, Statistical Bulletin 699, July 1981, http://babel.hathitrust.org/cgi/pt?id=uc1.32106011137699;view=1up;seq=1; Population data from "World Population Prospects: The 2012 Revision," United Nations Population Division, 2012, http://esa.un.org/wpp/Excel-Data/population.htm; "Undernourishment around the world in 2010," UN Food and Agriculture Organization, 2010, http://www.fao.org/docrep/013/i1683e/i1683e02.pdf, "FAO Statistical Yearbook 2013," UN FAO, http://www.fao.org/docrep/018/i3107e/i3107e00.htm, FAOSTAT, UN FAO, 2014, http://faostat3.fao.org/home/E; harvesting image from US Environmental Protection Agency

47. *Energy Transitions: History, Requirements, Prospects* by Vaclav Smil, (Praeger, 2010), appendix

48. "Key World Energy Statistics, 2012," International Energy Agency, http://www.iea.org/publications/freepublications/publication/kwes.pdf

49. Computed from US energy consumption data from the US Census Bureau, "Statistical Abstracts of the US," 2009 and 2011, and "Historical Statistics of the United States, Colonial Times to 1970," http://www.census.gov/prod/www/statistical_abstract.html

50. Robert Barro and Johg-Wha Lee, "A New Data Set of Educational Attainment in the World 1950-2010," Asian Development Bank and Korea University, Apr., 2010, http://www.nber.org/papers/w15902; Christian Morrisson and Fabrice Murtin, "The Century of Education," Centre for Economics Education, London School of Economics, Sep. 2009, http://cee.lse.ac.uk/ceedps/ceedp109.pdf

51. "World Illiteracy at Mid-Century," UNESCO, 1957, http://unesdoc.unesco.org/images/0000/000029/002930eo.pdf; "Adult and Youth Literacy: National, regional and global trends, 1985-2015," UNESCO, June 2013, http://www.uis.unesco.org/Education/Documents/literacy-statistics-trends-1985-2015.pdf

52. Vaclav Smil, (See no. 47); "Key World Energy Statistics, 2012," International Energy Agency, http://www.iea.org/publications/freepublications/publication/kwes.pdf; oil pump image by Antandrus under Creative Commons License

53. Educational Attainment (See no. 50); graduation cap image under Creative Commons License

54. *The First Global Revolution: A Report by the Club of Rome* by Alexander King and Bertrand Schneider, (Pantheon Books, 1991), p. 7; fist image by Worker

55. "The State of Food Insecurity in the World," Food and Agriculture Organization of the UN, 2014, http://www.fao.org/publications/sofi/2014/en/

56. "Human Development Report," (See no. 44)

57. "World Water Development Report 2016," United Nations, http://www.unesco.org/new/en/natural-sciences/environment/water/wwap/wwdr/2016-water-and-jobs/

58. "Energy Access Database," International Energy Agency, 2011, http://www.worldenergyoutlook.org/resources/energydevelopment/energyaccessdatabase/

59. Food Insecurity, (See no. 55)

60. "Progress on Drinking Water and Sanitation," World Health Organization, 2014, http://www.unwater.org/publications/publications-detail/

en/c/231531/

61.   Max Roser, "Our World in Data," 2014, http://www.ourworldindata.org/data/political-regimes/democratisation/; Center for Systemic Peace, 2014, http://www.systemicpeace.org/inscrdata.html; statue of liberty image by dzhingarov under Creative Commons License

62.   *The State of Humanity* by Julian Simon, (Wiley-Blackwell, 1996), p. 27

63.   Matt Ridley, 2014, http://www.rationaloptimist.com/biography

64.   World on the Edge: How to Prevent Environmental and Economic Collapse by Lester Brown, (W.W. Norton & Co., 2011), p. x

65.   Ellie Zolfagharifard, "Climate change and air pollution will lead to famine by 2050, study claims," *MailOnLine*, Jul. 28, 2014, http://www.dailymail.co.uk/sciencetech/article-2708296/Climate-change-air-pollution-lead-famine-2050-study-claims.html; image of warehouse fire by Petteri Sulonen under Creative Commons License

## Chapter 3: Overpopulation Fear

1.    *Essay on the Principle of Population* by Thomas Malthus, 1798, p. 4, http://www.esp.org/books/malthus/population/malthus.pdf

2.    Ibid

3.    Malthus, (See no. 1), p. 44

4.    Michael Kremer, "Population Growth and Technological Change: One Million B.C. to 1990," *Quarterly Journal of Economics*, Vol. 108, No. 3, Aug. 1993, p. 681-716, http://www.econ.ucdavis.edu/faculty/gclark/210a/readings/kremer1993.pdf;

5.    Stephanie Haensch et al., "Distinct Clones of Yersinia pestis Caused the Black Death, PLOS Pathogens, Oct. 07, 2010, http://www.plospathogens.org/article/info%3Adoi%2F10.1371%2Fjournal.ppat.1001134

6.    *Epidemics and Pandemics: Their Impacts on Human History* by J. N. Hays, (ABC-CLIO, 2005), p. 151

7.    *Guns, Germs, and Steel*, The Fates of Human Societies, by Jared Diamond, (W.W. Norton, 1999), p. 211

8.    Abbas Behbehani, "The Smallpox Story: Life and Death of an Old Disease," Microbiological Reviews, Dec. 1983, p. 455-509, http://www.ncbi.nlm.nih.gov/pmc/articles/PMC251588/

9.    1500-1940 data from Michael Kremer, "Population Growth and Technological Change: One Million B.C. to 1990," *Quarterly Journal of Economics*, Vol. 108, No. 3, Aug. 1993, p. 681-716, http://www.econ.ucdavis.edu/faculty/gclark/210a/readings/kremer1993.pdf; 1950-2010 data from United Nations Population Division, 2012, http://esa.un.org/unpd/wpp/Excel-Data/population.htm; Dhaka image by Ian Muttoo under Creative Commons License

10.   *Historical Statistics of the United States, Colonial Times to 1970, Part 1*, US Census Bureau, 1970, p.77, http://books.google.com/books?id=0YzOoHrvMPIC&q=dieases#v=onepage&q=dieases&f=false; Smallpox image by George Henry Fox

11.   *Our Plundered Planet* by Henry Fairfield Osborn, Jr., (Little, Brown, 1948)

12.   *The Limits of Earth* by Henry Fairfield Osborn, Jr., (Little, Brown, 1953)

13.   *Brave New World Revisited* by Aldous Huxley, (Chatto & Windus, 1959), http://www.huxley.net/bnw-revisited/

14.   *The Population Bomb* by Paul Ehrlich, (Sierra Club—Ballantine Books, 1968)

15.   Ibid, p. 152

16.   Kevin Begos, "The American Eugenics Movement after World War II," *IndyWeek*, May, 18, 2011, http://www.indyweek.com/indyweek/the-american-eugenics-movement-after-world-war-ii-part-2-of-3/Content?oid=2483521

17.   David Suzuki video on overpopulation, Dec. 20, 2010, https://www.youtube.com/watch?v=8x98KFcMJeo

18.   "The State of the World's Children 1992," UNICEF, 1992, http://www.unicef.org/sowc/archive/ENGLISH/The%20State%20of%20the%20World's%20Children%201992.pdf

19.   *Merchants of Despair: Radical Environmentalists, Criminal Pseudo-Scientists, and the Fatal Cult of Anti-Humanism* by Robert Zubrin, (Encounter Books, 2012), p. 158

20.   *Ecoscience: Population, Resources, Environment* by Paul Ehrlich, John Holdren, and Anne Ehrlich, (W.H. Freeman, 1977), p. 795-796

21.   Alaka Basu, "Family Planning and the Emergency," *Economic and Political Weekly*, Vol. 20, No. 10, Mar. 9, 1985, pp. 422-425, http://www.jstor.org/discover/10.2307/4374158?uid=3739656&uid=2129&uid=2&uid=70&uid=4&uid=3739256&sid=21104605658851

22.   *Merchants of Despair*, (See no. 19), p. 176

23.   Ma Jian, "China's barbaric one-child policy," Guardian, May 5, 2013, http://www.theguardian.com/books/2013/may/06/chinas-barbaric-one-child-policy

24.   "Total Population, CBR, CDR, NIR and TFR of China (1949-2000)," *China Daily*, Aug. 20, 2010, from China Statistical Yearbook 2000, http://www.chinadaily.com.cn/china/2010census/2010-08/20/content_11182379.htm

25.   Therese Hosketh et al., "The Effect of China's One-Child Family Policy after 25 Years," *New England Journal of Medicine*, Sep. 15, 2005, http://www.nejm.org/doi/full/10.1056/NEJMhpr051833

26.   Bahgat Elnadi and Adel Rifaat, "Interview with Jacques-Yves Cousteau," *UNESCO Courier*, Nov. 1991, http://unesdoc.unesco.org/images/0009/000902/090256eo.pdf; Matrioshka image from artefact

27.   *Merchants of Despair*, (See no. 19), p. 181

28.   China's One-Child Policy, (See no. 25)

29.   Ma Jian, "China's Brutal One-Child Policy, " *New York Times*, May 21, 2013, http://www.nytimes.com/2013/05/22/opinion/chinas-brutal-one-child-policy.html?_r=0

30.   "Anger as moderator says China's one-child policy good for planet," *Scotsman*, Oct. 21, 2014, http://www.scotsman.com/news/anger-as-moderator-says-china-s-one-child-policy-good-for-planet-1-1300869; question mark image from semjaza

31.   China's barbaric one-child policy, (See no. 23)

32.   China's Brutal One-Child Policy, (See no. 29)

33.   China's Brutal One-Child Policy, (See no. 29)

34.   *Merchants of Despair*, (See no. 19), p. 156

35.   *Merchants of Despair*, (See no. 19), p. 180

36.   Ronald Bailey, "Billions Served: Norman Borlaug interviewed by Ronald Bailey," *Reason.com*, Apr. 1, 2000, http://reason.com/archives/2000/04/01/billions-served-norman-borlaug

37.   1500-1940 data from Michael Kremer, "Population Growth and Technological Change: One Million B.C. to 1990," *Quarterly Journal of Economics*, Vol. 108, No. 3, Aug. 1993, p. 681-716, http://www.econ.ucdavis.edu/faculty/gclark/210a/readings/kremer1993.pdf; 1950-2010 data from United Nations Population Division, 2012, http://esa.un.org/unpd/wpp/; Tokyo image by Ian Muttoo under Creative Commons License

38.   "World Population Prospects: The 2012 Revision," United Nations Population Division, 2012, http://esa.un.org/wpp/

39.   World Population Prospects: The 2012 Revision, United Nations Population Division, 2012, http://esa.un.org/wpp/

40.   Robert Kunzig, "Population 7 Billion," National Geographic, January, 2011, http://ngm.nationalgeographic.com/2011/01/seven-billion/kunzig-text

41.   Gordon Chang, "Beijing Praises Its One-Child Policy as World Population Hits 7 Billion," *World Affairs Journal*, Nov. 1, 2011, http://www.worldaffairsjournal.org/blog/gordon-g-chang/beijing-praises-its-one-child-policy-world-population-hits-7-billion

42.   Soma Naoko, "South Korea's Explicit Family Policy and Japan's Implicit Approach," *Nippon.com*, Sep. 19, 2012, http://www.nippon.com/en/in-depth/a01003/

43.   World Population, (See no. 39)

44.   World Population, (See no. 39)

45.   Diagram modified from Max Roser, "Our World in Data," 2014, http://www.ourworldindata.org/data/population-growth-vital-statistics/world-population-growth/

46.   "Probabilistic Population Projections," United Nations Population Division, 2014, http://esa.un.org/unpd/ppp/

47.   *The Ultimate Resource II* by Julian Simon, (Princeton University Press, 1998), p. 315

48.   Kremer, (See no. 4)

49.   "World Population Prospects: The 2012 Revision," United Nations Population Division, 2012, http://esa.un.org/wpp/

50.   "Statistical Abstract of the United States," US Census Bureau, 2012, http://www.census.gov/compendia/statab/

51.   Valerie Richardson, "Climate-Change Activists Call for Tax Policies to Discourage Childbirth," *Washington Times*, Aug. 19, 2016, http://www.washingtontimes.com/news/2016/aug/19/climate-change-activists-tax-discourage-childbirth/; Thinker statue image by Frank Kovalcheck under Creative Commons License

52.   "Danish students to be taught to have more babies," *thelocal.dk*, Oct. 29, 2014, http://www.thelocal.dk/20141029/danish-students-to-be-taught-to-have-babies

53.   "Polish Government to Pay Families to Have More Children," *Associated Press*, Dec. 1, 2015, http://www.dailyherald.com/article/20151201/business/312019835/

54.   Michael Bastasch, "Environmentalists giving away Earth Day condoms to combat overpopulation," *Daily Caller*, Mar. 21, 2014, http://dailycaller.com/2014/03/21/environmentalists-giving-away-earth-day-condoms-to-combat-overpopulation/; image by Dan Rocha under Creative Commons license

55.   "State of World Population 2009," United Nations Population Fund, http://unfpa.org/swp/2009/

56.   Tim Radford, "The Whole World in Our Hands," *Guardian*, Sep. 16, 2000, http://www.theguardian.com/books/2000/sep/16/scienceandnature.books

57.   Pete Gunter, "Mental Inertia and Environmental Decay: The End of an Era," *The Living Wilderness*, 34, No. 109, Spring 1970, p. 3-5

## Chapter 4:  Our Polluted Planet?

1.    George Carlin, Sep. 29, 1972, https://www.youtube.com/watch?v=rtZXgfdauBY

2.    Jon Stone, "Air pollution to blame for 60,000 early deaths per year, Government to be warned," *Independent*, Nov. 30, 2014, http://www.independent.co.uk/news/uk/home-news/air-pollution-to-blame-for-60000-early-deaths-per-year-government-to-be-warned-9893810.html

3.    "Air quality deteriorating in many of the world's cities," World Health Organization, May 7, 2014, http://www.who.int/mediacentre/news/releases/2014/air-quality/en/

4.    "Key Findings for 2010-2012," American Lung Association, 2014, http://www.stateoftheair.org/2014/key-findings/

5.    Image of Nelson's column during the Great London Smog of December, 1952 by N.T. Stobbs under Creative Commons License

6.    *The Big Smoke* by Peter Brimblecombe, (Methuen, 1987)

7.    Ibid

8.    Eric Morris, "From Horse Power to Horsepower," University of California, *Access*, Spring 2007, http://www.uctc.net/access/30/Access%2030%20-%2002%20-%20Horse%20Power.pdf

9.    Ibid

10.   "The History of Urban Air Pollution," Atmosphere, Climate & Environment Information Programme, 2014, http://www.lordgrey.org.uk/~f014/usefulresources/aric/Resources/Teaching_Packs/Key_Stage_4/Air_Quality/01.html

11.   "A Brief History of Pollution," NOAA Ocean Service Education, 2015, http://oceanservice.noaa.gov/education/tutorial_pollution/02history.html

12.   "June 22, 1969: Cuyahoga River Catches Fire," This Day in Water History, June 22, 2014, https://thisdayinwaterhistory.wordpress.com/2014/06/22/june-22-1969-cuyahoga-river-catches-fire/

13.   Image of Cuyahoga River Fire, Nov. 3, 1952, Cleveland State University, Michael Schwartz Library

14.   *Tea in China: The History of China's National Drink* by John Evans, (Praeger, 1992)

15.   Glass of water image by Derek Jensen, public domain

16.   "World Water Development Report 2016," United Nations, http://www.unesco.org/new/en/natural-sciences/environment/water/wwap/wwdr/2016-water-and-jobs/

17.   Paul Ehrlich and John Holdren, "A bulletin dialogue on the 'Closing Circle' critique: One dimensional ecology," *Bulletin of the Atomic Scientists*, 28(5), pp. 16-27, 1972.

18.   Paul Ehrlich and John Holdren, "Human Population and the Global Environment," *American Scientist*, Vol. 62, pp. 282-292, 1974.

19.   "Special Report on Emissions Scenarios," Intergovernmental Panel on Climate Change, 2000, http://www.ipcc.ch/ipccreports/sres/emission/index.php?idp=50

20.   Alice Thomson and Rachel Sylvester, "Recession will be just the ticket, says Ryanair boss Michael O'Leary," *Circolo Luce Del Sud*, Aug. 2, 2008, http://www.circolocedelsud.it/?p=3158; faces image from Bryan Derksen

21.   Ed Driscoll, "Episcopal Church Replaces God with Gaia on Good Friday," pjmedia.com, Apr. 8, 2011, http://pjmedia.com/eddriscoll/2011/04/08/episcopal-church-replaces-god-with-gaia-on-good-friday/; image by TheByteMan

22.   "National Air Pollutant Emission Trends, 1900-1998," US Environmental Protection Agency, Mar. 2000, http://www.epa.gov/ttnchie1/trends/trends98/

23.   Image of Clark Avenue Bridge, Cleveland, OH, July 1973 by the US Environmental Protection Agency

24.   US Environmental Protection Agency, 2014, http://www.epa.gov/airtrends/; Image of World War II production plant by Alfred Palmer

25.   Ibid

26.   EPA, (See no. 24)

27.   Claus Hecking, "Environmental Protection: What became of the Dying Forests?," *SpiegelOnLine*, Mar. 1, 2015, http://translate.google.com/translate?hl=en&sl=de&tl=en&u=http%3A%2F%2Fwww.spiegel.de%2Fwissenschaft%2Fnatur%2Fumweltschutz-was-wurde-aus-dem-waldsterben-a-1009580.html;  8-ball image by nicubunu

28.   US Environmental Protection Agency, 2015, http://www.epa.gov/airtrends/aqtrends.html#comparison

29.   Wolfgang Schöpp et al., "Long-term development of aid deposition (1880-2030) in sensitive freshwater regions in Europe," Hydrology and Earth System Sciences, 7(4), pp. 436-446, (2003), http://hydrol-earth-syst-sci.net/7/436/2003/hess-7-436-2003.pdf

30.   John Skelly and John Innes, "Waldsterben in the Forests of Central Europe and Eastern North America: Fantasy or Reality?," *Plant Disease*, 1994, pp. 1021-1032, http://eurekamag.com/research/002/730/002730953.php

31.   *Acidic Deposition: State of Science and Technology, Summary Report of the U.S. National Acid Precipitation Assessment Program*, edited by Patricia Irving, (National Acid Precipitation Assessment Program, 1991)

32.   Donald Tobi et al., "The Conifer Swift Moth and Spruce-fir Decline,"United States Forest Service," 1989, http://www.fs.fed.us/ne/newtown_

square/publications/technical_reports/pdfs/scanned/OCR/ne_gtr120e.pdf

33. Acidic Deposition, (See no. 31)
34. Waldsterben, (See no. 30)
35. "National Acid Precipitation Assessment Program Report to Congress 2011," Office of the President of the United States, Dec. 28, 2011, https://www.whitehouse.gov/sites/default/files/microsites/ostp/2011_napap_508.pdf
36. Atle Hinder and Richard Wright, "Long-term records and modelling of acidification, recovery, and liming at Lake Hovvatn, Norway," *Canadian Journal of Fisheries and Aquatic Sciences*, Nov. 2005, http://www.nrcresearchpress.com/doi/abs/10.1139/f05-165#.VWCRUZXbJ9M
37. Gene Grossman and Alan Kruger, "Economic Growth and the Environment, *The Quarterly Journal of Economics*, May, 1995, pp. 353-377, http://www.econ.ku.dk/nguyen/teaching/Grossman%20and%20Krueger%201995.pdf
38. Matthew Cole et al., "The environmental Kuznets curve: an empirical analysis," *Environment and Development Economics*, Feb. 2001, http://www.researchgate.net/publication/4729022_The_environmental_Kuznets_curve_an_empirical_analysis
39. Economic Growth, (See no. 37)
40. Pekka Kauppi et al., "Returning forests analyzed with the forest identity," *Proceedings of the National Academy of Sciences*, Nov. 13, 2006, http://www.pnas.org/content/103/46/17574.short
41. Tatyana Soubbotina, "Beyond Economic Growth," World Bank, 2000, http://www.worldbank.org/depweb/beyond/beyondco/beg_all.pdf; World Health Organization Outdoor Pollution Database, 2008, http://www.who.int/phe/health_topics/outdoorair/databases/cities-2011/en/
42. *Air Quality in the Mexico Megacity* by Luisa Molina and Mario Molina (editors), (Springer, 2002), p. 4
43. Anne-Marie O'Connor, "Mexico City drastically reduced air pollutants since 1990s," *Washington Post*, Apr. 1, 2010, http://www.washingtonpost.com/wp-dyn/content/article/2010/03/31/AR2010033103614.html
44. "Beyond Economic Growth, (See no. 41)
45. *Monitoring Water Quality* by Santinder Ahuja (editor), (Elsevier, 2013), pp. 19-20
46. "Barrington School Keeps Students—and Parents—In the Dark," *Barrington Hills Observer*, Sep. 4, 2013, http://barringtonhillsobserver.com/2013/09/04/barrington-school-keeps-students-and-parents-in-the-dark/; flower image by HakanL
47. "National Rivers and Streams Assessment 2008–2009," US Environmental Protection Agency, Feb. 29, 2013, http://water.epa.gov/type/rsl/monitoring/riverssurvey/
48. "National Lakes Assessment: A Collaborative Survey of the Nation's Lakes," US Environmental Protection Agency, 2009, http://www.epa.gov/owow/LAKES/lakessurvey/pdf/nla_report_low_res.pdf
49. "National Coastal Condition Report IV, US Environmental Protection Agency, Sep. 2012, http://water.epa.gov/type/oceb/assessmonitor/nccr/upload/0_NCCR_4_Report_508_bookmarks.pdf
50. "European Waters—Current Status and Future Challenges," European Environment Agency, Nov. 26, 2012, http://www.eea.europa.eu/publications/european-waters-synthesis-2012
51. "Great Lakes," US Environmental Protection Agency, 2015, http://www.epa.gov/glnpo/basicinfo.html
52. "History of Wastewater Treatment in the United States," Macalester College, 2015, http://www.macalester.edu/academics/environmentalstudies/students/projects/urbanwastewaterwebsite/history.html
53. "State of the Great Lakes 2011," Environment Canada and the US Environmental Protection Agency, 2014, http://www.ec.gc.ca/grandslacs-greatlakes/DEA99937-E0B6-4F10-8F0A-993661A2F9CC/Highlights%20Report%20E%20130827%20FINAL.pdf
54. Barbara Froehlich-Schmitt, "Rhine Salmon 2020," International Commission for Protection of the Rhine, 2004, http://www.iksr.org/fileadmin/user_upload/Dokumente_en/rz_engl_lachs2020_net.pdf
55. Alexandre Kiss, "The Protection of the Rhine Against Pollution," *Natural Resources Journal*, July, 1985, pp. 613-637, http://lawschool.unm.edu/nrj/volumes/25/3/03_kiss_protection.pdf
56. "15 Years of Managing the Danube River Basin 1991–2006," Danube Regional Project, http://www.icpdr.org/main/publications/15-years-managing-danube-basin
57. Presentation by Anne Schulte-Wülwer-Leidig, "Rhine Salmon Revival," International River Symposium, 2014, http://riversymposium.com/wp-content/uploads/2014/10/A4_Anne-Schulte-W%C3%BClwer-Leidig.pdf
58. Presentation by Maarten Hofstra, "International Cooperation on the River Rhine, " UNESCO, 2010, http://www.unece.org/fileadmin/DAM/env/water/cadialogue/docs/Almaty_Oct2010/Eng/Hofstra_Eng.pdf
59. Rhine Salmon, (See no. 57)
60. Danube River Basin, (See no. 56)
61. Not a real headline; Newspaper image by baroquon; Comedy image by John Reid
62. E. Borsos et al., "Anthropogenic Air Pollution in the Ancient Times," 2003, http://www2.sci.u-szeged.hu/eghajlattan/akta03/005-015.pdf
63. David Krabbenhoft and Paul Schuster, "Glacial Ice Cores Reveal A Record of Natural and Anthropogenic Atmospheric Mercury Deposition for the Last 270 Years," US Geological Survey, Jun. 2002, http://toxics.usgs.gov/pubs/FS-051-02/pdf/fs-051-02.pdf
64. "Six Flags Great Adventure to Cut 18,000 Trees to Go Solar," *CBSNewYork/AP*, Mar. 27, 2015, http://newyork.cbslocal.com/2015/03/27/six-flags-great-adventure-to-cut-18000-trees-to-go-solar/; Eagle killed by wind turbine image by Stefan Hedgren
65. Glacial Ice Cores, (See no. 63)
66. Joseph McConnell and Ross Edwards, "Coal burning leaves toxic heavy metal legacy in the Arctic," *Proceedings of the National Academy of Sciences*, Aug. 26, 2008, http://www.pnas.org/content/105/34/12140.full; Image of liquid mercury by bionerd
67. Coal burning, (See no. 66)
68. Glacial Ice Cores, (See no. 63)
69. *Silent Spring* by Rachel Carson, (Houghton Mifflin, 1962), p. 15
70. David Tilman et al., "Agricultural sustainability and intensive production practices," *Nature*, Aug. 8, 2002, pp. 671–677, http://www.readcube.com/articles/10.1038%2Fnature01014
71. "Global Business of Chemistry," American Chemistry Council, 2015, http://www.americanchemistry.com/Jobs/EconomicStatistics/Industry-Profile/Global-Business-of-Chemistry
72. Mario Molina and F. S. Rowland, "Stratospheric sink for chlorofluoromethanes: chlorine atom-catalysed destruction of ozone," *Nature*, June 28, 1974, v. 249, no. 5460, pp. 810–812, http://www.unep.ch/ozone/pdf/stratospheric.pdf
73. J.C Farman et al., "Large losses of total ozone in Antarctica reveal seasonal $ClO_x/NO_x$ interaction," *Nature*, May 16, 1985, v. 315, pp.207–210, http://www.readcube.com/articles/10.1038%2F315207a0
74. "Ozone depletion: Uncovering the hidden hazard of hairspray," University of California Museum of Paleontology, 2007, http://undsci.berkeley.edu/lessons/pdfs/ozone_depletion_complex.pdf
75. *Earth in the Balance: Ecology and the Human Spirit* by Al Gore, (Houghton Mifflin, 1992), p. 85; Thinker statue image by Frank Kovalcheck under Creative Commons License
76. Ozone depletion, (See no. 74)
77. "Ozone Hole Watch," National Aeronautics and Space Adminstration, 2015, http://ozonewatch.gsfc.nasa.gov/
78. S. E. Strahan et al., "Inorganic chlorine variability in the Antarctic vortex and implications for ozone recovery," Journal of Geophysical Research: Atmospheres, Dec., 18, 2014, pp. 14098–14109, https://espo.nasa.gov/home/attrex/content/Inorganic_chlorine_variability_in_the_

Antarctic_vortex_and_implications_for_ozone_recovery

79.  Ozone Hole Watch, See no. 77; "Production and consumption of ozone-depleting substances," European Environment Agency, 2015, http://www.eea.europa.eu/data-and-maps/indicators/production-and-consumption-of-ozone-2/assessment; Image of record ozone hole over Antarctic on September 24, 2006 from NASA

80.  "Pollution Abatement and Control in OECD Countries," Organization for Economic Cooperation and Development, 2007, http://www.oecd.org/env/indicators-modelling-outlooks/38230860.pdf

81.  "Celebrate Bike to Work Week 2013 June 8-14, " City of Evanston, Jun. 7, 2013, http://www.cityofevanston.org/news/2013/06/celebrate-bike-to-work-week-2013-june-8-14/

82.  "Solid Oxide Electrolysers," University College London, Aug. 12, 2013, http://www.ucl.ac.uk/ucell/about/research-areas/electrolysers

83.  "Q+A: Burning Calories with HOK Washington, DC, Sustainable Design Specialist Sean Quinn," Life at HOK, Jun. 2, 2011, http://www.hoklife.com/2011/06/02/qa-burning-calories-with-hok-washington-dc-sustainable-design-specialist-sean-quinn/

84.  "How to Use CO2 When Growing Marijuana," *The Weed Blog*, Feb. 29, 2012, http://www.theweedblog.com/co2-and-marijuana-plants/; plant image by Tanheiheimandy under Creative Commons License

85.  "The Dirtiest Fuel on the Planet," *blog.algore.com*, http://blog.algore.com/2011/08/the_dirtiest_fuel_on_the_plane.html

86.  Harry Reid, "Reid Statement On Closure of Reid Gardner," De. 31, 2014, http://www.reid.senate.gov/press_releases/2014-31-12-reid-statement-on-closure-of-reid-gardner

87.  Paul Pearson and Martin Palmer, "Atmospheric carbon dioxide concentrations over the past 60 million years," *Nature*, Aug. 17, 2000, http://www.nature.com/nature/journal/v406/n6797/abs/406695a0.html

88.  Image of Dr. Sherwood Idso and pine trees with different levels of CO2 provided by Craig Idso, 1989

89.  Craig Idso, "Estimates of Global Food Production in the Year 2050," Center for the Study of Carbon Dioxide and Global Change, Jun. 15, 2011, http://www.co2science.org/education/reports/foodsecurity/GlobalFoodProductionEstimates2050.pdf

90.  Randall Donohue et al., "Impact of CO$_2$ fertilization on maximum foliage cover across the globe's warm, arid environments," *Geophysical Research Letters*, May 13, 2013, pp. 1-5, http://www.researchgate.net/profile/Tim_Mcvicar/publication/261541229_Impact_of_CO2_fertilization_on_maximum_foliage_cover_across_the_globe's_warm_arid_environments/links/00b49534c7b1a62b87000000.pdf

91.  Idso, (See no. 89); Image of sugar beet harvest in Germany from Sven Wusch under Creative Commons License

92.  Ben Cosgrove, "'Throwaway Living': When Tossing Out Everything Was All The Rage," *Time*, May 15, 2014, http://time.com/3879873/throwaway-living-when-tossing-it-all-was-all-the-rage/

93.  David Kohn, "A Disposable Society? Andy Rooney: Americans Generate Too Much Trash", *CBS News*, Aug. 30, 2001, http://www.cbsnews.com/news/a-disposable-society-30-08-2001/

94.  "ICC and UNEP Host Climate and Resource Efficiency Forum," United Nations Environment Programme, Oct. 23, 2008, http://www.unep.org/documents.multilingual/default.asp?DocumentID=548&ArticleID=5964&l=en

95.  *Our Final Century: A Scientists Warning: How Terror, Error, and Environmental Disaster Threaten Humankind's Future in This Century--On Earth and Beyond* by Martin Rees, (Heinemann, 2003); Image of Frankenstein's monster from Universal Studios

96.  "Municipal Solid Waste Generation, Recycling, and Disposal in the United States," US Environmental Protection Agency, Feb. 2014, http://www.epa.gov/solidwaste/nonhaz/municipal/pubs/2012_msw_dat_tbls.pdf; Image of Freshkills landfill at Staaten Island, New York City, from EPA, 1973

97.  Ibid

98.  Municipal Solid Waste, (See no. 96)

99.  Municipal solid waste and recycling figures from Eurostat database, European Commission, 2015, http://ec.europa.eu/eurostat/data/database; European population for EU-27 nations from "Key Figures on Europe," Eurostat 2014 Edition, http://ec.europa.eu/eurostat/en/web/products-pocketbooks/-/KS-EI-14-001

100. "The Truth About Recycling," *Economist*, Jun. 7, 2007, http://www.economist.com/node/9249262

101. Municipal Solid Waste, (See no. 96)

102. Clark Wiseman, "Are We Promoting Waste?," *Cato Journal*, Fall 1992, pp. 443-460, http://object.cato.org/sites/cato.org/files/serials/files/cato-journal/1992/11/cj12n2-9.pdf

103. "Integrated Science Assessment for Particulate Matter," US Environmental Protection Agency, Dec. 2009, http://cfpub.epa.gov/ncea/cfm/recordisplay.cfm?deid=216546

104. Presentation by Amanda Brown, "Health Effects of Particulates and Black Carbon," US Environmental Protection Agency, Dec. 2013, http://www2.epa.gov/sites/production/files/2014-05/documents/health-effects.pdf

105. Lisa Jackson, "Hearing on Regulatory Reform Series #7-The EPA's Regulatory Planning, Analysis, and Major Actions," US House of Representatives, Subcommittee on Oversight and Investigations, Sep. 22, 2011, http://democrats.energycommerce.house.gov/index.php?q=hearing/hearing-on-regulatory-reform-series-7-the-epas-regulatory-planning-analysis-and-major-action

106. "Household air pollution and health," World Health Organization, Mar. 2014, http://www.who.int/mediacentre/factsheets/fs292/en/

107. "Indoor Air Pollution from Biomass: A Global Health Disparities Challenge," Christopher Olopade, Jun. 19, 2014, https://www.youtube.com/watch?v=ShIboeA2Dc8

108. Image of Nigerian woman cooking indoors by Christopher Olopade, 2014

109. James Enstrom presentation at the Tenth International Conference on Climate Change, Washington DC, July 11, 2015, https://www.youtube.com/watch?v=r2iGWFTjoCQ&index=29&list=PLgnnPnL9OL7Gbzw8wdzgZs8SA9HdUfQn6

110. Douglas Dockery et al., "An Association between Air Pollution and Mortality in Six U.S. Cities," *New England Journal of Medicine*, De. 9, 1993, http://www.scientificintegrityinstitute.org/Dockery1993.pdf

111. Arden Pope et al., "Particulate Air Pollution as a Predictor of Mortality in a Prospective Study of U.S. Adults," American Journal of Respiratory and Critical Care Medicine, Vol. 151, pp. 669-674, 1995, http://www.ncbi.nlm.nih.gov/pubmed/7881654

112. An Association, (See no. 110)

113. Particulate Air Pollution, (See no. 111)

114. "Regulatory Impact Analysis for the Final Revisions to the National Ambient Air Quality Standards for Particulate Matter," US Environmental Protection Agency, Dec. 2012, http://www.epa.gov/ttn/ecas/regdata/RIAs/finalria.pdf

115. Michael Jerrett et al., "Spatiotemporal Analysis of Air Pollution and Mortality in California Based on the American Cancer Society Cohort," California Environmental Protection Agency, Nov. 2011, http://www.arb.ca.gov/research/apr/past/06-332.pdf

116. An Association, (See no. 101); Particulate Air Pollution, (See no. 102)

117. Michael Green et al., "Reference Guide on Epidemiology," *Reference Manual on Scientific Evidence: Third Edition*, National Academy of Sciences, 2011, http://www.fjc.gov/public/pdf.nsf/lookup/SciMan3D12.pdf/$file/SciMan3D12.pdf

118. Ibid

119. Richard Doll and Bradford Hill, "Lung Cancer and Other Causes of Death in Relation to Smoking," *British Medical Journal*, Nov. 10, 1956, http://www.ncbi.nlm.nih.gov/pmc/articles/PMC2035864/pdf/brmedj03180-0019.pdf

120. Reference Guide, (See no. 117)

121. Daniel Krewski et al., "Extended Follow-Up and Spatial Analysis of the American Cancer Society Study Linking Particulate Air Pollution and

Mortality," Health Effects Institute, May 2009, http://ephtracking.cdc.gov/docs/RR140-Krewski.pdf

122. James Enstrom, "Fine Particulate Air Pollution and Total Mortality Among Elderly Californians, 1973-2002," *Inhalation Toxicology*, Jun. 2005, http://www.scientificintegrityinstitute.org/IT121505.pdf

123. EPA Grant Awards Database, 2015, http://yosemite.epa.gov/oarm/igms_egf.nsf/Reports/Non-Profit+Grants?OpenView

124. Timothy Cama, "Senators Vote to Block EPA's Use of 'Secret Science'," *The Hill*, April 28, 2015, http://thehill.com/policy/energy-environment/240365-senators-vote-to-block-epas-use-of-secret-science; Spy image by Yuri Ribeiro Sucupira under Creative Commons license

125. Tim Berry, "Survey: What Are CEOs Thinking?," *Huffington Post*, Nov. 19, 2007, http://www.huffingtonpost.com/tim-berry/survey-what-are-ceos-thin_b_73313.html

126. Leigh Denault and Jennifer Landis, "Motion and Means: Mapping Opposition to Railways in Victorian Britain," Dec. 1999, https://www.mtholyoke.edu/courses/rschwart/ind_rev/rs/denault.htm

127. "Progress Cleaning the Air and Improving People's Health,"  US Environmental Protection Agency, 2015, http://www.epa.gov/air/caa/progress.html

128. Postcard image of the San Juan Express, a narrow-gauge passenger train operating in Colorado between 1937 and 1951

129. Progress Cleaning, (See no. 127)

130. C. Duranceau et al., "Vehicle Recycling, Reuse, and Recovery: Material Disposition from Current End-of-Life Vehicles," SAE International, Apr. 12, 2011, http://papers.sae.org/2011-01-1151/

131. "Reuse & Recycling at HP," HP, 2015, http://www8.hp.com/us/en/hp-information/environment/recycling-reuse.html#.VXDI45XbJ9M

132. "Dell Recyling," Dell, 2015, http://www.dell.com/learn/us/en/uscorp1/dell-environment-recycling

133. "National Emissions Inventory (NEI) Air Pollutant Emissions Trends Data," US Environmental Protection Agency, 2015, http://www.epa.gov/ttn/chief/trends/; US Federal Highway Administration, 2011 statistics; Image of Volvo by OSX

134. "BP Leak the World's Worst Accidental Oil Spill," *Telegraph*, Aug. 3, 2010, http://www.telegraph.co.uk/finance/newsbysector/energy/oilandgas/7924009/BP-leak-the-worlds-worst-accidental-oil-spill.html

135. International Tanker Owners Pollution Federation, 2015, http://www.itopf.com/knowledge-resources/data-statistics/statistics/

136. "Surface Mining for Coal in Missouri," Missouri Department of Natural Resources, 2016, http://dnr.mo.gov/geology/lrp/surface-mining.htm?/env/lrp/surface-mining.htm

137. Anthony Watts, "Center for Biological Diversity Petitions EPA to List CO2 as a 'Toxic Substance," WattsUpWithThat, July 1, 2015, https://wattsupwiththat.com/2015/07/01/climate-craziness-of-the-week-center-for-biological-diversity-petitions-epa-to-list-co2-as-a-toxic-substance/

## Chapter 5:  Climate Delusion

1. Bill Richardson, Henderson, Nevada, June 6, 2007, https://www.youtube.com/watch?v=7ShaW5ucSbl

2. Intergovernmental Panel on Climate Change, http://www.ipcc.ch/organization/organization.shtml, 2015

3. C40 Cities Climate Leadership Group, http://www.c40.org/, 2015

4. Presidents' Climate Commitment, http://www.presidentsclimatecommitment.org/about/commitment, 2015

5. *The Weather Makers: How Man is Changing the Climate and What It means for Life on Earth* by Tim Flannery, (Grove Press, 2001), p.17; Image of Frankenstein's monster from Universal Studios

6. "Manicured Lawns Contribute to Global Warming by Producing Greenhouse Gases," *Tribune India*, Jan. 18, 2015, http://www.tribuneindia.com/news/features/sci-tech-gadgets-env/manicured-lawns-contribute-to-global-warming-by-producing-greenhouse-gases/31521.html; Question mark image from semjaza

7. Whitehouse Press Release, Nov. 25, 2009, https://www.whitehouse.gov/the-press-office/president-attend-copenhagen-climate-talks

8. Camila Turner, "G7 Pledges to End Fossil Fuel Use This Century," *Telegraph*, Jun. 8, 2015, http://www.telegraph.co.uk/news/earth/environment/climatechange/11661162/G7-pledges-to-end-fossil-fuel-use-this-century.html

9. Rachel Cruz, "Ben & Jerry's 'Save Our Swirled': Company Seeks To Raise Global Warming Awareness with New Flavor," *hngn.com*, Jun. 01, 2015, http://www.hngn.com/articles/97130/20150601/ben-jerrys-new-flavor-seeks-to-raise-global-warming-awareness-video.htm; Lemonade image by Michael Fludkov under Creative Commons License

10. Sara Knapton, "Tepid Coffee Anyone? Europe Rules Percolators Must Shut Off After Five Minutes," *Telegraph*, Jan. 1, 2015, http://www.telegraph.co.uk/news/shopping-and-consumer-news/11320629/Tepid-coffee-anyone-Europe-rules-percolators-must-shut-off-after-five-minutes.html; Question mark image from semjaza

11. Climatic Research Unit, University of East Anglia, http://www.cru.uea.ac.uk/, 2015

12. Intergovernmental Panel on Climate Change, Fourth Assessment Report, Synthesis Report, 2007, p.39, http://www.ipcc.ch/publications_and_data/ar4/syr/en/contents.html

13. "Trends in Atmospheric Carbon Dioxide," Earth System Research Laboratory, NOAA, 2015, http://www.esrl.noaa.gov/gmd/ccgg/trends/

14. *A First Course in Atmospheric Radiation* by Grant Petty, (Sundog Publishing, 2006), p. 143

15. Richard Parncutt, "Death Penalty for Global Warming Deniers?," University of Graz, Oct. 25, 2012, http://www.webcitation.org/6D8yy8NUJ; Sign image from Cookiecaper under Creative Commons License; spoof by the author

16. Intergovernmental Panel on Climate Change, Fourth Assessment Report, Working Group I, Summary for Policy Makers, 2007, p.12, http://www.ipcc.ch/report/ar4/

17. *Unstoppable Global Warming Every 1500 Years* by S. Fred Singer and Dennis Avery, (Rowman & Littlefield, 2007), p. 239

18. Evan Halper, "Google Severs Ties with Conservative Group over Climate Change Stance," *Los Angeles Times*, Sep. 22, 2014, http://www.latimes.com/nation/politics/politicsnow/la-pn-google-conservative-20140922-story.html; Hippopotomus image by Jean-Pierre Dalbera, 2011 under Creative Commons License

19. *Canon of Insolation and the Ice-Age Problem* by Milutin Milankovic, 1941, (Agency for Textbooks, 1998)

20. *Unstoppable Global Warming*, (See no. 17)

21. "What is an El Niño?," National Oceanic and Atmospheric Administration, 2016, http://www.pmel.noaa.gov/tao/elnino/el-nino-story.html

22. "The Pacific Decadal Oscillation," Joint Institute for the Study of the Atmosphere and Ocean, University of Washington, 2016, http://research.jisao.washington.edu/pdo/

23. "Frequently Asked Questions About the Atlantic Multidecadal Oscillation (AMO)," National Oceanic and Atmospheric Administration, 2016, http://www.aoml.noaa.gov/phod/amo_faq.php

24. Richard Alley, "The Younger Dryas cold interval as viewed from central Greenland," *Quarternary Science Reviews* 19, 2000, pp. 213-226, http://www.sciencedirect.com/science/article/pii/S0277379199000621

25. *CO2Science.org*, Craig Idso, 2016, http://www.co2science.org/data/mwp/mwpp.php

26. Richard Alley, (See no. 24); Climate4you, 2016, http://www.climate4you.com/; image of Viking ship by Bruun Rasmussen, 2011

27. Kathryn Hansen, "NASA Study Illustrates How Global Peak Oil Production Could Impact Climate," National Aeronautics and Space Administration, Oct. 24, 2008, http://newslink.federallabs.org/2008/10/24/nasa-study-illustrates-how-global-peak-oil-production-could-impact-climate/

28.  "The Science," *350.org*, 2016, http://350.org/about/science/

29.  Hubertus Fischer et al., "Ice Core Records of Atmospheric CO2 Around the Last Three Glacial Terminations," *Science*, Mar. 12, 1999, http://www.sciencemag.org/content/283/5408/1712.abstract

30.  Paul Pearson and Martin Palmer, "Atmospheric carbon dioxide concentrations over the past 60 million years," *Nature*, Nov. 2, 1999, http://www.ldeo.columbia.edu/~peter/Resources/Seminar/readings/Pearson%20and%20Palmer%202000.pdf

31.  Gavin Schmidt et al., "The attribution of the present-day total greenhouse effect," NASA Goddard Institute for Space Studies, draft paper, Au. 10, 2010

32.  Intergovernmental Panel on Climate Change, Fifth Assessment Report, Working Group I, p. 471, http://www.ipcc.ch/report/ar5/wg1/

33.  *The Mad, Mad, Mad World of Climatism* by Steve Goreham, (New Lenox Books, 2012), pp. 83-86

34.  Richard Lindzen, "Understanding Common Climate Claims," proceedings of the 2005 ERICE Meeting of the World Federation of Scientists on Global Emergencies, 2005

35.  Syukuro Manabe and Richard Wetherald, "Thermal Equilibrium of the Atmosphere with a Given Distribution of Relative Humidity," *Journal of the Atmospheric Sciences*, May, 1967, pp. 241-259, http://ruby.fgcu.edu/courses/twimberley/EnviroPhilo/ThermalEqu.pdf

36.  "Working Group I: The Scientific Basis," The Intergovernmental Panel on Climate Change, 2016, http://www.ipcc.ch/ipccreports/tar/wg1/345.htm

37.  John Costella, "The Climategate Emails," The Lavoisier Group, March 2010, http://www.lavoisier.com.au/articles/greenhouse-science/climate-change/climategate-emails.pdf

38.  J. T. Houghton, "Climate Change: The IPCC Scientific Assessment," IPCC Working Group I, 1990, p. XXII, http://www.ipcc.ch/publications_and_data/publications_and_data_reports.shtml#1

39.  "Use of NOAA ESRL DATA," 2016, ftp://aftp.cmdl.noaa.gov/products/trends/co2/co2_annmean_mlo.txt

40.  John Christy testimony before the US House of Representatives, Feb. 2, 2016, https://science.house.gov/sites/republicans.science.house.gov/files/documents/HHRG-114-SY-WState-JChristy-20160202.pdf; weather balloon image by Harold Linden under GNU General Public License

41.  Richard Lindzen and Yong-Sang Choi, "On the Observational Determination of Climate Sensitivity and Its Implications," *Asia-Pacific Journal of Atmospheric Sciences*, May 22, 2011, pp. 377-390, http://www-eaps.mit.edu/faculty/lindzen/236-Lindzen-Choi-2011.pdf

42.  *An Inconvenient Truth: The Planetary Emergency of Global Warming and What We Can Do About It* by Al Gore, (Rodale Books, 2006), p. 10

43.  James Hansen et al., "Ice melt, sea level rise and superstorms: evidence from paleoclimate data, climate modeling, and modern observations that 2°C global warming is highly dangerous," *Atmospheric Chemistry and Physics Discussions*, July 23, 2015, http://www.atmos-chem-phys-discuss.net/15/20059/2015/acpd-15-20059-2015.html

44.  Peter Cochrane, "Going under the sea ice - Getting to the bottom of Antarctic mystery," University of Tasmania, 2016, http://www.utas.edu.au/o2t/current-issue/articles/going-under-the-sea-ice-getting-to-the-bottom-of-antarctic-mystery

45.  "Will Earth Get Warmer?," *Launceston Examiner*, Apr. 25, 1939, http://trove.nla.gov.au/ndp/del/article/52305165; Book image by dear theophilus

46.  "Cryosphere Today," University of Illinois Polar Research Group, 2016, http://arctic.atmos.uiuc.edu/cryosphere/

47.  Ibid

48.  "Antarctic monthly surface air temperatures south of 70S," *Climate4you*, 2016, http://www.climate4you.com/

49.  Photo of Amundsen-Scott South Pole Station by National Science Foundation, 2010

50.  "Polar Meteorology: Understanding Global Impacts," World Meteorological Organization, 2007, http://www.wmo.int/worldmetday/sites/default/files/WMD2007_web_brochure_E.pdf

51.  Daniel Greenfield, "Global Warming Expedition to Prove Antarctic Ice is Melting Trapped by Ice," *Front Page Magazine*, Dec. 29, 2013, http://www.frontpagemag.com/point/214101/global-warming-expedition-prove-antarctic-ice-daniel-greenfield; Image of icebreaker Polar Star from US Coast Guard

52.  "Amundsen-Scott South Pole Station," National Science Foundation, 2016, https://www.nsf.gov/geo/plr/support/southp.jsp

53.  "Early Warning Signs of Global Warming: Glaciers Melting," Union of Concerned Scientists, 2016, http://www.ucsusa.org/global_warming/science_and_impacts/impacts/early-warning-signs-of-global-5.html#.Vofx8cZIh9M

54.  S. Fred Singer, "Nature, Not Human Activity, rules the Climate," *The Heartland Institute*, 2008, https://www.heartland.org/policy-documents/nature-not-human-activity-rules-climate-pdf

55.  Gary Braasch, "Mendenhall Glacier, Now and Then," *National Geographic*, Sep. 15, 2011, http://voices.nationalgeographic.com/2011/09/15/mendenhall-glacier-now-and-then/

56.  Mary Catharine Martin, "Ancient trees emerge from frozen forest 'tomb'," *Juneau Empire*, Sep. 12, 2013, http://juneauempire.com/outdoors/2013-09-13/ancient-trees-emerge-frozen-forest-tomb; Image by Abby Lowell

57.  Steve Nolan, "Ancient forest revealed 1,000 years after being 'entombed' in gravel as Alaskan glacier melts," *DailyMail*, Oct. 10, 2013, http://www.dailymail.co.uk/sciencetech/article-2451640/Mendenhall-Glacier-melting-reveals-ancient-forest.html

58.  *San Jose Mercury News*, June 30, 1989, http://nl.newsbank.com/nl-search/we/Archives?p_product=SJ&s_site=mercurynews&p_multi=SJ&p_theme=realcities&p_action=search&p_maxdocs=200&p_topdoc=1&p_text_direct-0=0EB7304FF9A84273&p_field_direct-0=document_id&p_perpage=10&p_sort=YMD_date:D&s_trackval=GooglePM; Stop Falsch image from Andrikkos under Creative Commons Attribution-Share Alike License

59.  Vivian Gornitz, "Sea Level Rise, After the Ice Melted and Today," NASA, Goddard Institute for Space Studies, Jan. 2007, http://www.giss.nasa.gov/research/briefs/gornitz_09/

60.  Arthur Robinson et al., "Environmental Effects of Increased Atmospheric Carbon Dioxide," *Journal of American Physicians and Surgeons*, 2007, pp. 79-90, http://www.oism.org/pproject/s33p36.htm

61.  "Climate Change Impacts in the United States," US Global Change Research Program, May, 2014, http://nca2014.globalchange.gov/downloads

62.  "Hurricane/Post-Tropical Cyclone Sandy, October 22–29, 2012," NOAA, http://www.nws.noaa.gov/os/assessments/pdfs/Sandy13.pdf

63.  Bernie Sanders, "Global Warming and Hurricane Sandy," Nov. 1, 2012, http://www.sanders.senate.gov/newsroom/press-releases/global-warming-and-hurricane-sandy

64.  Ian Schwartz, "Obama: "Climate Change Didn't Cause Hurricane Sandy, But May Have Made It Stronger," *RealClearPolitics*, May 28, 2015, http://www.realclearpolitics.com/video/2015/05/28/obama_climate_change_didnt_cause_hurricane_sandy_but_may_have_made_it_stronger.html

65.  "1821 Norfolk and Long Island Hurricane," World Public Library, 2016, http://www.worldlibrary.org/articles/1821_Norfolk_and_Long_Island_Hurricane

66.  "Chronological List of All Hurricanes: 1851 - 2014," Hurricane Research Division, National Oceanic and Atmospheric Administration, 2016, http://www.aoml.noaa.gov/hrd/hurdat/All_U.S._Hurricanes.html

67.  Ibid

68.  Hurricanes, (See no. 66); Image of Hurricane Fran in 1996 from the National Climatic Data Center, NOAA

69.  Sheldon Whitehouse, "Time to Wake Up: GOP Opposition to Climate Science," May 20, 2013, http://www.whitehouse.senate.gov/news/speeches/time-to-wake-up-gop-opposition-to-climate-science

70. "US Tornado Climatology," National Climatic Data Center, NOAA, 2016, https://www.ncdc.noaa.gov/climate-information/extreme-events/us-tornado-climatology

71. "Climate Watch, April 1999," National Climatic Data Center, NOAA, Apr. 23, 1999, http://www.ncdc.noaa.gov/extremeevents/specialreports/Climate-Watch-April-1999.pdf

72. Eric Niiler, "Is Air Conditioning Killing the Planet?," Discovery News, July 28, 2015, http://news.discovery.com/earth/weather-extreme-events/is-air-conditioning-killing-the-planet-150728.htm; ghost image by netalloy

73. NCDC, (See no. 70)

74. Timothy Cama, "Oil giants call for global carbon pollution fees," The Hill, June 1, 2015, http://thehill.com/policy/energy-environment/243588-oil-giants-call-for-worldwide-carbon-pollution-fees; foot image by Lior Golgher under GNU Free Documentation License

75. Climate Change: The Facts, edited by Alan Moran, (Stockdale Books, 2015), p.52

76. Roy Spencer, "MORE Tornadoes from Global Warming? That's a Joke, Right?" Apr. 29, 2011, http://www.drroyspencer.com/2011/04/more-tornadoes-from-global-warming-thats-a-joke-right/

77. Ryan Maue, "Weather Bell Models," 2015, http://models.weatherbell.com/tropical.php; Image of Cyclone Catarina, 2004 from NASA

78. Steve Crutchfield, "US Drought 2012: Farm and Food Impacts," US Department of Agriculture, July 26, 2013, http://www.ers.usda.gov/topics/in-the-news/us-drought-2012-farm-and-food-impacts.aspx

79. Seth Borenstein, "This US summer is 'what global warming looks like': scientists," The Associated Press, July 3, 2012, http://phys.org/news/2012-07-summer-global-scientists.html

80. Lee Scott, "Twenty First Century Leadership," Wal Mart Executive Viewpoints, Oct. 23, 2005, http://corporate.walmart.com/_news_/executive-viewpoints/twenty-first-century-leadership; Hippopotomus image by Jean-Pierre Dalbera, 2011 under Creative Commons License

81. "US Percentage Areas (Very Warm/Cold, Very Wet/Dry)," National Climatic Data Center, NOAA, 2015, https://www.ncdc.noaa.gov/temp-and-precip/uspa/

82. "The wet autumn of 2000," UK Meteorological Office, 2016, http://www.metoffice.gov.uk/climate/uk/interesting/autumn2000.html

83. Pardeep Pall et al., "Anthropogenic greenhouse gas contribution to flood risk in England and Wales in autumn 2000," Nature, Feb. 17, 2011, http://www.nature.com/nature/journal/v470/n7334/full/nature09762.html

84. "UK temperature, rainfall, and sunshine anomaly graphs," UK Meteorology Office, 2016, http://www.metoffice.gov.uk/climate/uk/summaries/anomalygraphs

85. "Climate Change 2014: Impacts, Adaptation, and Vulnerability," The Intergovernmental Panel on Climate Change, Fourth Assessment Report, Working Group II, http://www.ipcc.ch/publications_and_data/publications_and_data_reports.shtml#1

86. Xan Rice, "Severe drought causes hunger for 10 million in west Africa," Guardian, June 3, 2010, http://www.theguardian.com/environment/2010/jun/03/drought-hunger-west-africa

87. David Martosko, "Video shows Hillary Clinton boarding private jet just hours after launching global-warming push - and she's using a french aircraft that burns 347 gallons of fuel every hour!," DailyMail, Aug. 5th, 2015, http://www.dailymail.co.uk/news/article-3176630/Video-shows-Hillary-Clinton-boarding-private-jet-just-hours-launching-global-warming-push-s-using-FRENCH-aircraft-burns-347-gallons-fuel-hour.html; faces image from Bryan Derksen

88. Yen-Ting Hwang et al., "Anthropogenic sulfate aerosol and the southward shift of tropical precipitation in the late 20th century," Geophysical Research Letters, Apr. 22, 2013, pp1-6, http://www.atmos.washington.edu/~dargan/papers/hfk13.pdf

89. T. M. Shanahan, et al., "Atlantic Forcing of Persistent Drought in West Africa," Science, Apr. 17, 2009, http://www.sciencemag.org/content/324/5925/377.abstract

90. Philipp Mueller, "The Sahel is Greening," Global Warming Policy Foundation, Aug. 12, 2011, http://www.thegwpf.org/images/stories/gwpf-reports/mueller-sahel.pdf

91. John Holdren, "The Polar Vortex Explained in 2 Minutes," video by the White House Briefing Room, Jan. 8, 2014 https://www.youtube.com/watch?v=5eDTzV6a9F4; Image of Brooklyn Bridge by User: Postdlf under GNU Free Documentation License

92. Climate Change, (See no. 75), p. 52

93. Samantha Kramer, "Aztec Human Sacrifice," Michigan State University, Apr. 25, 2013, http://anthropology.msu.edu/anp264-ss13/2013/04/25/aztec-human-sacrifice/

94. Michael Northcott lecture at Wheaton College, Apr. 8, 2015

95. Emily Oster, "Witchcraft, Weather and Economic Growth in Renaissance Europe," Journal of Economic Perspectives, vol. 18, no. 1, Winter 2004, pp. 215-228, http://home.uchicago.edu/eoster/witchec.pdf

96. Climate Change 2014, (See no. 85), p. 301

97. "Scientists Speak Out: The New IPCC Report," Polar Bears International, Apr. 14, 2014, http://www.polarbearsinternational.org/news-room/pbi-blog/scientists-speak-out-new-ipcc-report

98. "Agreement on Conservation of Polar Bears," Environmental Treaties and Resource Indicators, Nov. 15, 1973, http://sedac.ciesin.org/entri/texts/polar.bears.1973.html

99. Ryu Spaeth, "Climate change is causing polar bears to eat dolphins," The Week, June 12, 2015, http://theweek.com/speedreads/560258/climate-change-causing-polar-bears-eat-dolphins, Looney Tunes image from Warner Brothers

100. "Adopt a Polar Bear," World Wildlife Fund, 2016, http://gifts.worldwildlife.org/gift-center/gifts/Species-Adoptions/Polar-Bear.aspx

101. Emma Juner, "Protecting the polar bears' Arctic home," Coca-Cola, 2016, http://www.coca-cola.co.uk/stories/sustainability/environment/protecting-the-polar-bears-arctic-home/

102. "Coca-Cola- 'Saving the Polar Bears (Arctic Home)'," Cream, 2016, https://www.creamglobal.com/17798/34200/coca-cola-saving-the-polar-bears-(arctic-home)

103. "Climate Change in the American Mind," Yale University and George Mason University, Nov. 2013, http://environment.yale.edu/climate-communication/files/Climate-Beliefs-November-2013.pdf

104. Edward Maibach and Matthew Nisbet, "The Health Community Should Reframe Climate Change as a Human Health Issue," Cornerstone, George Mason University, May 9, 2011, http://cornerstone.gmu.edu/articles/2927

105. "Climate Change and Health Effects," US Environmental Protection Agency, Apr. 2010, http://www3.epa.gov/climatechange/downloads/Climate_Change_Health.pdf

106. Image of Stewart Beach on Galveston Island, Texas, 1973 by Blair Pittman

107. W. R. Keating et al., "Heat Related Mortality in Warm and Cold Regions of Europe: Observational Study," British Medical Journal, v. 321, Sep. 16, 2000, pp. 670-673, http://www.ncbi.nlm.nih.gov/pubmed/10987770

108. Matthew Falagas et al., "Seasonality of Mortality: The September Phenomenon in Mediterranean Countries," Canadian Medical Association Journal, Oct. 13, 2009, http://www.cmaj.ca/content/181/8/484.abstract

109. Kristen Gelineau, "US Scientist: Ocean Acidity Major Threat to Reefs," Associated Press, July 9, 2012, http://myhero.com/hero.asp?hero=ocean_acidity_threatens_reefs_AP

110. Sigourney Weaver testimony to the US Senate, Apr. 22, 2010, http://www.commerce.senate.gov/public/index.cfm/hearings?Id=9ED82F3D-E66F-4214-891C-4E8C32543919&Statement_id=F41B4980-B15C-42C3-A0A1-682C334FC521

111. "Ocean Acidification due to increasing atmospheric carbon dioxide," The Royal Society, June, 2005, http://www.us-ocb.org/publications/

Royal_Soc_OA.pdf
112.    Jonathan Watts, "Stern: Rich nations will have to forget about growth to stop climate change," *Guardian*, Sep. 11, 2009, http://www.theguardian.com/environment/2009/sep/11/stern-economic-growth-emissions; question mark image from semjaza
113.    "1932 Shock News: Melting Polar Ice Caps to Drown the Planet," *stevengoddard.wordpress*, Jan. 24, 2014, https://stevengoddard.wordpress.com/2014/01/24/1932-shock-news-melting-polar-ice-caps-to-drown-the-planet/
114.    Hannes, Baumann et al., "Large Natural pH, CO2, and O2 Fluctuations in a Temperate Tidal Salt Marsh on Diel, Seasonal, and Interannual Time Scales," *Estuaries and Coasts*, Feb. 28, 2014, http://www.msrc.sunysb.edu/~conover/Baumann%20etal%20ESCO2014.pdf
115.    Gretchen Hofmann et al., "High-Frequency Dynamics of Ocean pH: A Multi-Ecosystem Comparison," *PLoS ONE*, Dec. 2011, http://journals.plos.org/plosone/article?id=10.1371/journal.pone.0028983
116.    "Ocean Acidification (The Phenomenon)," *CO2Science.org*, http://www.co2science.org/subject/o/acidificationphenom.php
117.    Image of healthy reef and CO2 vents from Bob Halsted
118.    "Advice to the New Administration and Congress: Actions to make our nation resilient to severe weather and climate change," University Corporation for Atmospheric Research and other organizations, 2009, http://www.ucar.edu/td/transition.pdf
119.    Hal Lewis resignation letter to the American Physical Society, Oct. 6, 2010, http://wattsupwiththat.com/2010/10/16/hal-lewis-my-resignation-from-the-american-physical-society/; money image from *deviantart.com* under Creative Commons License
120.    Ryan Van Velzer, "Does climate change impact national security? ASU gets $20M to find out," *Republic*, July 3, 2014, http://www.azcentral.com/story/news/local/tempe/2014/07/02/asu-researching-national-security-risks-of-climate-change/12082781/; money image from *deviantart.com* under Creative Commons License
121.    Judith Curry, "Scientists and motivated reasoning," *Climate Etc.*, Aug. 20, 2013, http://judithcurry.com/2013/08/20/scientists-and-motivated-reasoning/
122.    The Climategate E-mails, (See no. 38)
123.    "California Targets Dairy Cows to Combat Global Warning," *FoxNews*, Nov. 29, 2016, http://www.foxnews.com/us/2016/11/29/california-targets-dairy-cows-to-combat-global-warming.html; cow image by Andrew Duffell under Creative Commons License

## Chapter 6:  Resource Shortage?

1.      David Boyd, "Sustainability Within a Generation," David Suzuki Foundation, 2004, http://www.davidsuzuki.org/publications/downloads/2004/DSF-GG-En-Final.pdf
2.      *The Greenhouse Trap: What We Are Doing to the Atmosphere and How We Can Slow Global Warming* by Francesca Lyman, (Beacon Press, 1989), p.108
3.      "Green-Works Helping to Save the Planet," *UK Government News*, Mar. 8, 2005, http://www.gov-news.org/gov/uk/news/green_works_helping_to_save_the_planet/17494.html
4.      Thomas Friedman, "The Inflection Is Near?," *New York Times*, Mar. 7, 2009, http://www.nytimes.com/2009/03/08/opinion/08friedman.html?_r=0
5.      *Handbook of Chemistry and Physics, 81st Edition* by David Lide, (CRC Press, 2000)
6.      *Sustainable Development: Constraints and Opportunities* by Mostafa Tolba, (Butterworth-Heinemann, 1987), p. 20; explosion image is US Navy photo
7.      Bauxite image from Saphon under Creative Commons Generic License; Aluminum image from Image of Elements, photographer unknown
8.      Chemistry of the Elements, 2nd Edition, by Greenwood and Earnshaw, (Elsevier, 2012), p. 1174-1175
9.      *Minerals: An Expanding or a Dwindling Resource?* by David Brooks, (La Direction, Ministere de l'energie, des mines et des ressources, 1973), p. 4
10.     David Harvey et al., "The Prebisch-Singer Hypothesis: Four Centuries of Evidence," *Review of Economics and Statistics*, May, 2010, http://www.mitpressjournals.org/doi/abs/10.1162/rest.2010.12184?journalCode=rest#.VpO4K8ZIh9M
11.     Blake Clayton, "Bad news for Pessimists Everywhere: Malthus Was Wrong," *Council on Foreign Relations*, Mar. 22, 2013, http://blogs.cfr.org/levi/2013/03/22/bad-news-for-pessimists-everywhere-malthus-was-wrong/
12.     World Bank historical commodity price data, 2016, http://data.worldbank.org/data-catalog/commodity-price-data
13.     Ibid; Lumber image of Foildarrig, UK from Nigel Cox under Creative Commons License
14.     World Mineral Production and Statistical Summary reports, 1960-2013, British Geological Survey, https://www.bgs.ac.uk/mineralsUk/statistics/worldArchive.html; "Mineral Commodity Summaries 2015," US Geological Survey, http://minerals.usgs.gov/minerals/pubs/mcs/
15.     Price data, (See no. 12)
16.     Price data, (See no. 12); World Mineral Production, (See no. 14); Nickel image by Materialscientist under GNU Free Documentation License
17.     Price data, (See no. 12)
18.     Kenneth Medlock and Amy Jaffe, "Who Is In the Oil Futures Market and How Has It Changed?," James Baker Institute for Public Policy, Rice University, Aug. 26, 2009, http://bakerinstitute.org/files/1412/
19.     "Resources for Freedom, Volume II," The President's Materials Policy Commission, June 1952, http://catalog.hathitrust.org/Record/001313143; *United States Mineral Resources* by Donald Brobst and Walden Pratt, (US Government Printing Office, 1973, pp. 21-23; US Geological Survey, "Mineral Commodity Summaries," 2006-2011, http://minerals.usgs.gov/minerals/pubs/mcs/; Copper mineral image from Daniel Stucht under GNU Free Document License
20.     US Geological Survey, "Mineral Commodity Summaries," 1995-2015, http://minerals.usgs.gov/minerals/pubs/mcs/
21.     Cassandra Sweet, "The $2.2 Billion Bird-Scorching Solar Project at California's Ivanpah Plant, Mirrors Produce Heat and Electricity--And Kill Wildlife," *Wall Street Journal*, Feb. 13, 2014, http://www.wsj.com/articles/SB10001424052702304703804579379230641329484; Eagle killed by wind turbine image by Stefan Hedgren
22.     "The Scrap Recycling Industry: Iron and Steel, American Iron and Steel Institute, 2016, http://www.isri.org/docs/default-source/recycling-industry/fact-sheet---iron-and-steel.pdf
23.     "Mineral Commodity Summaries 2015," US Geological Survey, http://minerals.usgs.gov/minerals/pubs/mcs/
24.     *The Ultimate Resource 2* by Julian Simon, (Princeton University Press, 1996), p. 12
25.     "BP Statistical Review of World Energy," BP Corporation, June 2015, http://www.bp.com/en/global/corporate/energy-economics/statistical-review-of-world-energy.html
26.     "Monthly Energy Review, " US Energy Information Agency, Dec. 2015, https://www.eia.gov/totalenergy/data/monthly/
27.     "Petroleum and Other Liquids--Spot Prices," US Energy Information Agency, 2016, https://www.eia.gov/dnav/pet/pet_pri_spt_s1_d.htm
28.     M. King Hubbert, "Nuclear Energy and the Fossil Fuels," Shell Development Company, June 1956
29.     Monthly Energy Review, (See no. 26)
30.     Monthly Energy Review, (See no. 26)
31.     Petroleum and Other Liquids, (See no. 27)
32.     Monthly Energy Review, (See no. 25); California oil pump image from CGP Grey under Creative Commons License
33.     President Jimmy Carter, address to the nation, Apr. 18, 1977, https://www.youtube.com/watch?v=J8HwVeSMuhE; Stop Falsch image from

Andrikkos under Creative Commons License
34. "International Energy Statistics," US Energy Information Agency, 2016, http://www.eia.gov/cfapps/ipdbproject/IEDIndex3.
cfm?tid=5&pid=53&aid=1
35. Ibid
36. Ibid, Gasoline pump image from Nevit Dilmen under Creative Commons License
37. Mike Bowlin, CEO of Atlantic Richfield Company, ARCO, presentation at the Cambridge Energy Research Associates, 18th Annual Executive
Conference, Houston, TX, Feb. 9, 1999; Lemonade image by Michael Fludkov under Creative Commons License
38. International Energy Statistics, (See no. 34)
39. International Energy Statistics, (See no. 34); Gas flame image by George Shuklin
40. Bruno Waterfield and Emily Gosden, "EU to ban high-energy hair dryers, smartphones and kettles," *Telegraph*, Aug. 28, 2014, http://www.
telegraph.co.uk/news/worldnews/europe/eu/11061538/EU-to-ban-high-energy-hair-dryers-smartphones-and-kettles.html; Hairdryer image from
Batholith; Graveyard silhouette image by naoshika
41. George Monbiot, "We Were Wrong on Peak Oil. There's Enough to Fry Us All," *Guardian*, Jul. 2, 2012, http://www.theguardian.com/
commentisfree/2012/jul/02/peak-oil-we-we-wrong; Crying child image by Crimfants under Creative Commons License
42. International Energy Statistics, (See no. 34)
43. International Energy Statistics, (See no. 34); "Technically Recoverable Shale Oil and Shale Gas Resources: An Assessment of 137 Shale
Formations in 41 Countries Outside the United States," US Department of Energy, June, 2013, https://www.eia.gov/analysis/studies/
worldshalegas/; *Energy Transitions: History, Requirements, Prospects* by Vaclav Smil, (Praeger, 2010), appendix
44. BP Review, (See no. 24); "Key Energy World Statistics," International Energy Agency, 2011, http://www.etiea.cn/data/
upfiles/201110/2011102509440252.pdf
45. International Energy Statistics, (See no. 34)
46. Dan Fletcher, "Top 10 Odd Environmental Ideas," *Time*, Apr. 2009, http://content.time.com/time/specials/packages/
article/0,28804,1882682_1882680_1882665,00.html; flower image by Hakani

## Chapter 7:  Renewable Energy Myths

1. *At Home: A Short History of Private Life* by Bill Bryson, (Knopf Doubleday, 2010)
2. Steve Goreham, "Using Energy and Happy about it," *Energy Tribune*, Mar. 4, 2013, http://www.energytribune.com/74559/using-energy-and-
happy-about-it#sthash.DvblZN8W.dpbs
3. Sean Alfano, "Gore Defends Mansion's Power Consumption," *CBS News*, Feb. 28, 2007,
4. Estimates made from "EIA Wind 2014 Annual Report," International Energy Agency, Aug. 2015, http://www.ieawind.org/annual_reports_
PDF/2014.html
5. Sean Alfano, (See no. 2)
6. Robert Bryce, "Renewable Energy's Incurable Scale Problem," *Energy Tribune*, Jul. 13, 2012, http://www.robertbryce.com/articles/56-
renewable-energy-s-incurable-scale-problem
7. "BP Statistical Review of World Energy," BP Corporation, June 2015, http://www.bp.com/en/global/corporate/energy-economics/statistical-
review-of-world-energy.html; "Hoover Dam," US Bureau of Land Reclamation, 2016, http://www.usbr.gov/lc/hooverdam/faqs/powerfaq.html
8. BP Statistical Review, (See no. 7)
9. BP Statistical Review, (See no. 7); Image of Three Gorges Dam from Rehman under Creative Commons License
10. *Solar Power Your Home for Dummies*, by Rik DeGunther, (For Dummies, 2010), p. 251; Model in hat image from Australian National Maritime
Museum
11. BP Statistical Review, (See no. 7)
12. Image of California Valley Solar Ranch from Sarah Swenty under Creative Commons License
13. "California Valley Solar Ranch Fact Sheet," Sunpower, 2014, http://us.sunpower.com/sites/sunpower/files/media-library/fact-sheets/fs-
california-valley-solar-ranch-factsheet.pdf
14. "The Betz Limit and the Maximum Efficiency for Horizontal Axis Wind Turbines," WindPower Program, 2016; http://www.wind-power-program.
com/betz.htm
15. *Blue Planet in Green Shackles* by Václav Klaus, (Competitive Enterprise Institute, 2008), p.86
16. "World Energy Assessment: Energy and the Challenge of Sustainability," United Nations Development Programme, 2000; Vampire image by
Alejandro Lunadei under Creative Commons License
17. "London Array: The Project," londonarray.com, http://www.londonarray.com/the-project-3/
18. *The Mad, Mad, Mad World of Climatism* by Steve Goreham, (New Lenox Books, 2012), p. 195
19. "IEA Wind 2014 Annual Report," International Energy Agency, Aug. 2015, p. 5; https://www.ieawind.org/annual_reports_PDF/2014/2014%20
AR_smallfile.pdf
20. Image of solar rooftop covered in snow, Dec. 12, 2012, by Asurnipal under Creative Commons License
21. UK National Grid, 2016; http://www.gridwatch.templar.co.uk/
22. Ibid; Image of Scroby Sands wind farm, Bury St. Edmunds, UK, by Martin Pettitt under Creative Commons License
23. Kimball Rasmussen, "A Rational Look at Renewable Energy," Deseret Power, Nov. 2010, https://www.heartland.org/sites/default/files/rational-
look-renewables.pdf
24. Nancy Pfotenhauer, "Big Wind's Bogus Subsidies," *US News & World Report*, May 12, 2014, http://www.usnews.com/opinion/blogs/nancy-
pfotenhauer/2014/05/12/even-warren-buffet-admits-wind-energy-is-a-bad-investment; Currency image from US Treasury Department
25. "Levelized Cost and Levelized Avoided Cost of New Generation Resources in the Annual Energy Outlook 2015," US Energy Information
Administration, June 2015, https://www.eia.gov/forecasts/aeo/pdf/electricity_generation.pdf
26. Ibid
27. "Levelized Cost and Levelized Avoided Cost of New Generation Resources in the Annual Energy Outlook 2014," US Energy Information
Administration, Apr. 2014, http://large.stanford.edu/courses/2014/ph240/suresh2/docs/electricity_generation.pdf
28. Thomas Stacy and George Taylor, "The Levelized Cost of Electricity from Existing Generation Resources," Institute for Energy Research, June
2015, http://instituteforenergyresearch.org/wp-content/uploads/2015/06/ier_lcoe_2015.pdf
29. Levelized costs, (See no. 27)
30. Jonathan Cook and Cynthia Lin, "Wind Turbine Shutdowns and Upgrades in Denmanrk: Timing Decisions and the Impact of Government
Policy," University of California Davis, July, 2015,http://www.des.ucdavis.edu/faculty/Lin/DKwind_paper.pdf
31. DirK Jordan and Sarah Kurtz, "Photovoltaic Degradation Rates—An Analytical Review," National Renewable Energy Laboratory, June 2012,
32. Stacy and Taylor, (See no. 28)
33. Levelized costs, (See no. 27)
34. Levelized costs, (See no. 27); Stacy and Taylor, (See no. 28)
35. "Wholesale Electricity and Natural Gas Market Data," US Energy Information Administration, 2016, http://www.eia.gov/electricity/

wholesale/#history

36. Database of State Incentives for Renewables and Efficiency, 2016, http://www.dsireusa.org/
37. Jacobsen and Delucci, "A Path to Sustainable Energy by 2030," *Scientific American*, Nov. 2009, http://www.scientificamerican.com/article/a-path-to-sustainable-energy-by-2030/; Image of Brooklyn Bridge by User: Postdlf under GNU Free Documentation License
38. Ibid
39. Kate Connolly, "G7 Leaders Agree to Phase Out Fossil Fuel Use by End of Century," *Guardian*, June 8, 2015, http://www.theguardian.com/world/2015/jun/08/g7-leaders-agree-phase-out-fossil-fuel-use-end-of-century
40. "Corporate Renewable Energy Buyers' Principles," World Wildlife Fund, Sep. 2015, http://www.worldwildlife.org/pages/powering-businesses-on-renewable-energy
41. Tom Bawden, "Global Warming: Data Centres to Consume Three Times as Much Energy in Next Decade, Experts Warn," *Independent*, Jan. 23, 2016, http://www.independent.co.uk/environment/global-warming-data-centres-to-consume-three-times-as-much-energy-in-next-decade-experts-warn-a6830086.html; Vampire image by Alejandro Lunadei under Creative Commons License
42. "Global Coal Plant Tracker," EndCoal.org, Dec. 2015, http://endcoal.org/global-coal-plant-tracker/
43. "First European Climate Change Programme," European Commission, 2016, http://ec.europa.eu/clima/policies/eccp/first/index_en.htm
44. Ibid
45. Directive 2009/28/EC of the European Parliament and of the Council, Apr. 23, 2009, http://eur-lex.europa.eu/legal-content/EN/TXT/?uri=URISERV%3Aen0009
46. Benny Peiser, "Testimony to the Committee on Environment and Public Works of the United States Senate, Dec. 2, 2014, http://www.thegwpf.com/content/uploads/2014/12/Peiser-Senate-Testimony-2.pdf
47. Gabrial Calzada et al., "Study of the Effects on Employment of Public Aid to Renewable Energy Sources," University of Rey Juan Carlos, Mar. 2009, http://instituteforenergyresearch.org/wp-content/uploads/2015/05/090327-employment-public-aid-renewable.pdf
48. "Economic Impacts from the Promotion of Renewable Energies: The German Experience," Rheinisch-Westfälisches Institut für Wirtschaftsforschung, Oct. 2009, http://instituteforenergyresearch.org/media/germany/Germany_Study_-_FINAL.pdf
49. "Renewables 2010 Global Status Report," REN21, Sep. 2010, http://www.ren21.net/Portals/0/documents/activities/gsr/REN21_GSR_2010_full_revised%20Sept2010.pdf
50. Ibid
51. Directive 2009/28/EC, (See no. 46)
52. Eurostat Energy Statistics, 1990-2013, EU Commission, http://ec.europa.eu/eurostat/data/database; Eurostat Energy Statistics, Apr. 15, 2015, http://ec.europa.eu/eurostat/statistics-explained/index.php/Electricity_production,_consumption_and_market_overview; wind and solar data from EurObserv'ER Barometer 2015 reports, http://www.eurobserv-er.org/
53. EurObserv'ER Wind and Solar Barometer 2015 reports, http://www.eurobserv-er.org/
54. EurObserv'ER Wind Barometer 2015 report, http://www.eurobserv-er.org/
55. "Household Electricity Prices in the EU Rose by 2.9% in 2014," Eurostat, May 27, 2015, http://ec.europa.eu/eurostat/documents/2995521/6849826/8-27052015-AP-EN.pdf/4f9f295f-bb31-4962-a7a9-b6c4365a5deb
56. Dimitri Pescia et al., "Agora Energiewende (2015): Understanding the Energiewende. FAQ on the Ongoing Transition of the German Power System," Oct., 2015, www.agora-energiewende.de
57. Lindsay McIntosh, "Millions of Trees Felled in Pursuit of Energy Targets," *Times*, Jan. 2, 2014, http://www.thetimes.co.uk/tto/news/article3963129.ece; Eagle killed by wind turbine image by Stefan Hedgren
58. EurObserv'ER Solar Barometer 2015 report, http://www.eurobserv-er.org/
59. Hans Poser et al., "Development and Integration of Renewable Energy: Lessons Learned from Germany," Finadvice, July 2014, http://www.finadvice.ch/files/germany_lessonslearned_final_071014.pdf
60. Matthias Luedecke, "Energy Revolution Could Cost Up to One Trillion Euros," *Frankfurter Allgemaine Zeitung*, Feb. 19, 2013, https://translate.google.com/translate?hl=en&sl=de&u=http://www.faz.net/aktuell/politik/energiepolitik/umweltminister-altmaier-energiewende-koennte-bis-zu-einer-billion-euro-kosten-12086525.html&prev=search
61. Andrew Orlowski, "Snow Blankets London for Global Warming Debate," *Register*, Oct. 29,2008, http://www.theregister.co.uk/2008/10/29/commons_climate_change_bill/
62. IEA Wind, (See no. 19)
63. EurObserv'ER Solar Barometer 2015 report, http://www.eurobserv-er.org/
64. "Energy from Renewable Sources," Eurostat, Feb. 15, 2015, http://ec.europa.eu/eurostat/statistics-explained/index.php/Main_Page
65. Michael Liebreich presentation at the Bloomberg New Energy Finance Summit 2014, http://about.bnef.com/presentations/bnef-summit-2014-keynote-presentation-michael-liebreich/; "Clean Energy Defies Fossil Fuel Price Crash to Attract Record $329BN Global Investment in 2015," Bloomberg New Energy Finance, Jan. 14, 2016, http://about.bnef.com/press-releases/clean-energy-defies-fossil-fuel-price-crash-to-attract-record-329bn-global-investment-in-2015/
66. Energy from Renewable Sources, (See no. 64)
67. Drax power station, North Yorkshire, England image by Paul Glazzard under Creative Commons License
68. Christopher Booker, "Eco Madness and How Our Future is Going Up in Smoke as We Pay Billions to Switch from Burning Coal to Wood Chips at Britain's Biggest Power Station," *DailyMail*, Mar. 8, 2013, http://www.dailymail.co.uk/news/article-2290444/Madness-How-pay-billions-electricity-bills-Britains-biggest-power-station-switch-coal-wood-chips--wont-help-planet-jot.html
69. Ibid
70. Thomas Barth, presentation at the 5th Conference ELECPOR, Nov. 1, 2013, http://www.elecpor.pt/pdf/Thomas%20Barth_ELECPOR_Nov2013.pdf
71. Household electricity price data from Eurostat database, 2015, http://ec.europa.eu/eurostat/data/database?p_p_id=NavTreeportletprod_WAR_NavTreeportletprod_INSTANCE_nPqeVbPXRmWQ&p_p_lifecycle=0&p_p_state=normal&p_p_mode=view&p_p_col_id=column-2&p_p_col_count=1
72. Ibid
73. Household Electricity Prices, (See no. 55); EurObserv'ER Wind and Solar, (See no. 54); "World Development Indicators," World Bank, Dec. 22, 2015, http://data.worldbank.org/news/release-of-world-development-indicators-2015; "Electric power Monthly," Feb. 2015, US Energy Information Administration, https://www.eia.gov/electricity/monthly/; Wind turbine and solar cell image from the island of Zirje, Croatia by Nenad Veneko under Creative Commons License
74. Industrial electricity price data from Eurostat database, 2015, http://ec.europa.eu/eurostat/data/database?p_p_id=NavTreeportletprod_WAR_NavTreeportletprod_INSTANCE_nPqeVbPXRmWQ&p_p_lifecycle=0&p_p_state=normal&p_p_mode=view&p_p_col_id=column-2&p_p_col_count=1;
75. Poser, (See no. 59)
76. BP Statistical Review, (See no. 7)
77. Eurostat data, (See no. 74); "Electric Power Monthly," US Energy Information Administration, 2008 to 2016, https://www.eia.gov/electricity/monthly/; Power line image from Huhu Uet under GNU Free Documentation License

78. "Unlocking Industrial Opportunities," Accenture, 2013, http://www.cpwerx.de/SiteCollectionDocuments/PDF/Accenture-EBS-2013-Unlocking-Industrial-Opportunities.pdf; Green bus image from Alan Sansbury under Creative Commons License

79. Matthew Elliott and Oliver Lewis, "Energy Policy and the EU," Business for Britain, 2014, http://businessforbritain.org/BFBEnergyPaper.pdf

80. "World Energy Outlook" presentation, International Energy Agency, Nov. 2013, http://www.worldenergyoutlook.org/weo2013/

81. Poser, (See no. 59)

82. Lakshmi Mittal, "Rewrite Energy Policy and Re-Industrialise Europe," Financial Times, Jan. 20, 2014, http://www.ft.com/cms/s/0/af5859b0-81c8-11e3-87d5-00144feab7de.html#axzz44bJ9l0Wz

83. Chris Bryant, "High European Energy Prices Drive BMW to US," Financial Times, May 27, 2013, http://www.ft.com/intl/cms/s/0/be69a732-ab5a-11e2-8c63-00144feabdc0.html#axzz44bJ9l0Wz

84. "RWE Posts First Net Loss in 60 Years," RWE press release, Mar. 4, 2014, http://www.rwe.com/web/cms/de/37110/rwe/presse-news/pressemitteilungen/pressemitteilungen/?pmid=4010679

85. Pierre Gosselin, "Bleeding to Death…Germany's Largest Power Company E.ON Loses Whopping $7.8 Billion…Collapse Accelerates," NoTricksZone, Nov. 11, 2015, http://notrickszone.com/2015/11/11/bleeding-to-death-germanys-largest-power-company-e-on-loses-whopping-7-8-billion-collapse-accelerates/#sthash.IQofTsGc.dpbs

86. Matthew Gray, "Coal: Caught in the EU Utility Death Spiral," Carbon Tracker, June 2015, http://www.carbontracker.org/wp-content/uploads/2015/06/CTI-EU-Utilities-Report-v6-080615.pdf

87. "How to Lose Half a Trillion Euros," Economist, Oct. 12, 2013, http://www.economist.com/news/briefing/21587782-europes-electricity-providers-face-existential-threat-how-lose-half-trillion-euros

88. "Energy Prices and Costs Report," European Commission, Mar. 17, 2014, http://ec.europa.eu/energy/sites/ener/files/documents/20140122_swd_prices.pdf; "Quarterly Report on European Electricity Markets," European Commission, Q3 2015, https://ec.europa.eu/energy/sites/ener/files/documents/quarterly_report_on_european_electricity_markets_q3_2015.pdf

89. Diarmaid Williams, "E.ON Opts to Close Irsching Gas-Fired Power Plant," Power Engineering International, Mar. 30, 2015, http://www.powerengineeringint.com/articles/2015/03/e-on-opts-to-close-irsching-gas-fired-power-plant.html

90. Sonja van Renssen and Hughes Belin, "New Vattenfall CEO Magnus Hall: 'What is True for Eon, is Pretty Much True for Us'," EnergyPost, Dec. 10, 2014, http://www.energypost.eu/vattenfalls-new-ceo-magnus-hall-true-e-pretty-much-true-us/; Currency image from US Treasury Department

91. "Power Capacity Payments are Coming Across Europe," Timera Energy, Mar. 2, 2015, http://www.timera-energy.com/power-capacity-payments-are-coming-across-europe/

92. Giles Parkinson, "EU's Biggest Utility Dumps Conventional Generation to Focus on Renewables," RenewEconomy.com, Dec. 2, 2014, http://reneweconomy.com.au/2014/eus-biggest-utility-dumps-conventional-generation-to-focus-on-renewables-41244

93. "The State of Renewable Energies in Europe," Eurobserv'er, 2013-2014, http://www.eurobserv-er.org/

94. Bloomberg New Energy Finance, (See no. 65); Image of solar park in Kreis Düren, Germany by EnergieAgentur.NRW under Creative Commons License

95. State of Renewable Energies in Europe, (See no. 93)

96. Bloomberg New Energy Finance, (See no. 65)

97. Gabrial Calzada, (See no. 47)

98. Pierre Gosselin, "Spain's Great Photovoltaic Bust—30,000 Jobs Lost Since 2008, NoTricksZone, Jan., 13, 2011, http://notrickszone.com/2011/01/13/spains-great-photovoltaic-bust-30000-jobs-lost-since-2008/#sthash.GHUwF5Gr.dpbs; Mary Hutzler, "Renewable Subsidies in Europe," Energyskeptic.com, Jul. 22, 2014, http://energyskeptic.com/2015/renewable-subsidies-in-spain-germany-italy-and-the-uk/

99. Stephen Jewkes and Massimo Gaia, "Italy's Planned Solar Subsidy Cuts Risk Scaring Off Investors," Reuters, June 23, 2014, http://uk.reuters.com/article/italy-solar-subsidies-idUKL6N0P41TW201406

100. "A Sector in Transformation: Electricity Industry Trends and Figures," Eurelectric, Jan. 2015, http://www.eurelectric.org/media/161808/electricityindustrytrendsandfigures2015_lr-2015-030-0064-01-e.pdf

101. "Era of Constant Electricity at Home is Ending, Says Power Chief," Daily Telegraph, Mar. 2, 2011, http://wattsupwiththat.com/2011/03/04/the-empire-strikes-out/; Candle image from ehiner1 uner Creative Commons License

102. Peter Campbell, "Blackout Alert: Offices and Factories to Undergo 1970s-Style Electricity Rationing This Winter to Stop Households Being Plunged Into Darkness," MailOnLine, Sep. 2, 2014, http://www.dailymail.co.uk/news/article-2741039/Blackout-alert-Offices-factories-undergo-1970s-style-electricity-rationing-winter-stop-households-plunged-darkness.html

103. "Petroleum and Other Liquids--Spot Prices," US Energy Information Agency, 2016, https://www.eia.gov/dnav/pet/pet_pri_spt_s1_d.htm

104. Mark Mills, "Forget OPEC: Shale 2.0 Will bounce Back & Even Stronger," Wall Street Journal, Jan. 19, 2016, http://www.wsj.com/articles/after-the-carnage-shale-will-rise-again-1453162664

105. "Technically Recoverable Shale Oil and Sale Gas Resources," US Energy Information Agency, June, 2013, http://www.eia.gov/pressroom/releases/press391.cfm

106. Ambrose Evans-Pritchard, "Saudis 'Will Not Destroy the US Shale Industry,'" Telegraph, Jan. 24, 2016, http://www.telegraph.co.uk/finance/newsbysector/energy/oilandgas/12118594/Saudis-will-not-destroy-the-US-shale-industry.html

107. "Statement by the President on the Keystone XL Pipeline," Whitehouse.gov, Nov. 6, 2015, https://www.whitehouse.gov/the-press-office/2015/11/06/statement-president-keystone-xl-pipeline

108. Timothy Cama, "Union: Obama Threw Workers 'Under the Bus' in Keystone Decision," Hill, Nov. 6, 2015, http://thehill.com/policy/energy-environment/259395-union-obama-threw-workers-under-the-bus; green bus image from Alan Sansbury under Creative Commons License

109. "Beyond Coal," Sierra Club, 2016, http://content.sierraclub.org/coal/about-the-campaign

110. "Gas Firm Funded Sierra Club Campaign," Charleston Gazette-Mail, Feb. 15, 2012, http://www.wvgazettemail.com/Opinion/DonSurber/201202140156; Crocodile image by DrBartje under Creative Commons License

111. Not an actual headline; Newspaper image by baroquon; Comedy image by John Reid

112. Jeremy Fisher et al., "The Carbon Footprint of Electricity from Biomass," Synapse Energy Economics, June 11, 2012, http://www.synapse-energy.com/sites/default/files/Carbon-Footprint-of-Biomass-11-056.pdf

113. Revised 1996 IPCC Guidelines for National Greenhouse Gas Inventories, Intergovernmental Panel on Climate Change, 2016, http://www.ipcc-nggip.iges.or.jp/public/gl/guidelin/ch1wb1.pdf

114. "Biofuels," European Commission, 2016, https://ec.europa.eu/energy/en/topics/renewable-energy/biofuels

115. "US Bioenergy Statistics," US Department of Agriculture, Feb. 2016, http://www.ers.usda.gov/data-products/us-bioenergy-statistics.aspx

116. Lester Brown, "Starving the People to Feed the Cars," Washington Post, Sep. 10, 2006, http://www.washingtonpost.com/wp-dyn/content/article/2006/09/08/AR2006090801596_pf.html

117. The Mad, Mad, Mad World of Climatism: Mankind and Climate Change Mania by Steve Goreham, (New Lenox Books, 2012), p. 207

118. Image of children in Africa by FrontierEnviro under Creative Commons License

119. Nithin Coca, "Indonesia Doubles Down on Palm Oil," Equal Times, July 27, 2015, http://www.equaltimes.org/indonesia-doubles-down-on-palm-oil?lang=en#.VwFaTsYo59M

120. "Opinion of the EEA Scientific Committee on Greenhouse Gas Accounting in Relation to Bioenergy," European Environment Agency, Sep.

15, 2011, http://www.eea.europa.eu/about-us/governance/scientific-committee/sc-opinions/opinions-on-scientific-issues/sc-opinion-on-greenhouse-gas/view

121.  "Renewable Fuel Standard: Potential Economic and Environmental Effects of U.S. Biofuel Policy," National Academy of Sciences, 2011, http://www.nap.edu/catalog/13105/renewable-fuel-standard-potential-economic-and-environmental-effects-of-us

122.  "FACT SHEET: President Obama's Plan to Make the U.S. the First Country to Put 1 Million Advanced Technology Vehicles on the Road," White House Press Release, Jan. 25, 2011 https://www.whitehouse.gov/sites/default/files/other/fact-sheet-one-million-advanced-technology-vehicles.pdf

123.  "2017 and Later Model Year Light-Duty Vehicle Greenhouse Gas Emissions and Corporate Average Fuel Economy Standards," Environmental Protections Agency and Department of Transportation, Federal Register, v. 76, no. 231 Dec. 1, 2011, https://www.federalregister.gov/articles/2012/10/15/2012-21972/2017-and-later-model-year-light-duty-vehicle-greenhouse-gas-emissions-and-corporate-average-fuel

124.  *The Mad, Mad, Mad World of Climatism*, (See no. 117), p. 212

125.  Nathan Bomey, "Average Age of Cars on U.S. Roads Breaks Record," *USA Today*, July 29, 2015, http://www.usatoday.com/money/

126.  Tesla Model S New Vehicle Limited Warranty, 2012, https://www.teslamotors.com/sites/default/files/blog_attachments/ms_vehicle_warranty.pdf

127.  David Noland, "Tesla Model S Battery Life: How Much Range Loss for Electric Car Over Time?," *Green Car Reports*, Feb. 17, 2015, http://www.greencarreports.com/news/1096801_tesla-model-s-battery-life-how-much-range-loss-for-electric-car-over-time

128.  "Monthly Sales Plug-in Scorecard," InsideEVs.com, March 2016, http://insideevs.com/monthly-plug-in-sales-scorecard/

129.  "Impact of Next Generation Storage on the Electrical Grid," George Crabtree, lecture and University of Chicago, Dec. 9, 2016

130.  Lois Fran, "Germany Wants All Europe to Ban Non-Electric New Cars by 2030," *Itechpost*, Oct. 31, 2016, http://www.itechpost.com/articles/38376/20161009/germany-non-electric-cars-gas-powered-europe.htm; engine image by Olli1800 under Creative Commons license; stove image by hatalar205

131.  Julian Hattem, "EPA Releases Draft Rules to Cut Emissions from Power Plants," *Hill*, Sep. 20, 2013, http://thehill.com/regulation/energy-environment/323597-epa-chief-emissions-limits-wont-kill-coal-industry

132.  Mayer Hillman, "Your Planet: The Case for Rationing," *Independent*, Sep. 19, 2005, http://www.independent.co.uk/environment/your-planet-the-case-for-rationing-507513.html; image by TheByteMan

133.  Christopher Smith, testimony before the US House of Representatives, July 25, 2013, https://science.house.gov/legislation/hearings/subcommittee-energy-future-coal-utilizing-america-s-abundant-energy-resources

134.  "Quest Fact Sheet: Carbon Dioxide Capture and Storage Project," Massachusetts Institute of Technology, Mar. 30, 2016, https://sequestration.mit.edu/tools/projects/quest.html

135.  "The Global Status of CCS," Global CCS Institute, 2015, https://www.globalccsinstitute.com/publications/global-status-ccs-2015-summary-report

## Chapter 8: Agriculture Under Attack

1.   "Quotations on Agriculture," Thomas Jefferson Encyclopedia, Aug. 23, 1785, http://wiki.monticello.org/mediawiki/index.php/Quotations_on_Agriculture

2.   "World Development Indicators," World Bank, 2016, http://data.worldbank.org/data-catalog/world-development-indicators

3.   Agriculture production index, 1961-2013, United Nations Food and Agriculture Organization, 2016, http://faostat3.fao.org/browse/Q/*/E

4.   "The State of Food Insecurity in the World," United Nations Food and Agriculture Organization, 2014, http://www.fao.org/publications/sofi/2014/en/

5.   *The World of Coffee: The Science and Culture of the World's Most Popular Drug* by Bennett Alan Weinberg and Bonnie K. Bealer, (Psychology Press, 2001), p. 3–4

6.   Gene McKenzie, "A Little Bit of History," *Journal of the Bromeliad Society*, July 1, 2010, https://www.highbeam.com/doc/1G1-248734304.html

7.   Amy Grant, "Varieties of Orange Fruit: Learn About Different Types of Oranges," *Gardening Know How*, Jan. 11, 2016, http://www.gardeningknowhow.com/edible/fruits/oranges/different-types-of-oranges.htm

8.   Patrik Lindenfors et al., "An Empirical Study of Cultural Evolution: The Development of European Cookery form Medieval to Modern Times," *Cliodynamics: The Journal of Quantitative History and Cultural Evolution*, 2015, http://www.academia.edu/22378002/An_Empirical_Study_of_Cultural_Evolution_The_Development_of_European_Cookery_from_Medieval_to_Modern_Times

9.   "Assessing the Environmental Impacts of Consumption and Production: Priority Products and Materials," United Nations Environment Programme, 2010, http://www.unep.org/resourcepanel/Portals/24102/PDFs/PriorityProductsAndMaterials_Report.pdf

10.  US Department of Agriculture database, 2016, https://apps.fas.usda.gov/psdonline/psdQuery.aspx; Image of rice planting in Iran by Mostafa Saeednejad under Creative Commons License

11.  "Climate Change 2014: Impacts, Adaptation, and Vulnerability, Part A," Fifth Assessment Report of the Intergovernmental Panel on Climate Change, Working Group II, 2014, http://www.ipcc.ch/report/ar5/wg2/

12.  Jeremy Rifkin, "There's a Bone to Pick With Meat Eaters," *LATimes*, May 27, 2002, http://articles.latimes.com/2002/may/27/opinion/oe-rifkin27

13.  Food and Agriculture Organization of the United Nations, FAOSTAT database, 2016, http://faostat3.fao.org/home/E

14.  Jelle Bruinsma, "The Resource Outlook to 2050," Food and Agriculture Organization of the United Nations, 2009, ftp://ftp.fao.org/agl/aglw/docs/ResourceOutlookto2050.pdf

15.  Naria Rulli et al., "The Water-Land-Food Nexus of First-Generation Biofuels," *Nature.com*, Mar. 3, 2016, http://www.nature.com/articles/srep22521

16.  Jo Confino, "James Cameron and Wife to Launch Campaign Advocating Sustainable Plant-Only Based Diet," *Guardian*, July 4, 2014, http://www.rawstory.com/2014/07/james-cameron-and-wife-to-launch-campaign-advocating-sustainable-plant-only-based-diet/; Meat image by Rainer Zenz under GNU Free Documentation License; graveyard silhouette image by naoshika

17.  Ronald Phillips, "Mobilizing Science to Break Yield Barriers," *Crop Science*, Mar.-Apr. 2010, pp. 99-108, https://dl.sciencesocieties.org/publications/cs/articles/50/Supplement_1/S-99

18.  *The Population Bomb* by Paul Ehrlich, (Sierra Club—Ballantine Books, 1968), p. 40

19.  US Department of Agriculture feed grains database, 2016, http://www.ers.usda.gov/data-products/feed-grains-database.aspx; Maize image by burgkirsch under Creative Commons License

20.  Food and Agriculture Organization of the United Nations, FAOSTAT database, 2016, http://faostat3.fao.org/home/E

21.  Igor Shiklomanov, "World Water Resources," United Nations Educational, Scientific, and Cultural Organization, 1998, http://biosinfonet.yolasite.com/resources/World%20water%20resources.pdf

22.  "The World's Water: Is There Enough?," World Meteorological Organization, 1997, http://www.bvsde.paho.org/bvsaca/fulltext/worldwater.pdf

23.  "UNEP Launches Definitive Study of Global Environmental Crisis," United Nations press release, Sep. 15, 1999, http://www.un.org/press/en/1999/19990915.unep47.doc.html

24.  United Nations Human Development Report 2006, http://hdr.undp.org/sites/default/files/reports/267/hdr06-complete.pdf

25.  A. Y. Hoekstra, "Virtual Water Trade," Proceedings of the International Expert Meeting on Virtual Water Trade, Feb. 2003, http://waterfootprint.org/media/downloads/Report12.pdf

26.  Shiklomanov, (See no. 21)
27.  Food and Agriculture Organization of the United Nations, FAOSTAT database, 2016, http://faostat3.fao.org/home/E
28.  Shiklomanov, (See no. 21)
29.  Sean Martin, "Earth to RUN OUT of Water by 2050: Leaked Report Shows 'Catastropic' Fate Facing World," *Daily Express*, Apr. 30, 2016, http://www.express.co.uk/news/science/665779/water-shortage-nestle-wikileaks-meat; image of warehouse fire by Petteri Sulonen under Creative Commons License
30.  "Water and Jobs," United Nations World Water Development Report 2016, http://www.unesco.org/new/en/natural-sciences/environment/water/wwap/wwdr/2016-water-and-jobs/
31.  Food and Agriculture Organization of the United Nations, FAOSTAT database, 2016, http://faostat3.fao.org/home/E
32.  Water and Jobs, (See no. 30)
33.  Food and Agriculture Organization of the United Nations, FAOSTAT database, 2016, http://faostat3.fao.org/home/E
34.  Water and Jobs, (See no. 30)
35.  "Progress on Drinking Water and Sanitation," World Health Organization, 2014, http://www.unwater.org/publications/publications-detail/en/c/231531/
36.  International Desalination Association, 2016, http://idadesal.org/desalination-101/desalination-by-the-numbers/
37.  Sede Boqer, "ADAPTATION: Israel is Creating a Water Surplus Using Desalination," *EENews.net*, Feb. 7, 2014, http://www.eenews.net/stories/1059994202
38.  Gary Hergert et al., "A Historical Overview of Fertilizer Use," Mar. 2015, http://cropwatch.unl.edu/fertilizer-history-p1
39.  *Enriching the Earth: Fritz Haber, Carl Bosch, and the Transformation of World Food Production* by Vaclav Smil, (MIT Press, 2001)
40.  Hergert, (See no. 38)
41.  Food and Agriculture Organization of the United Nations, FAOSTAT database, 2016, http://faostat.fao.org/site/422/DesktopDefault.aspx?PageID=422#ancor
42.  W. Stewart et al., "The Contribution of Commercial Fertilizer Nutrients to Food Production," American Society of Agronomy, 2005, https://dl.sciencesocieties.org/publications/aj/abstracts/97/1/0001
43.  Tom Philpott, "A Brief History of Our Deadly Addiction to Nitrogen Fertilizer," *MotherJones*, Apr. 19, 2013, http://www.motherjones.com/tom-philpott/2013/04/history-nitrogen-fertilizer-ammonium-nitrate
44.  "Intensive Farming," Greenpeace New Zealand, 2016, http://www.greenpeace.org/new-zealand/en/campaigns/climate-change/smart-farming/the-bad/
45.  Dan Charles, "Fertilized World," *National Geographic*, May, 2013, http://ngm.nationalgeographic.com/2013/05/fertilized-world/charles-text; Church image by TheByteMan
46.  *Enriching the Earth*, (See no. 39), p. xiv
47.  *Enriching the Earth*, (See no. 39), p. 60
48.  *Enriching the Earth*, (See no. 39), p.160
49.  *Enriching the Earth*, (See no. 39), p.186
50.  Food and Agriculture Organization of the United Nations, FAOSTAT database, 2016, http://faostat.fao.org/site/422/DesktopDefault.aspx?PageID=422#ancor
51.  Joy Adamonis, "Is Your Lawn Accelerating Climate Change," CleanAirLawnCare, http://www.cleanairlawncareboston.com/lawn-accelerating-climate-change/; question mark image from semjaza
52.  "Data Center - Food and Agriculture," Earth Policy Institute from International Fertilizer Industry Association, Dec. 2013, http://www.earth-policy.org/data_center/C24; fertilizer application image by USDA
53.  Ibid
54.  "Sick Water: The Central Role of Wastewater Management in Sustainable Development," UN Environmental Programme, 2010, http://www.unep.org/pdf/SickWater_screen.pdf
55.  John Unsworth, "History of Pesticide Use," International Union of Pure and Applied Chemistry, May 10, 2010, http://agrochemicals.iupac.org/index.php?option=com_sobi2&sobi2Task=sobi2Details&catid=3&sobi2Id=31
56.  *Silent Spring* by Rachel Carson, (Houghton-Mifflin, 1962), p. 7–8
57.  *Climatism! Science, Common Sense, and the 21st Century's Hottest Topic* by Steve Goreham, (New Lenox Books, 2010), p. 301-302
58.  Ibid, p. 303
59.  K. Bassil et al., "Cancer Health Effects of Pesticides," *Canadian Family Physician*, Oct. 2007, http://www.ncbi.nlm.nih.gov/pmc/articles/PMC2231435/pdf/0531704.pdf
60.  M. Sanborn et al., "Non-Cancer Health Effects of Pesticides," *Canadian Family Physician*, Oct. 2007, http://www.ncbi.nlm.nih.gov/pmc/articles/PMC2231436/
61.  "Pesticide Data Program," US Department of Agriculture, 2014, https://www.ams.usda.gov/sites/default/files/media/2014%20PDP%20Annual%20Summary.pdf
62.  Bruce Ames and Lois Gold, "The Causes and Prevention of Cancer: The Role of Environment," *Biotherapy*, 1998, https://toxnet.nlm.nih.gov/cpdb/pdfs/Biotherapy1998.pdf
63.  "Harvest of Fear," Jeremy Rifkin interview with *PBS*, Aug. 2000, http://www.pbs.org/wgbh/harvest/interviews/rifkin.html; Ghost image by netalloy
64.  "FAO Statistical Yearbook, 2013," Food and Agriculture Organization of the United Nations, http://www.fao.org/docrep/018/i3107e/i3107e00.htm
65.  "Genetic Engineering," Greenpeace website, 2016, http://www.greenpeace.org/international/en/campaigns/agriculture/problem/genetic-engineering/
66.  Clive James, "Global Status of Commercialized Biotech GM Crops: 2015," ISAAA, 2015, http://isaaa.org/resources/publications/briefs/51/executivesummary/default.asp
67.  Wilhelm Klümper and Matin Qaim, "A Meta-Analysis of the Impacts of Genetically Modified Crops," PLOS ONE, Nov. 2014, http://journals.plos.org/plosone/article?id=10.1371/journal.pone.0111629
68.  Benjamin Goad, "Groups Press Costco to Reject 'Frankenfish,'" *The Hill*, Mar. 18, 2014, http://thehill.com/regulation/technology/201094-groups-press-costco-to-reject-gmo-frankenfish; Judy Garland image from *The Wizard of Oz*
69.  "Transgenic Crops by Trait," GMO Compass, Jan. 19, 2007, http://www.gmo-compass.org/eng/agri_biotechnology/gmo_planting/145.gmo_cultivation_trait_statistics.html
70.  Clive, (See no. 66)
71.  Amy Dean and Jennifer Armstrong, "Genetically Modified Foods," American Academy of Environmental Medicine, May 8, 2009, https://www.aaemonline.org/gmo.php
72.  "A Decade of EU-Funded GMO Research," European Commission, 2010, https://ec.europa.eu/research/biosociety/pdf/a_decade_of_eu-funded_gmo_research.pdf
73.  "Vitamin A Deficiency," World Health Organization, 2016, http://www.who.int/nutrition/topics/vad/en/

74.    "The Beginnings of Golden Rice," GoldenRice.org, 2016, http://www.goldenrice.org/Content2-How/how1_sci.php
75.    Ibid
76.    Matt McGrath, "'Golden Rice' GM Trial Vandalised in the Philippines," *BBC News*, Aug. 9, 2013, http://www.bbc.com/news/science-environment-23632042
77.    Clive, (See no. 66)
78.    Clive, (See no. 66)
79.    "Did You Know Organic Underwear Could Look This Good?," *Natural Living for Women*, 2016, http://www.natural-living-for-women.com/organic-underwear.html; flower image by Hakani
80.    "Agricultural Marketing Service's National Organic Program," US Department of Agriculture, 2016, https://www.ams.usda.gov/sites/default/files/media/About%20the%20National%20Organic%20Program.pdf
81.    "Systematic Review of Differences in Nutrient Content of Organically and Conventionally Produced Food, " UK Food Standards Agency, Apr. 27, 2010, http://tna.europarchive.org/20100929190231/http://www.food.gov.uk/science/research/choiceandstandardsresearch/consumerchoicestandards/l01list/organicreview/
82.    Brian Caldwell et al., "Resource Guide for Organic Insect and Disease Management," Cornell University, 2013, http://www.sare.org/Learning-Center/SARE-Project-Products/Northeast-SARE-Project-Products/Resource-Guide-for-Organic-Insect-and-Disease-Management
83.    "The National List of Allowed and Prohibited Substances," US Dept. of Agriculture, 2016, https://www.ams.usda.gov/rules-regulations/organic/national-list
84.    Christie Wilcox, "Mythbusting 101: Organic Farming > Conventional Agriculture," *Scientific American*, July 18, 2011, http://blogs.scientificamerican.com/science-sushi/httpblogsscientificamericancomscience-sushi20110718mythbusting-101-organic-farming-conventional-agriculture/
85.    Ibid
86.    Theodore Roosevelt address to the Deep Waterway Convention, Memphis, TN, Oct. 4, 1907
87.    "REDD+," UN Food and Agriculture Organization, 2016, http://en.openei.org/wiki/UN-REDD_Programme
88.    "The State of the World's Forests 2012," UN Food and Agriculture Organization, http://www.fao.org/docrep/016/i3010e/i3010e.pdf
89.    "Global Forest Resource Assessment 2015," UN Food and Agriculture Organization, http://www.fao.org/resources/infographics/infographics-details/en/c/325836/
90.    Food and Agriculture Organization of the UN, FAOSTAT database, 2016, http://faostat3.fao.org/download/G2/GL/E
91.    Food and Agriculture Organization of the UN, FAOSTAT database, 2016, http://faostat3.fao.org/download/G2/GL/E; World Bank database 2016, http://data.worldbank.org/indicator/NY.GDP.PCAP.CD; Exceptions with shrinking forests are Argentina, Brunei, Equatorial Guinea, Panama, Portugal, and Venezuela
92.    "The State of World Fisheries and Aquaculture 2016," UN Food and Agriculture Organization; http://www.fao.org/fishery/sofia/en
93.    Gaia Vince, "How the World's Oceans Could Be Running Out of Fish," *BBC*, Sep. 21, 2013, http://www.bbc.com/future/story/20120920-are-we-running-out-of-fish
94.    The State of World Fisheries, (See no. 92)
95.    The State of World Fisheries, (See no. 92)
96.    Robert Zubrin, "The Pacific's Salmon Are Back—Thank Human Ingenuity," *National Review*, Apr. 22, 2014, http://www.nationalreview.com/article/376258/pacifics-salmon-are-back-thank-human-ingenuity-robert-zubrin
97.    Ibid
98.    "Controversial BC Salmon Project Pits Haida members Against Feds," *Huffpost British Columbia*, Dec. 18, 2012, http://www.huffingtonpost.ca/2012/10/18/controversial-bc-salmon-project-iron_n_1982530.html?utm_hp_ref=food&ir=Food
99.    "The Promise of a Blue Revolution," *Economist*, Aug. 7, 2003; http://www.economist.com/node/1974103

## Chapter 9:  Business Environmental Policy—Sensibly Green

1.     Quote by Peter Drucker, http://www.brainyquote.com/quotes/quotes/p/peterdruck105338.html
2.     Miranda Marquit, "Green Ideas: Making Concrete from Rice," *PhysOrg.com*, July 21, 2009, http://phys.org/news/2009-07-green-ideas-concrete-rice.html; tree image by Cruiser under GNU Free Documentation License
3.     Stefano Valentino, "Belgian "CO2 Champion" Plant Bought Off Forged Chinese Carbon Credits," *Mobile Reporter*, Sep. 23, 2015, http://www.voxeurop.eu/en/content/article/4987300-belgian-co2-champion-plant-bought-forged-chinese-carbon-credits; Lemonade image by Michael Fludkov under Creative Commons License
4.     "Steel's Contribution to a Low Carbon Future and Climate Resilient Societies," World Steel Association, 2015, https://www.worldsteel.org/steel-by-topic/climate-change.html
5.     "Climate Action," World Steel Association, 2016, https://www.worldsteel.org/steel-by-topic/climate-change.html
6.     "Steel Statistical Yearbook, 2015," World Steel Association, http://www.worldsteel.org/statistics/statistics-archive/yearbook-archive.html
7.     Thomas Gibson and Chuck Schmitt, "The Crisis Facing the U.S. Steel Industry," *CNN.com*, Mar. 23, 2016, http://www.cnn.com/2016/03/23/opinions/american-steel-industry-gibson-schmitt/
8.     Kate Connolly, "G7 Leaders Agree to Phase Out Fossil Fuel Use by End of Century," *Guardian*, June 8, 2015, https://www.theguardian.com/world/2015/jun/08/g7-leaders-agree-phase-out-fossil-fuel-use-end-of-century
9.     *Conversations with Norman Mailer* by Michael Lennon, (Univ. Press of Mississippi, 1988), p. 321; explosion image is US Navy photo
10.    "Plastics-the Facts 2015," Plastics*Europe*, 2015, http://www.plasticseurope.org/Document/plastics---the-facts-2015.aspx
11.    Plastic bag use from "Plastic Bags Fact Sheet," Earth Policy Institute, Oct. 2014, http://www.earth-policy.org/press_room/C68/plastic_bags_fact_sheet; Plastic bottle use estimated from numerous sources, including Rick LeBlanc, "Plastic Recycling Facts and Figures," *The Balance*, June 1, 2016, https://www.thebalance.com/plastic-recycling-facts-and-figures-2877886
12.    "The New Plastics Economy Rethinking the Future of Plastics," World Economic Forum, 2016, https://www.weforum.org/reports/the-new-plastics-economy-rethinking-the-future-of-plastics/
13.    "World on the Edge: How to Prevent Environmental and Economic Collapse, Chapter 8. Building and Energy Efficient Economy," Earth Policy Institute, 2016, http://www.earth-policy.org/books/wote/wotech8
14.    "How Much Oil is Used to Make PET Plastic Water Bottles?," *GlaciaNova*, Feb. 1, 2014, https://glacianova.wordpress.com/2014/02/01/how-much-oil-is-used-to-make-pet-plastic-water-bottles/
15.    Jenna Jambeck et al., "Plastic Waste Inputs from Land into the Ocean," *Sciencemag.org*, Feb. 2015, http://www.iswa.org/fileadmin/user_upload/Calendar_2011_03_AMERICANA/Science-2015-Jambeck-768-71__2_.pdf
16.    World Economic Forum, (see no. 12)
17.    Michael Casey, "World's Oceans "Plagued" by 269,000 Tons of Plastic Pollution," *CBS News*, Dec. 11, 2014, http://www.cbsnews.com/news/worlds-oceans-plagued-by-269000-tons-of-plastic-pollution/
18.    "France Bands All Plastic Dishware Starting in 2020," *Fortune*, Sep. 17, 2016, http://fortune.com/2016/09/17/france-bans-plastic-dishware-2020/; flower image by Hakani

19. Mackenzie Anderson, "Great Things Come in Innovative Packaging: An Introduction to PlantBottle™ Packaging," Coca-Cola Company, June 3, 2015, http://www.coca-colacompany.com/stories/great-things-come-in-innovative-packaging-an-introduction-to-plantbottle-packaging

20. Donnella Meadows, "Can We Avoid a New Silent Spring?: Endocrine Disrupters—Chemicals Mimicking Hormones—May Be the Cause of Widespread Reproduction Anomalies," *Los Angeles Times*, Mar. 10, 1996, http://articles.latimes.com/1996-03-10/opinion/op-45336_1_endocrine-disrupters

21. Ron Way, "Toxic Dangers in Plastic Baby Bottles," Minnpost, Feb. 7, 2008, https://www.minnpost.com/environment/2008/02/toxic-dangers-plastic-baby-bottles; Judy Garland image from *The Wizard of Oz*

22. "What Does That Number Mean?," Ecology's Water Quality Policy Forum, Feb. 8, 2013, http://www.ecy.wa.gov/programs/wq/swqs/HelpfulTerminologyAnalogies.pdf

23. Lisa Brown and Bill Finkbeiner, "Our Polluted Bodies," *Seattle Times*, July 18, 2006, http://old.seattletimes.com/html/opinion/2003104819_toxics05.html; ghost image by netalloy

24. Dennis Avery, "FDA: No Low-Dose Chemical Dangers," Hudson Institute, May 20, 2014, http://www.hudson.org/research/10307-fda-no-low-dose-chemical-dangers

25. Ames, "Pollution, Pesticides, and Cancer Prevention: Misconceptions," 1997, http://spot.colorado.edu/~gravesp/ec3545handout10.html

26. Ibid

27. Ruth Kava, "Why the 'War on Cancer' is Oversimplified," American Council on Science and Health, May 11, 2016, http://acsh.org/news/2016/05/11/why-the-war-on-cancer-is-oversimplified

28. Bruce Ames and Lois Swirsky Gold, "Paracelsus to Parascience: the Environmental Cancer Distraction," *Mutation Research*, 2000, https://toxnet.nlm.nih.gov/cpdb/pdfs/Paracelsus.pdf

29. Ibid

30. Nathan Berger et al., "Cancer in the Elderly," Transactions of the American Clinical and Climatological Association, 2006, https://www.ncbi.nlm.nih.gov/pmc/articles/PMC1500929/

31. "Focus on Phthalates: Myth vs. Fact," Chemical Fabrics and Film Association, Feb. 2013, http://www.enduratex.com/pdf/Focus%20on%20Phthalates.pdf

32. "Scientific Opinion on Bisphenol A," European Food Safety Authority, 2015, http://www.efsa.europa.eu/sites/default/files/corporate_publications/files/factsheetbpa150121.pdf

33. Tunga Salthammer et al., "Formaldehyde in the Indoor Environment," *Chemical Reviews*, 2010, https://www.ncbi.nlm.nih.gov/pmc/articles/PMC2855181/

34. Joseph Rosen, "Much Ado About Alar," *Issues in Science and Technology*, Fall 1990, http://courses.washington.edu/alisonta/pbaf590/pdf/Rosen_Alar.pdf

35. National Cancer Institute SEER data, 2016, http://seer.cancer.gov/faststats/selections.php?#Output; image of human lung cancer by Emmanuelm under Creative Commons license

36. Ibid

37. Mark Carney presentation to Lloyds of London, Sep. 29, 2015, https://www.youtube.com/watch?v=V5c-eqNxeSQ

38. "ExtremWetterKongress," 2014, http://extremwetterkongress.de/

39. Roger Pielke Jr., "The Precipitous Decline in US Flood Damage as a Percentage of GDP," *The Climate Fix*, Feb. 5, 2015 https://theclimatefix.wordpress.com/2015/02/05/the-precipitous-decline-in-us-flood-damage-as-a-percentage-of-gdp/

40. John Roach, "Insurer's Message: Prepare for Climate Change or Get Sued," *NBC News*, June 4, 2014, http://www.nbcnews.com/science/environment/insurers-message-prepare-climate-change-or-get-sued-n122856

41. Steven Thomas, "Price of Oceanfront Property up More than 20 Percent This Year," *Veronews*, Oct. 16, 2014, http://www.veronews.com/32963_features/price-of-oceanfront-property-up-more-than-percent-this-year/article_169a642e-5496-11e4-afc6-001a4bcf6878.html; Wave image by Shalom Jacobovitz under Creative Commons License

42. Benjamin Gaddy et al., "Venture Capital and Cleantech: The Wrong Model for Clean Energy Innovation," MIT Energy, July, 2016, https://energy.mit.edu/wp-content/uploads/2016/07/MITEI-WP-2016-06.pdf; Thinker statue image by Frank Kovalcheck under Creative Commons License

43. Ibid

44. *Climatism: Science, Common Sense, and the 21st Century's Hottest Topic* by Steve Goreham, (New Lenox Books, 2010), pp. 308-312

## Chapter 10: Upheaval—Coming Changes in Energy and Climate Regulation

1. Paul Samuelson, "Economics of Forestry in an Evolving Society," *Economic Inquiry*, Vol. XIV, Dec. 1976, p. 467

2. "China Cannot Afford to Follow US Example in Economic Development," People's Daily Online, Sep. 8, 2005, http://en.people.cn/200509/08/eng20050908_207306.html; ghost image by netalloy

3. "Vision 2050: The New Agenda for Business," World Business Council for Sustainable Development, Feb. 2010, http://www.wbcsd.org/pages/edocument/edocumentdetails.aspx?id=219; Thinker statue image by Frank Kovalcheck under Creative Commons License

4. James Hansen, "Coal-fired Power Stations are Death Factories. Close Them,," *Guardian*, Feb. 14, 2009, https://www.theguardian.com/commentisfree/2009/feb/15/james-hansen-power-plants-coal; Vampire image by Alejandro Lunadei under Creative Commons License

5. Valerie Richardson, "Sheldon Whitehouse Calls for News Outlets to Suppress 'Extreme' Op-Eds by Climate Skeptics," *Washington Times*, July 14, 2016, http://www.washingtontimes.com/news/2016/jul/14/sheldon-whitehouse-calls-news-outlets-suppress-ext/; Stalin image public domain

6. RENIXX World Index, *Financial Times*, 2016, http://markets.ft.com/data/indices/tearsheet/summary?s=RENX:GER; Burning money image by Vmenkov under Creative Commons license

7. Ibid

8. "State and Trends of the Carbon Market 2011," "State and Trends of the Carbon Market 2012," World Bank, 2011, 2012, http://documents.worldbank.org/curated/en/749521468179970954/State-and-trends-of-the-carbon-market-2012; "Carbon Market Monitor," Thomson Reuters, Jan. 11, 2016, https://climateobserver.org/wp-content/uploads/2016/01/Carbon-Market-Review-2016.pdf

9. Ibid

10. Jason Scott, "Aussie Leader Slams Renewables 'Obsession' as Energy Chiefs Meet," *Bloomberg*, Oct. 6, 2016, http://www.bloomberg.com/news/articles/2016-10-06/aussie-leader-slams-renewables-obsession-as-energy-chiefs-meet

11. Daniel Wetzel, "Renewable Energy Cost Explosion: €25,000 Euros for Each German Family of Four," *Welt*, Oct. 10, 2016, http://www.thegwpf.com/germanys-renewable-energy-cost-explosion-25000-euros-for-each-family-of-four/

12. "Global Trends in Sustainable Energy Investment 2008," UN Environment Programme, 2008, http://fs-unep-centre.org/sites/default/files/media/globaltrends2008_0.pdf; eight ball image by nicubunu

13. "Global Trends in Renewable Energy Investment 2016, " UN Environment Programme, Boomberg New Energy Finance, Mar. 2016, http://fs-unep-centre.org/publications/global-trends-renewable-energy-investment-2016

14. "The Pacific Decadal Oscillation (PDO)," Joint Institute for the Study of the Atmosphere and the Ocean, 2016, http://research.jisao.washington.edu/pdo/

15.  "Atlantic Multi-decadal Oscillation (AMO)," National Center for Atmospheric Research, 2016, http://www.cgd.ucar.edu/cas/catalog/climind/AMO.html

16.  Global Trends, (See no. 13); wind farm image by Visitor7 under Creative Commons License

17.  P. Gosselin, "Current Solar Cycle Fades, Continues to be Weakest in 200 Years…Likely Foretelling Global Cooling," *NoTricksZone*, Oct. 18, 2016, http://notrickszone.com/2016/10/18/current-solar-cycle-fades-continues-to-be-weakest-in-200-years-likely-foretelling-global-cooling/#sthash.7ixpn6tA.dpbs

18.  *The Mad, Mad, Mad World of Climatism:  Mankind and Climate Change Mania* by Steve Goreham (New Lenox Books, 2012), p. 97

19.  Justin Haskins, "EPA Wants to Monitor Your Hotel Showers," *Daily Caller*, Apr. 9, 2015, http://dailycaller.com/2015/04/09/epa-wants-to-monitor-your-hotel-showers/; Binoculars with eyes image by Juhele

20.  Stuart Rintoul, "Town of Beaufort Changed Tony Abbott's View on Climate Change," *Australian*, Dec. 12, 2009, http://www.theaustralian.com.au/archive/politics/the-town-that-turned-up-the-temperature/story-e6frgczf-1225809567009

21.  Peter Hannam, "CSIRO Climate Cuts 'Devastating', Almost 3000 Scientists Tell Malcolm Turnbull," *Sydney Morning Herald*, Feb. 12, 2016; http://www.smh.com.au/environment/climate-change/csiro-climate-cuts-devastating-almost-3000-scientists-tell-malcolm-turnbull-20160211-gms3ea.html

22.  Simon Kent, "Aussie PM Tony Abbott Cancels All Government Wind Farm Subsidies," *Breitbart*, July 12, 2015, http://www.breitbart.com/big-government/2015/07/12/aussie-pm-tony-abbott-cancels-all-government-wind-farm-subsidies/

23.  Ian Johnston, "Climate Change Department Closed by Theresa May in 'Plain Stupid' and 'Deeply Worrying' Move, *Independent*, July 14, 2016, http://www.independent.co.uk/environment/climate-change-department-killed-off-by-theresa-may-in-plain-stupid-and-deeply-worrying-move-a7137166.html

24.  "Sarkozy Comes Out of the Closet as a Climate Skeptic," *Local*, Sep. 15, 2016, http://www.thelocal.fr/20160915/sarkozy-turns-climate-sceptic-in-battle-for-the-elyse

25.  Brad Plumer, "There's No Way Around It: Donald Trump Looks Like a Disaster for the Planet," *Vox*, Nov. 9, 2016,http://www.vox.com/2016/11/9/13571318/donald-trump-disaster-climate; Crying child image by Crimfants under Creative Commons License

26.  Rollo May, "Living Your Wild Creativity," 2017, https://www.livingyourwildcreativity.com/courage-to-create-may/

# INDEX

# X

# Y

# Z

# ABOUT THE AUTHOR

Steve Goreham is a speaker, author, and researcher on environmental issues and a former engineer and business executive. He is an independent columnist and an invited guest on radio and television, including Fox Business Channel, The 700 Club, Jim Bohannon, Lou Dobbs, Sean Hannity, Dennis Miller, Lars Larson, and Janet Parshall. He's the Executive Director of the Climate Science Coalition of America, a non-political association of scientists, engineers, and citizens dedicated to informing about the realities of climate science and energy economics.

*Outside the Green Box* is Steve's third book. Over 100,000 copies of his previous two books, *The Mad, Mad, Mad World of Climatism: Mankind and Climate Change Mania* and *Climatism! Science, Common Sense, and the 21st Century's Hottest Topic*, are now in print. Steve's full-time efforts are devoted to correcting misconceptions about energy, resources, climate change, and the environment, including resultant negative impacts on business, industry, agriculture, and public policy. He wrote this book to bring the facts about sustainable development to business and to change commonly-held, but mistaken, beliefs about the environment.

Steve holds an MS in Electrical Engineering from the University of Illinois and an MBA from the University of Chicago. He has more than 30 years of experience at Fortune 100 and private companies in engineering and executive roles. He is husband and father of three and resides in Illinois in the United States of America.

# Steve
# Goreham

### Speaker/Author/Researcher
### Environment, Business, and Public Policy

Informative and engaging speaker, delivering compelling and provocative programs to businesses, universities, and other organizations. Effective communicator in the boardroom, conference hall, and on the debate panel regarding:

- The Environment
- Sustainable Development
- Economic Trends
- Energy
- Climate Change
- Corporate Environmental Policy

### www.stevegoreham.com

## Enjoy Steve's Other Books

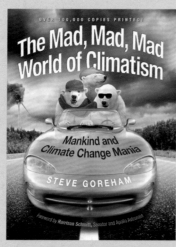

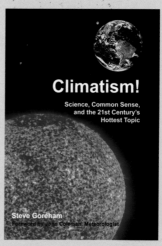

"An amusing and colorful, yet science-based, look at mankind's obsession with global warming." —*Publishers Weekly*

300-Page Color Soft Cover
150 Sidebars, 113 Figures,13 Cartoons
New Lenox Books (2012)

The complete discussion of the science, politics, and policy implications of the global warming debate.

480-Page Black & White Hard Cover
135 Figures
New Lenox Books (2010)